POST-COLONIAL LITERATURES

Reconfigurations – Critical readings in Post-colonialism
(Series editors: Faith Pullin, Lee Spinks and Karina Williamson;
University of Edinburgh)

Reconfigurations will discuss the diverse relationships between literary production and theories of post-colonial culture. Particular attention will be paid to the ways in which post-colonial literatures reconfigure the insights of post-colonial and postmodern theory within their own signifying practices.

Post-Colonial Literatures

Expanding the Canon

Edited by

Deborah L. Madsen

Pluto Press
LONDON • STERLING, VIRGINIA

First published 1999 by Pluto Press
345 Archway Road, London N6 5AA
and 22883 Quicksilver Drive,
Sterling, VA 20166–2012, USA

Copyright © Deborah L. Madsen 1999

The right of the individual contributors to be identified as
the authors of this work has been asserted by them in accordance
with the Copyright, Designs and Patents Act 1988.

British Library Cataloguing in Publication Data
A catalogue record for this book is available from the British Library

ISBN 0 7453 1515 1 hbk

Library of Congress Cataloging in Publication Data
Post-colonial literatures : expanding the canon / edited by Deborah L.
Madsen.
   p.   cm.
Includes index.
ISBN 0–7453–1515–1 (hbk)
1. Commonwealth literature (English)—History and criticism.
2. Literature and society—English-speaking countries—History—20th
century. 3. American literature—Minority authors—History and
criticism. 4. English literature—Foreign countries—History and
criticism. 5. English literature—20th century—History and
criticism. 6. Decolonization in literature. 7. Ethnic groups in
literature. 8. Minorities in literature. 9. Canon (Literature)
I. Madsen, Deborah L.
PR9080.P55   1999
820.9'9171241—dc21   99–21628
                                                                                      CIP

Designed and produced for Pluto Press by
Chase Production Services, Chadlington, OX7 3LN
Typeset from disk by Stanford DTP Services, Northampton
Printed in the EC by TJ International, Padstow

Contents

1. Beyond the Commonwealth: Post-Colonialism and American Literature 1
   Deborah L. Madsen

2. Post-Colonialism in the United States: Diversity or Hybridity? 14
   Karen Piper

3. Ethical Reading and Resistant Texts 29
   Patricia Linton

4. Fractures: Written Displacements in Canadian/US Literary Relations 45
   Richard J. Lane

5. The Rhythm of Difference: Language and Silence in *The Chant of Jimmie Blacksmith* and *The Piano* 58
   Marion Wynne-Davies

6. Locating and Celebrating Difference: Writing by South African and Aboriginal Women Writers 72
   Gina Wisker

7. Coming in From the Margins: Gender in Contemporary Zimbabwean Writing 88
   Pauline Dodgson

8. The Memory of Slavery in Fred D'Aguiar's *Feeding the Ghosts* 104
   Gail Low

9. 'Versioning' the Revolution: Gender and Politics in Merle Collins's *Angel* 120
   Suzanne Scafe

10 Erupting Funk: The Political Style of Toni Morrison's *Tar Baby*
    and *The Bluest Eye* 133
    Alan Rice

11 Afro-Hispanic Literature and Feminist Theories: Thinking
    Ethics 148
    Rosemary Geisdorfer Feal

12 Chicano/a Literature: 'An Active Interanimating of
    Competing Discourses' 164
    Candida N. Hepworth

13 Border Theory and the Canon 180
    Debra A. Castillo

14 Racialism and Liberation in Native American Literature 206
    Lee Schweninger

15 Ants in the System: 'Thinking Strongly' about Native
    American Stories 218
    Robert Gregory

List of Contributors 226
Index 229

Acknowledgements

The editor and publishers are grateful to Baobab Press for permission to quote from Chenjerai Hove's novel *Bones* (Harare, 1988) and Yvonne Vera's novel *Without a Name* (Harare, 1994), and HarperCollins Publishers Inc. for permission to quote from Barre Toelken's essay 'Seeing with a Native Eye' in *Seeing with a Native Eye*, ed. Walter Holden Capps, copyright Walter Holden Capps, 1976.

1

Beyond the Commonwealth: Post-Colonialism and American Literature

Deborah L. Madsen

Despite a great deal of discussion about metaphors of centre versus margin and metropolis versus outpost or offshoots, the post-colonial canon remains comprised both of privileged texts and also of privileged national and regional literatures: the English-language literatures of Africa, India, Canada, Australia, New Zealand, South-East Asia, and the Caribbean. It is obvious from its geo-literary composition that the development of this body of writing as 'post-colonialism' arose out of earlier models of 'Commonwealth Literature' and the 'New Literatures in English' and 'World Literature in English' paradigms. The reinvention of these models under the term 'post-colonialism' has, then, involved the negotiation of a very considerable historical legacy. Contemporary post-colonial theory and criticism comprises a diverse field which does, however, reveal two dominant approaches: the text-led criticism deriving from Commonwealth literary studies and the highly theoretical discourses that are indebted to poststructuralism in particular and in general a whole range of contemporary critical theorizing. It is the criticism of texts that has come to operate largely within an inherited definition of what constitutes the post-colonial, with theory operating as a kind of meta-discourse that assumes a given canon of post-colonial texts. This inherited definition, derived as it is from Commonwealth literary study, omits reference to the ethnic literatures of the United States as making a significant impact upon thinking about and representations of post-coloniality as a transnational condition. These issues are taken up in more detail below in terms of the state of post-colonial study and the potential of a comparative literary methodology to offer a fruitful way forward.

I should hasten to say that it is not only 'Commonwealth' or 'post-colonial' critics but Americanists as well who seek to distinguish American literature from the emerging canon of post-colonial literature and keep the two quite distinct as areas of knowledge. I have heard expressed repeatedly the objection that there is nothing 'post'-colonial about the situation of Native American peoples, who remain as thoroughly colonized now as at any time in the past. However, it seems to me that in this respect Native Americans have much in common with Australian Aboriginal peoples and New Zealand Maoris, who in exactly the same ways are threatened with erasure by a dominant white settler culture. It is this kind of comparative thinking that informs this volume. The writings gathered here cover a range of issues, authors and national literatures in order to contextualize the ethnic literatures of the United States as part of the developing field of post-colonial studies. Each chapter deals with a specific area, problem or theme, providing coverage of the post-colonial field and also working to integrate a broader conception of North American literatures (beyond only the Canadian) into the existing post-colonial paradigm and incidentally to enrich conceptions of what is American literary expression.

The motive driving these individual writings and the book as a whole, then, is the desire to revise and expand the post-colonial paradigm to accommodate the contributions of such colonized peoples as Native Americans, Chicano/as, Afro-Hispanic and African-American peoples. The chapters are arranged in a sequence that develops its own logic to emphasize precisely this project. Abstract theoretical issues around multiculturalism, reading practices and resistant texts that are so much a part of contemporary thinking about post-colonialism are raised by Karen Piper and Patricia Linton in the opening chapters. The chapters that follow then pursue the particularity of post-colonial writing through consideration of key national and ethnic literatures, and the most significant writers within each of these areas: Patricia Linton's discussion of the Native Canadian writer Thomas King is followed by Richard Lane's consideration of US–Canadian literary relations. Marion Wynne-Davies then turns to key 'white' Australian and New Zealand texts and Gina Wisker takes up the 'black' post-colonial in her chapter on Australian Aboriginal and black South African women writers. Zimbabwean women writers provide the focus of Pauline Dodgson's chapter; the issues of slavery and the black diaspora are taken up first by Gail Low in her discussion of Fred D'Aguiar's work, then Suzanne Scafe in her chapter on Merle Collins, and then in Alan Rice's chapter on Toni Morrison. The focus of the book shifts perceptibly to America in the chapters that follow Alan Rice. Rosemary Feal links the black and Hispanic discourses of America in her discussion of Afro-Hispanic writing. The position of the colonized Hispanic peoples of the United

States is considered in the two chapters that follow: Candida Hepworth on Chicano/a writing and Debra Castillo on the theory and writing of the US–Mexican border. The collection concludes with an appropriate focus on the most obviously colonized ethnic group within America: the indigenous peoples who, we are reminded, do not form a homogenous group. The comparative methodology offered by post-colonialism provides a challenging point of departure for consideration of the nature of Native American literary expression. Lee Schweninger looks at the issue of racialism as a part of the substance of Gerald Vizenor's Chippewa expression, and Robert Gregory offers an overview of story-telling as a Native, as opposed to Western, expressive form. Gregory ends his discussion with the example of Thomas King, the Native North American writer with whom Patricia Linton began, thus bringing the argument of this book full circle, uniting the Canadian Commonwealth with the American post-colonial and demonstrating the power of this union.

The design of the book attempts to represent the post-colonial literatures of North America in relation to more familiar (British Commonwealth) post-colonial areas, such as Caribbean, Australasian and African writing, and in relation to the theoretical framework of post-colonial studies. In what follows I would like to consider some of the details of this theoretical framework, especially issues that appear as motifs throughout the book, beginning with the rationale offered for the exclusion of the United States from the paradigm of post-colonial studies.

THE EXCLUSION OF US TEXTS FROM THE POST-COLONIAL CANON

The title of this introduction, 'Beyond the Commonwealth', has a double significance in relation to the contributions that follows. First, the intention is to explore ways of expanding the post-colonial canon by pursuing points of comparison between Commonwealth writings and the ethnic literatures of the United States. This comparativist approach is much favoured by post-colonial critics and I will discuss this in more detail below. Second, the book is motivated by the idea that it is precisely the American literary canon that developed from the original Commonwealth – the New England colonies – that excludes from the privileged category of American Literature those multiethnic writings that do in fact fit a post-colonial paradigm. It is my conviction, demonstrated by the writings in this volume, that if we are to create an authentic post-colonial canon then we need to lift our critical sights higher than the restricted field of ex-British Commonwealth literatures but at the same time we must refuse the powerful literary legacy of the New England Commonwealth as well.

The exclusion of American literature from the category of the post-colonial has not gone unnoticed and indeed critics who provide general accounts of post-colonialism also provide reasons for this exclusion. For example, in the introduction to their now classic introduction to post-colonial writing, *The Empire Writes Back*, Bill Ashcroft, Gareth Griffiths and Helen Tiffin describe the post-colonial as being identical with the former British Empire; the post-colonial then describes the condition of a national culture once the imperial rulers have departed and the effect upon the totality of the culture as a consequence of the experience of imperial domination (Ashcroft et al., 1989, p. 2). The example of the US is described as paradigmatic of this condition yet American literature contributes nothing to the examples of post-colonial expression discussed in the book. These examples, like the writings represented in the comprehensive and informative *Arnold Anthology of Post-Colonial Literatures in English*, are drawn from Africa, Australia, Canada, the Caribbean, New Zealand and the South Pacific, South Asia and South-East Asia (Thieme, 1996). Helen Tiffin and Diana Brydon, in the introduction to their book *Decolonising Fictions*, carefully distinguish the various post-colonial conditions of neo-colonial, independent and neo-imperial nations and remark that:

> The United States, in particular, as the only ex-British colony fully to become an imperial power in its own right, can no longer easily be grouped with countries whose cultures are still largely determined by dependency. While its earlier literature displays patterns comparable to those of other post-colonial literatures, developments since the end of the First World War have meant that American literature is no longer peripheralised. (Brydon and Tiffin, 1993, pp. 13–14)

The weakness of reasoning such as this is that the image of American literature invoked in this connection is the white Anglo male-dominated canon that has been so thoroughly discredited by feminism and writers of colour – most notably African American, Native American and Hispanic critics. This is the conception of American literature embodied in the old-style early editions of the *Norton Anthology of American Literature* as opposed to the more recent editions of that same anthology or the racially diverse representation of American literary expression published as the *Heath Anthology of American Literature*. So an obsolete conception of American literature, as originating in Massachusetts with the Winthrop and Bradford settlements and developing through the American Renaissance of the 1850s to a twentieth-century Modernist-Postmodernist literature, is used to justify the exclusion of texts by

Native American, Chicano/a, and African American writers from the canon of colonial and post-colonial literature. This to me seems untenable. Writers of colour, publishing in America, face precisely the problems of marginalization and cultural erasure that confront post-colonial writers of Africa and the Caribbean, and indigenous post-colonial writers of Canada and Australia and New Zealand. Yet the latter are permitted recognition under the banner of the post-colonial.

The commonality of post-colonial experience is a starting point for many discussions of the field. For instance, Elleke Boehmer describes her book on colonial and post-colonial literature as being about the 'making of the globalized culture of the late twentieth century; about the entry of once-colonized Others into the West' (Boehmer, 1995, p. 7). Bruce King in his essay 'The Commonwealth Writer in Exile' argues that 'Commonwealth and other post-colonial literatures are the result of European expansion overseas and the meeting and conflict of two or more cultures' (King, cited in Rutherford, 1992, p. 39). Helen Tiffin, in the introduction to the collection of essays she edited with Ian Adam, *Past the Last Post*, describes post-colonialism as both a body of writing and a set of discursive practices that are grounded in the experience of colonial domination (Adam and Tiffin, 1991, p. vii). It is this concept of commonality, of issues and experiences that cut across national, racial and chronological divisions, and its methodological relevance to the post-colonial study of American ethnic writing that I want to consider in more detail.

COMPARATIVITY AS A POST-COLONIAL METHODOLOGY

Ashcroft, Griffiths and Tiffin offer a comparativist methodological framework among several models for post-colonial criticism, based upon national or regional, racial, or comparative principles. In fact, however, comparison provides the basis for each of these models: whether they are comparing two or more nations or regions (perhaps invader-settler or indigenous cultures); or shared ethnic subjectivities, as in the study of the black diaspora or Négritude; or whether they are comparing the sense of place, the experience of exile or dispossession or cultural erasure, the choice of language, the construction of colonial identity, and other themes common to the literatures of colonial and post-colonial societies. Comparison may constructively be made of the literary techniques used by colonial and post-colonial writers: the violation of Western principles of realism by use of allegory, magic realism, discontinuous narrative, irony, multiple languages, and so on.

The activity of writing itself in post-colonial cultures becomes the object of critical comparison. In the foundational work of Frantz Fanon and Albert Memmi the act of writing in a colonized culture is subject to both imaginative and social control that is mediated by the dialectic relationship between the colonizer and the colonized (Ashcroft et al., 1989, p. 29). This means then that the possibility of 'decolonizing' the culture, of moving beyond a culture of domination and submission, resides primarily in the activity of writing. One powerful strategy of resistance is to embrace the hybridity, the mixed cultural legacy, of post-colonial societies. Hybrid texts deliberately violate inherited Western conceptions of time and of received history, the perspective of the colonized 'Other' is installed and endowed with an authoritative voice. Racial, ethnic and cultural differences are, in this way, superficially foregrounded in order to challenge and resist the false concepts of cultural purity and authenticity that serve the interests of the colonizer. This powerful concept of hybridity is used by Karen Piper to question the claims of the US to be a 'multicultural' society; in Piper's analysis, claims to multiculturalism obscure the genuinely hybrid nature of United States culture while legitimizing the ongoing colonization of marginal ethnic groups. Piper thus makes the idea of hybridity available to other contributors, such as Marion Wynne-Davies, Gail Low, Debra Castillo and Candida Hepworth, and across the literatures they discuss – of America, Australia, New Zealand and the Caribbean.

In their powerful book *Decolonising Fictions*, Diana Brydon and Helen Tiffin offer a comparative study of post-coloniality in Australian, Canadian and Caribbean writing. While they acknowledge that every post-colonial situation is different, they emphasize the importance of comparison among post-colonial cultures if we are to study 'the transformations undergone by the English language and literary traditions' in these diverse locations (Brydon and Tiffin, 1993, p. 12). This emphasis moves away from previous attempts to discover points of difference between the metropolitan centre and its post-colonial outposts; attempts that must remain enmeshed in the discursive constructions of the metropolis that is the primary object of study. Brydon and Tiffin seek to replace the centre/margin model of post-colonial inquiry with a model based upon the matrix comprised of multiple lines of communication, each of equal privilege. It is a difficult but necessary endeavour and one that depends crucially upon the principle of informed comparativity as its prime method. The comparative methodology formulated by Diana Brydon and Helen Tiffin resists the danger of falling in with either one of the two major impulses that characterize contemporary post-colonial studies: old-style humanistic literary approaches and excessively theoretical discursive approaches. Gareth

Griffiths begins his essay 'The Post-Colonial Project: Critical Approaches and Problems' with an incisive description of these twin impulses that is worth quoting at some length:

> The study of post-coloniality has recently moved away from earlier literary models towards models of discourse analysis and textuality, in which the literary text is seen as only one kind of document in the larger archive ... of the post-colonial. Nevertheless, the literary text, and the emergence of literatures in English in post-colonial countries, even in these readings, continue to be viewed as crucial evidence, since writing, literacy, and the control of literary representations are vital in determining how the colonizers and colonized viewed each other, and how the colonized established or renewed their claims to a separate and distinctive cultural identity. (Griffiths, in King, 1996, p. 164)

Theories of colonial discourse analysis and textuality inform the basic assumptions of Elleke Boehmer's account of colonial and post-colonial literature. She discusses at length the common experiences of colonialism and post-colonialism that can form the basis of comparative study and the representation of these experiences, in her account, is through what she calls 'colonialist discourse', defined as 'that collection of symbolic practices, including textual codes and conventions and implied meanings, which Europe deployed in the process of its colonial expansion' to explain the strangeness of newly colonized lands and peoples (Boehmer, 1995, p. 50). The key feature of this discourse is the transferability of its organizing metaphors – the same images were used in different colonies to create the impression of a global space that was the colonized world of Empire (Boehmer, 1995, p. 52). Key themes inform this colonialist discourse: 'the introversion of the colonial mission, or colonial drama; the masculine aspect of that drama; the representation of other peoples; and the resistant incomprehensibility or unreadability of the colonized beyond' (Boehmer, 1995, p. 60). These themes are reinforced by motifs repeated in the writings of invaders and settlers: the mistranslation by colonials of metropolitan meanings and cultural practices; their fear of contamination, of the primitive; their colonial gaze fixed upon investigating, researching, and studying the different peoples and lands they encountered (Boehmer, 1995, pp. 69–71). This colonialist discourse and the dynamic textual strategies of dominance and submission to which it gave rise forms the basis for post-colonial strategies of resistance and for critical comparisons among these texts.

Colonial writing ignored the 'agency, diversity, resistance, thinking, voices' of native peoples. Colonized peoples are relegated to the category of the 'other' that, in Boehmer's words, signifies that which is unfamiliar and extraneous to a dominant subjectivity, the opposite or negative against which an authority is defined. The West thus conceived of its superiority relative to the perceived lack of power, self-consciousness, or ability to think and rule, of colonized peoples.

The colonial relationship, mediated through discourse, is not then a simple opposition between the colonizer and the colonized but a complex network of discursive, power, relationships (Boehmer, 1995, p. 23). Frantz Fanon, whose name appears insistently among the chapters in this collection, called upon the colonized to resist the psychological complexes, inferiority and paranoia that are created by the colonial system in order to perpetuate itself. The creation of a literature that would represent and be a part of the nationalist struggle, which would effectively call for the transformation of consciousness, would then be an authentically post-colonial literature. This style of post-colonial writing would be used 'to project autonomous identity, to re-create traditional, communal relationships within new national formations, or otherwise to promote socialist or collectivist forms of social bonding' (Boehmer, 1995, pp. 184–85). The literary forms taken by post-colonial resistance are many; contributors discuss some of the literary strategies used by canonical post-colonial writers such as Bessie Head, Miriam Tlali, Sally Morgan, Thomas Keneally, Fred D'Aguiar, Merle Collins, Yvonne Vera, Dambudzo Marechera, Tsitsi Dangarembga, and by American writers such as Toni Morrison, Gerald Vizenor, Thomas King, Gloria Anzaldúa, Sandra Cisneros, Denise Chávez.

The colonialist discourse described above offers a prescription of native peoples as abject, weak, feminine, above all 'other' to western European culture (Boehmer, 1995, p. 80). Colonial discourses deal with the 'otherness' or unreadability of native peoples in one of two primary ways: by projecting on to them inappropriate or irrelevant European images in disregard of their reality, or by displacing the experience of intransigence and inscrutability on to representations of the native (Boehmer, 1995, p. 95). Nativist resistance to these strategies depended in large part upon the inversion of imperial values in what are referred to as 'reverse' or 'counter' discourses that appropriate and reverse oppressive symbolic systems (Boehmer, 1995, p. 104). How Native counter-discourses turn colonial identities into positive self-images is discussed by Patricia Linton, Gina Wisker and Lee Schweninger. This strategy of 'writing back' against oppressive colonial discourses was a primary response to what Fanon described as the condition of the colonized: the subjective double vision or split cultural perception in relation to the metropolitan and local cultures to neither of which the colonized belonged. Counter-discursive strategies empowered the colonized to convert damaging stereotypes into positive images: to intrude upon and convert colonialist genres, to recover a displaced and fragmented native cultural integrity (Boehmer, 1995, pp. 119, 122), and Marion Wynne-Davies, Gina Wisker and Lee Schweninger demonstrate how this happens in relation to the indigenous peoples of Australia, New Zealand and the United States.

The issue of post-colonial voice, of whom is speaking in and through post-colonial writings – the colonizer or the colonized? – brings to prominence the field of subaltern studies, though specifically it is Gayatri Chakravorty Spivak's critique to which the present chapters address themselves. In her much-quoted essay 'Can the Subaltern Speak?' Spivak makes the case that subaltern studies start from a set of Western preconceptions concerning the nature of the historical subject it seeks to retrieve from colonialist discourses. She notes, 'The object of the group's investigation is itself defined as a difference from the elite. It is towards this structure that the research is oriented' (Spivak, 1988, p. 286). The difficulty of understanding colonized peoples as agents in their own histories when those histories come to us mediated by colonial texts is rivalled only by the difficulty faced by native writers who would represent subaltern subjectivity and history knowing that the primary audience for these writings is the colonizing West. Spivak concludes that this kind of historical retrieval is impossible; the subaltern cannot speak. Subaltern subjectivity, once represented in language, is enmeshed in a Western colonial discourse. Authenticity can be preserved only in the medium of silence, once articulated that authenticity is lost. Yet indigenous peoples do attempt to make that communication; writers like Gerald Vizenor and Thomas King and others seek that difficult historical understanding. The subaltern does strain to speak.

It is through complex manipulation of language that native writers make the attempt to speak and yet preserve their authenticity. Techniques of appropriation and subversion are used by native, and also creole, writers based upon a denial of the authority and purity of the discourse of the colonizers. To deny the power of the English language is to deny the control of communication that is exerted by the metropolitan centre. Dialect, allusions, narrative intrusions, the refusal to translate key words, the strategic use of vernacular expression, the switching between languages or 'code switching' – all serve to undermine the assumption that English is an especially privileged agent of colonial control (see Ashcroft et al., 1989, pp. 55–72). By subverting the access to meaning through English, these techniques represent a subversion of the imperial capacity to dictate cultural meaning. These techniques, then, create resistant texts, texts that resist easy assimilation to a Western perspective. This is the starting point for the chapters by Patricia Linton and Robert Gregory as they discuss the subversive narrative techniques used by Native American writers to produce resistant texts.

Across national, regional and ethnic boundaries, native counter-discourses criticize the colonial legacy but also accommodate and reinterpret it within the terms of a recuperated native cultural context (Boehmer, 1995, p. 187). This body of native writing does the crucial cultural work of mending historical ruptures and repairing historical memories; reclaiming the native right to name; representing native peoples 'as subjects of their own past'; and filling in the historical blank that represented the pre-conquest past in the terms of the colonizer (Boehmer, 1995, pp. 190-94). To take control of the narratives of the past is of obvious importance but equally important is the choice of the language in which this work of reclamation is performed. The language of the English colonizer carries a great deal of political as well as historical freight – for instance, in Aboriginal and Native American cultures the prohibition, last century, of native language use in government schools is remembered as a key strategy in the deliberate destruction of native cultures. 'Englishes' is the term used by the authors of *The Empire Writes Back* to describe the multiplicity of versions of the English language created and used by post-colonial writers. These various Englishes demand that we read from a cross-cultural perspective and learn to translate from one to another without recourse to some authoritative standard of linguistic measurement. But in *Decolonising Fictions* Diana Brydon and Helen Tiffin extend the significance of this term to encompass not just standard English linguistic meanings but the whole concept of standard meanings for texts as well. They write:

> Instead of arguing for a universal meaning for each of the texts we examine here, we show how each text takes on a new significance in light of the comparative context in which it is placed. ... We need a comparative perspective to maintain polyphony as a challenge to the universalising impetus of imperialism and to the homogenising drive of nationalism in its dominant form. (Brydon and Tiffin, 1993, p. 20)

The definition of American literature as synonymous with the literature of the American invader-settler culture seems to me to represent a triumph of the 'universalising impetus of imperialism' and the 'homogenising drive of [American] nationalism' as well. Only in a comparative framework can the colonial and post-colonial condition of ethnic communities within the borders of the United States, communities such as the Native American tribes, Chicano/as, Afro-Hispanic and African American communities, be recognized for precisely what they are. In comparison with the post-colonial expression of Australian Aboriginal writers, Canadian First Nations writers, New Zealand Maori writers, indigenous African writers, the work of American Indian writers assumes a new set of significances that is derived from a matrix of indigenous experience, and not from the stifling paradigm of sophisticated metropolitan centre versus primitive post-colonial margin. This is important, because the values assigned to literary expression in native cultures may share more in common with each other than with the values of Western literary representation. This is even more important than the shared experiences of imperial domination, cultural catastrophe, genocide, and erasure. That the voices should speak is more important, ultimately, than that of which they speak.

I would like to conclude with a reference to Arnold Krupat's work on indigenous writing and the canon, *The Voice in the Margin* (1989). Krupat observes that the political relationship between America and Native America has been one of avoidance while in cultural terms this relationship has been represented as one of absence, where America occupies the status of 'virgin land' untouched by native influence. Since its beginnings, then, American 'civilization' has been defined in opposition to the 'other', the Indian 'savage' (Krupat, 1989, p. 3). Correspondingly, the category of 'indigenous literature' is constructed out of the interaction between local, traditional, tribal 'Indian' literary modes and the dominant literary modes of the nation states in which it appears (Krupat, 1989, p. 214). Krupat goes on to describe 'ethnic literatures' as the product of the same dynamic but involving a minority group that is not historically indigenous; national literatures, he goes on, are then comprised of local and indigenous and national literary production within the territory of national formation, and the national canon is a selection from the available texts of these kinds (Krupat, 1989, p. 215). The distinctive nature of the national canon (and Krupat wants to argue further for a canon of international or, his preferred term, 'cosmopolitan' literature which as yet does not exist) is its representation of 'collective autobiography' (Krupat, 1989, p. 33). This crystallizes his approach to the issue of indigenous voice and the post-colonial canon. The literary canon is a symptom of a common culture and so expresses part of our selves as collective selves, contributing to a collective subjectivity. Krupat presents this common self not as accommodating or as opposing others but as informed by others and their experiences dialogically. This dialogic relationship has important social as well as literary implications, because the whole concept of the canon as a function of prior cultural values implies a social dimension.

For Krupat the difference between essentialist and instrumentalist views of the canon

> is the willingness of the former to produce knowledge coercively in the interest of perpetrating an order whose material effect – doubtless undesired, doubtless inevitable, and resolutely denied – is further suffering and degradation for the many. This is what is at stake in the argument over literature and the literary canon. (Krupat, 1989, p. 49)

High stakes indeed. Krupat calls for an approach to canon construction – the writing of this collective autobiography – that is informed by a commitment to heterodoxy and 'unity-in-difference' (Krupat, 1989, p. 52). His call to dialogism and polyphony is a 'refusal of imperial domination, and so of the West's claim legitimately to speak for all the rest' (Krupat, 1989, pp. 16–17). The comparative approach to the literatures of colonized and post-colonial peoples would seem to serve precisely this agenda; by opening the discourses of post-colonialism to all who share the experiences it describes, all who want to contribute to that collective post-colonial autobiography, we expand not only the post-colonial canon but also our collective human community.

The writings gathered here attempt to move this project forward by representing an expanded conception of the post-colonial that includes invader-settler cultures, indigenous cultures, and 'ethnic' cultures, of the United States and the ex-British Empire or British Commonwealth. They show, through the insistent repetition of key issues, problems and terminology of post-colonial theory and criticism, that here is a body of works, a polyphony, that speaks the voice of heterodoxy and makes sense as 'unity-in-difference'.

Works Cited

Adam, Ian and Helen Tiffin (eds), 1991. *Past the Last Post: Theorizing Post-Colonialism and Post-Modernism*, New York and London: Harvester Wheatsheaf.

Ashcroft, Bill, Gareth Griffiths and Helen Tiffin (eds), 1989. *The Empire Writes Back: Theory and Practice in Post-Colonial Literatures*, London & New York: Routledge.

Boehmer, Elleke, 1995. *Colonial and Postcolonial Literature: Migrant Metaphors*, Oxford and New York: Oxford University Press.

Brydon, Diana and Helen Tiffin, 1993. *Decolonising Fictions*, Sydney, Mundelstrup and Hebden Bridge: Dangeroo Press.

King, Bruce, 1996. *New National and Post-Colonial Literatures*, Oxford: Clarendon Press.

Krupat, Arnold, 1989. *The Voice in the Margin: Native American Literature and the Canon*, Berkeley, Los Angeles and Oxford: University of California Press.

Rutherford, Anna (ed.), 1992. *From Commonwealth to Post-Colonial*, Sydney, Mundelstrup and Coventry: Dangeroo Press.

Spivak, Gayatri Chakravorty, 1988. 'Can the Subaltern Speak?', in Cary Nelson and Lawrence Grossberg (eds), *Marxism and the Interpretation of Culture*, Urbana: University of Illinois Press, pp. 271–313.

Thieme, John (ed.), 1996. *The Arnold Anthology of Post-Colonial Literatures in English*, London: Edward Arnold.

2

Post-Colonialism in the United States: Diversity or Hybridity?

Karen Piper

In 1994, Fauziya Kassindja came to the United States at the age of 17, seeking asylum from the ritual of female genital mutilation in her West African home of Togo. Kassindja's case was denied, and she was thrown into prison as an illegal immigrant for nearly two years until her case was appealed. While in prison she survived prison riots, repeated strip-searches, and arbitrarily imposed periods of solitary confinement. The reason for her imprisonment? The judge did not believe her story 'to be credible', though Kassindja had supplied proof of widespread genital mutilation practices in Togo as well as evidence that there were no laws in Togo protecting women from this practice (see BIA, 1996). The judge, however, found Kassindja 'not credible' because, though she had testified that female genital mutilation was pervasive in Togo, 'she herself had not yet been mutilated' (BIA, 1996). The only acceptable evidence, it would appear, would be the very thing that Kassindja was trying to avoid; the only evidence the judge would allow was evidence written on her body. The logic of this argument may well have read, 'How can murder be pervasive if you are not dead?'

Kassindja's experience with US Immigration would seem to support Gayatri Spivak's assertion, 'There is no space from which the sexed subaltern subject can speak' (Spivak, 1988, p. 307). Spivak uses the example of suttee to demonstrate that there are two choices available to the subaltern woman: native patriarchy or colonial regime. Spivak addresses the problematic position of having either to reject a traditional practice condemned by the colonizers (and thus embrace colonial rule) or to accept this practice (and thus embrace patriarchy). With only these two options available to her, Spivak says, the subaltern woman must necessarily be co-opted into one symbolic order or another, neither of which suits her own experience. However, shall we say that she 'cannot speak' or rather that her voice is rewritten into a larger colonial or patriarchal narrative? And if it is written into a narrative that cannot comprehend her intentions, does that then not create a point of weakness in that very narrative? The judge's response to Kassindja, I propose, is indicative of the failure of the discourse of 'multiculturalism' within the US. His response to difference is that it must be either absolute or it is unrecognizable. The question, then, is why did her cultural difference – being from a culture that practises mutilation – become invisible to the judge? Kassindja, as a woman rebelling against her own cultural traditions, failed to be recognized by the judge – similarly, 'multiculturalism', in the academy, too often fails to accept the hybridity and fruitful cross-pollination of cultures. The reason for this failure, I propose, is the failure of the US to recognize its own *post-colonial* status – only by erasing its own colonial history has the US created a space for 'multiculturalism'. I will address the problematic nature of this space and suggest the ways in which reading minority literature as *post-colonial* may ultimately create a space in which the 'subaltern' can be heard.

Homi Bhabha has suggested that the voice of the colonized continually disrupts colonial discourse, producing a kind of 'hybridization' and disrupting 'the silent repression of native traditions'. This hybridization

> reveals the ambivalence at the source of traditional discourses on authority and enables a form of subversion, founded on that uncertainty, that turns the discursive conditions of dominance into the grounds of intervention. (Bhabha, 1994, p. 145)

In the case of Kassindja, rather than suggesting that there is 'no space' from which the subaltern can speak, we may instead examine the variety of problematic spaces from which she never stopped speaking and resisting. In other words, we must examine the site of her articulation rather than her silence. Where is she speaking? How is it received? The complex parameters of the space in which Kassindja chose to speak, her reasons for choosing this space, and its failure to assimilate her discourse are all revelatory of the nature of the humanitarian and multicultural ideals of the US. In the case of Kassindja, it was not that she was mute; rather, it was that the Board of Immigration was deaf. And this particular deafness is revealing of the 'ambivalence at the source of traditional [legal] discourses' in the US. The inability to hear anything other than Kassindja's *own* mutilation, which would cancel her reason for requesting refuge, reveals an essential and destabilizing ambivalence at the heart of this discourse. Bringing together the concepts of immigration, sexuality and hybridity, I will ultimately try to argue that the US – and its literature – should be read as 'post-colonial' rather than 'multicultural' in order to create a space where its immigrant and minority literatures may be better heard.

Is the US Post-Colonial?

There is a problematic separation, within post-colonial theory, between notions of 'diversity' and 'hybridity'. The nature of this division is easily analysed in the context of the US. Bhabha has advocated conceptualizing 'an *inter*-national culture, based not on the exoticism or multiculturalism of the *diversity* of cultures, but on the inscription and articulation of culture's *hybridity*' (Bhabha, 1994, p. 209). Bhabha equates 'diversity' with a kind of 'multiculturalism'; conversely 'hybridity' is equated with 'inter-' or 'transnationalism'. But beyond this simple equation, Bhabha's argument for the acknowledgment of *hybrid* cultures and subjectivities comes dangerously close to rearticulating the 'melting pot' ideology that was prevalent prior to the emergence of the term 'multiculturalism' in the 1980s, a term that was coined by the Before Columbus Foundation. 'Multiculturalism', in direct conflict with the concept of hybridity, is often discussed as a 'celebration' of ethnic diversity or a 'struggle to keep cultural identity intact' in a *hybrid* environment; in contrast, cultures are never *intact* (Stovall).

Bhabha claims that *multiculturalism* is a form of *exoticism*, and I propose that it is because of this exoticism that Kassindja's judge failed to hear her. Because Kassindja was not marked as different by participating in the exotic practice of clitoridectomy, the judge failed to accept her difference. While, on the one hand, we can read this misapprehension as an inability to recognize difference, we can also read the judge's reaction as containing a certain fascination with the acts of 'barbarism' that he associates with Africa – a sublimated desire to witness a clitoridectomy. David Spurr, in *The Rhetoric of Empire*, has suggested that a certain fascination and attraction toward acts considered 'barbaric' continually occurs within colonial discourse. Spurr claims that as areas that were traditionally viewed as 'savage' or 'wild' were discovered, mapped and settled, a 'progressive despatialization of the concept of wildness' (Spurr, 1993, p. 77) occurred, so that 'an interiorization of savagery' in the unconscious took place. In this sense, cultural practices that are considered 'savage' become a part of the Euro-American unconscious to the point that this very 'savagery' or 'wildness' became, in many ways, a metaphor for sexuality. Interestingly, the association of clitoridectomy with Africa is entirely a false one, for it is a Muslim rather than a tribal practice; however, the judge's complete lack of awareness about the issues surrounding female genital mutilation make this distinction a mute point. The judge, after supposedly reading the case file, asked, 'What is FGM?' (the initials that are commonly used for female genital mutilation). The appeals lawyer stated, 'It is inconceivable that any judge that could have read this record could ask what is FGM? FGM is all over this record' (see BIA, 1996).

This desire for 'savagery', then, could be mixed with an aversion to the qualities of the 'savage – dishonesty, suspicion, superstition, lack of self-discipline' (BIA, 1996). Though the judge repeatedly calls her story 'incredible', he does not provide reasons for his disbelief. Besides finding the pervasiveness of female genital mutilation 'incredible', the judge also did not believe that Kassindja could have been forcibly separated from her mother after her father's death and thus become victim to an arranged marriage by her aunt. The judge never gave a reason for why this separation was incredible, and the appeals lawyer suggested,

> One can only assume that the Immigration Judge did not believe Ms. Kasinga on this point because that's not how family life usually works in the United States ... . But Togo is not the United States and the judge's reliance upon US cultural norms to judge Ms. Kasinga's credibility regarding the whereabouts of her mother was totally improper. (BIA, 1996)

The judge, I propose, projects a kind of 'savagery' upon Kassindja through his interest in clitoridectomy; failing to supply evidence to fulfil his desire, he instead views her as American. The evidence against her is that her family does not follow the mandates of American 'family values'. If she does not want to be African and suffer genital mutilation, she must be already American at heart. However, this conflicted approach to Kassindja's presence places her in a position where anything she may say will automatically be suspect. Not yet American, but not *really* African, Kassindja is exiled to the only space the judge saw available to her: a detention centre.

Kassindja's story brings up problems within the rhetoric of multiculturalism. There is, on the one hand, the problem that multiculturalism threatens to create a kind of ethnic essentialism, where the supposed *purity* of cultural practices – even genital mutilation – must be maintained and supported in order for that culture to be recognized as *authentic*. This kind of essentialism has been criticized by Salman Rushdie, who wrote,

> 'Authenticity' is the respectable child of old-fashioned exoticism. It demands that sources, forms, style, language and symbol all derive from a supposedly unbroken and homogenous tradition. Or else. (Rushdie, 1991, p. 67)

Ironically, the kind of essentialism that 'multiculturalism' often demands runs in direct contrast to the economic and property demands of capitalism in the US. It is not as if, upon entering the US, immigrants are told, 'Okay, we are a multicultural democracy ... here is an equal share of our land base and economy.' Instead, while cultural rituals and holidays may be maintained, they are entirely deterritorialized. 'Multiculturalism', in fact, is based upon the notion of equal representation and so is easily adapted to the supposed 'democratic' ideals of the US. Precluding alternative forms of land tenure, multiculturalism instead maintains individualistic forms of private property, essentially leaving the land 'barons' intact while labelling, and thereby creating, a labour force of 'serfs'. These alternative land tenures, however, may be the basis of cultures and therefore essential to their preservation. 'Multiculturalism', therefore, places the non-Anglo subject in the impossible position of having to preserve difference without a land base or means of survival – besides working at Taco Bell. 'Multiculturalism' maintains a labour force, a literature, and a form of discursive celebration. It is what Gilles Deleuze and Félix Guattari have called a form of 'reterritorialization', or an artificially resurrected control or check to the deterritorialized flows of capitalism. The *idea* of culture is resurrected, in all its difference, to keep in check any resistance to the material reality of the 'deterritorialized' landscape of capitalism (Deleuze and Guattari, 1983, pp. 145–261).

This is why the US has such trouble with its own indigenous subjects: the material reality of the reservation resists the simple reading of Native American literature as 'ethnic' or 'multicultural'. Reservations are separated from American culture, giving Native Americans an alternative economic system and communal identity that cannot be co-opted into the US system of multiculturalism. Because it cannot be co-opted, Native Americans are often preserved and representationally frozen in time (in headdress and moccasins) while their real presence is forgotten or ignored. Deleuze and Guattari have suggested that reservations function as sites of reterritorialization – or codes of cultural confinement – but even this limited land base is threatening to the ideals of multiculturalism, which requires an 'equality' (i.e. segregation) of individuals and so cannot accept the communal space of the reservation.

And here is the paradox of multiculturalism in the US: while attempting to maintain minority literatures as intact cultural sites, the discourse of multiculturalism is based upon 'equal representation' in its own literary canon. Based upon the model of democratic representation, multiculturalism maintains a deterritorialized individualism that limits the means to cultural expression. That is, diversity in the US can *only* be expressed through rituals or holidays – ceremonial dances, Kwanzaa, Cinco de Mayo. Literature also becomes a kind of coinage for expressing cultural difference; in the controlled space of the academy, difference can be celebrated without threatening established territorial or economic divisions between indigenous or Anglo or 'other' – these, in multicultural terms, are all *equal*. The US can pride itself in these exhibitions of 'multiculturalism', whereas, in reality, the only thing the US will tolerate is individual contributions to a rising gross national product. Multiculturalism, therefore, is a dangerous term for two reasons: first, it attempts to preserve cultures in a primordial state as objects for analysis; and second, it demands, conversely, that immigrants to the US adapt to its market needs. In ignoring the territorial divisions created by its colonial history, America's version of 'multiculturalism' becomes problematic and, at best, superficial. The US is *not* a multicultural environment; it is a settler-invader territory that has taken property from the indigenous inhabitants and moulded it to the needs of global capitalism. The literature of the US, therefore, should be read as a part of the global 'post-colonial canon' rather than as an internalized expression of multicultural difference.

The issue of whether or not the US should be defined as 'post-colonial', however, revolves less around the status of the US than the definition of the term. 'Post-colonial', in my definition, does not mean simply 'after colonialism' or 'resisting colonialism'. There is no 'after' to the territorial, judicial and economic codes generated by colonization. Rather, I define 'post-colonialism' as 'after the imprint of colonialism'. In this sense, post-colonialism began the moment the colonizer established his presence on foreign soil and continues through to today. 'Colonialism' in this respect may seem to be a useless term. On the contrary, I would suggest that colonialism involves all the machinations of power that lead to a post-colonial environment: it is the economic, social, and military policy which subjects one territory to another through the institution of foreign dependencies. 'Colonialism' in this sense is the agent; 'post-colonialism' is the result. The US, then, is post-colonial in the sense that its fundamental identity is wrapped in a colonizing project – whether settler or indigenous, the inhabitants of the US have been impacted by the colonial ideal of resource 'development' or exploitation. This is how Deleuze and Guattari describe America: 'It proceeds both by internal exterminations and liquidations (not only the Indians but also the farmers, etc.), and by successive waves of immigration from the outside' (Deleuze and Guattari, 1983, p. 20). It is only in forgetting these exterminations that a kind of immigrant 'multiculturalism' becomes a reality.

Discussions of the US as 'post-colonial' have either focused on its independence from Britain or examined its neo-colonial empire in the form of multinational corporations. In *The Empire Writes Back*, Bill Ashcroft, Gareth Griffiths and Helen Tiffin suggest that the US may be considered post-colonial only to the extent that it has established its own cultural identity. They write, 'The first task seems to be to establish that the texts can be shown to constitute a literature separate from that of the metropolitan culture', thus demonstrating an 'independent cultural identity' (Ashcroft et al., 1989, p. 133).

Ashcroft, Griffiths and Tiffin claim that in the settler colonies (the United States, Canada, Australia and New Zealand) the critical questions raised in literary texts 'highlight some of the basic tensions which exist in all post-colonial literatures' (Ashcroft et al., 1989, p. 135). Edward Said, in *Culture and Imperialism*, advocates the alternate position of treating the US as an imperial power to the extent that it has forced and maintained a dominant position in global politics. Similarly, Jenny Sharpe, in her essay 'Is the United States Postcolonial?', describes the US as a part of a transnational discourse on 'global capitalism and the international division of labor' (Sharpe, 1995). And Anne McClintock, in 'The Angel of Progress: Pitfalls of the Term 'Post-colonialism', claims that the US performs a kind of 'imperialism-without-colonies' by which 'the power of US finance capital and huge multi-nationals to direct the flows of capital, commodities, armaments and media information around the world can have an impact as massive as any colonial regime' (McClintock, 1993, p. 296). This concept of 'imperialism-without-colonies', however, does not take into account either the actual dependencies of the US in the form of Puerto Rico, the Marshall Islands, and Guam, or the internal colonization of its indigenous inhabitants. Both of these readings – post-colonial or neo-colonial – make light of the fact that the US is still actively displacing indigenous people and is therefore actively colonial. The US does not suddenly become 'post-colonial' simply by virtue of redefining its overseas connections with England. However, the US is postcolonial in the sense that it is largely defined by 'internal exterminations' and 'successive waves of immigration'. The US is post-colonial if the term is used (as Ashcroft, Griffiths and Tiffin have done) to designate the time period 'from the moment of colonisation to the present day' (Ashcroft et al., 1989, p. xv).

Immigration as a Masculine Enterprise

The notion of 'assimilation' was, for centuries, the focal point for American immigrants. Whether Swedish, Irish, French or British, the idea of 'becoming American' meant leaving behind ethnic distinctions in order to embrace 'American' identity. Frederick Jackson Turner, in 'The Significance of the Frontier in American History', suggests that this 'American' identity could be achieved only by a process of literally stripping the European clothes from the body. He wrote,

> The wilderness masters the colonist. It finds him a European in dress, industries, tolls, modes of travel, and thought. ... It strips off the garments of civilization and arrays him in the hunting shirt and moccasin. (Turner, 1921, p. 3)

The notion of 'wilderness' would prove to be essential in creating national identity, providing a site reason and a site to forsake European identity in favour of indigeneity. Although Native Americans were excluded from citizenship and ownership because they did not fence or develop their land, they were considered essential in providing the foundations for American identity. Turner described the relation of the colonist to the wilderness: 'He [the colonist] must accept the conditions which it [the wilderness] furnishes, or perish, and so he fits himself into the Indian clearings and follows the Indians trails' (Turner, 1921, p. 3). If Indians provided guides to America, however, they were also considered dispensable once 'America' was achieved. Indians were treated as that scaffolding or support that would be abolished once the building was erect. In this sense, hybridity became erased from the construct of American identity.

If 'whiteness' or ethnic erasure was ultimately the ideal of immigration, the space of the immigrant was also distinctly gendered as male. The 'wilderness' or 'frontier' became a kind of production line for a masculine form of national identity. Theodore Roosevelt claimed that 'the only national life which is really worth leading' would be one without 'the over-civilized man, who has lost the great fighting, masterful virtues' and 'the man of dull mind, whose soul is incapable of feeling the mighty lift that thrills "stern men with empires in their brains"' (Roosevelt, 1998, vol. VIII, p. 5). Only by entering the wilderness, killing the Indians and fencing the land could this kind of 'virile' Americanism be achieved; ironically, the loss of wilderness was perpetually threatening to eliminate this masculinity. Roosevelt wrote, 'Hardy outdoor sports, like hunting, are in themselves of no small value to the National character and should be encouraged in every way' (Roosevelt, 1998, vol. V, p. 8). For Roosevelt, the way of preserving the 'wilderness experience', which he believed made *men*, was to preserve National Parks and Monuments. These areas, however, were closed to settlement, and so this frontier-generated identity became a kind of permanent homelessness. According to Turner, the frontier was a 'death to localism', creating a form of mobility that could only be circumscribed by the rhetoric of nationalism.

Roosevelt defined the *Übermensch* of the American frontier. The genocide of American Indians became, for him, a necessary component of a national identity wrapped in virility:

> Every submersion or displacement of an inferior race ... by a superior race, means the infliction and sufferings of hideous woes and misery. It is a sad and dreadful thing that there should be of necessity such throes of agony; and yet they are the birth-pangs of a new and vigorous people. (Roosevelt, 1968, p. 19)

In Europe, Friedrich Nietzsche was also describing these birth-pangs:

> Let Europe relieve itself of the fourth part of its inhabitants! What at home began to degenerate into dangerous discontent and criminal tendencies will, once outside, gain a wild and beautiful naturalness and be called heroism. (Nietzsche, 1980, p. 91)

Europe is spoken of in this passage as in need of ritual expulsion; in this way, the degenerate elements of society would be purged or excreted. Only 'outside' would these criminal elements be put to good use – in the colonies? The 'outsideness' of this place would suggest going abroad into a new and untamed continent ready to absorb (untamed) criminality within its own 'wild' borders. What Roosevelt's 'new and vigorous people' and Nietzsche's 'heroes' have in common is the necessity of 'wild' places for acts of heroism. When the 'inferior races' can no longer be 'displaced' because there is no land left to move them on to, Roosevelt begins to take the opposite tactic of preserving lands where Indians cannot live, wilderness preserves that also functions as sites for the preservation of 'whiteness'.

Immigration, at the turn of the century, meant a loss of ethnic history, an assimilation that would be forced by the wilderness itself; multiculturalism today, in contrast, has attempted to preserve difference. And yet, preserving an enforceable difference ('or else') that refuses to recognize hybridity leads to an oppressive environment and a 'deafened' history. On the other hand, there is a dangerously fine line in the US between 'hybridity' and 'assimilation'. Multicultural differences, I propose, cannot be maintained without an acknowledgment of post-colonial territoriality. Individually owned, private, fenced land is the only kind of culture in the US – aside from detention camps, reservations, squatter societies and 'public' lands. And, as I have just demonstrated, 'public' lands are either for the purpose of resource extraction or for maintaining the 'frontier' experience that produced masculine Americanism. Do public lands preserve the wilderness, or do they preserve the concept of 'whiteness'? One need only look at the statistics on the use of National Parks by African Americans, Mexican Americans, or Native Americans to answer this question.

The 'immigration = virility' equation that people like Turner, Nietzsche and Roosevelt have created works against Kassindja as a female immigrant. If becoming-American, historically, has been tied to a rhetoric of becoming-male, then the occupation of this space by a woman becomes doubly difficult. This is interesting when we contemplate the judge's interest in the 'mutilation' of Kassindja's genitals. I propose that this bizarre reference by the judge reveals the impossible space created for Kassindja as a refugee from genital mutilation. The judge can only accept Kassindja as a *desexualized* subject and thus nearer to the masculine ideal. For this reason, she would only be allowed to speak through her own clitoridectomy. The closest that a woman can come to occupying the space of an American subject, this would suggest, is to be genderless.

THE PLEASURE PRINCIPLE

Hélène Cixous has written, 'Too bad for them if they fall apart upon discovering that women aren't men … . But isn't this fear convenient for them? Wouldn't the worst be, isn't the worst, in truth that women aren't castrated?' (Cixous, 1986, p. 317). It was precisely at the moment of discovering that Kassindja was a *woman*, I propose, that the rhetoric of the judge 'fell apart' – the American legal system was literally disassembled by Kassindja's claim to her own sexuality. 'Now, I-woman am going to blow up the Law', Cixous wrote, 'an explosion henceforth possible and ineluctable' (Cixous, 1986, p. 320). Kassindja, in coming to America, refused to give up her body – even though it would not be accepted even on American shores. 'So few women have as yet won back their body', Cixous wrote, but Kassindja refused to give up the right to her own pleasure. And this was a victory not only for women and their sexuality, but also for a discourse that was unable to create a space for Kassindja. Caught between assimilation and authenticity, Kassindja fought to occupy that hybrid space that is not male and still is wild. Kassindja's body split the legal discourse that would entrap her, revealing its bankrupt lack of hearing and forcing it to recognize, instead, the language of her bodily needs.

Kassindja's story has an interesting ending. In 1996, the 23-year-old lawyer Layli Miller Bashir took up Kassindja's case, and she was released from prison. But in that same year Bill Clinton signed into law an immigration bill that would restrict people like Kassindja from again succeeding. A New York lawyer, Stanley Mailman, explained: 'The law sets us back 100 years. ... Decades of reasonable court decisions have been overturned in the effort to remove from immigration judges the discretion to administer the immigration law with mercy' (Lewis, 1997). The new law prohibits people who arrive in the US without proper papers to seek asylum from persecution. According to Anthony Lewis, 'It will have devastating effects on asylum applicants like Fauziya Kassindja' (Lewis, 1997). Kassindja has gone on to write a very successful book and now lives in Alexandria, Virginia; but for women 'like Fauziya' more repressive laws now make it even more impossible for their stories to be heard.

Benita Parry wrote of the moment 'when the scenario written by colonialism is given a performance by the native that estranges and undermines the colonialist script' (Parry, 1995, p. 42). Kassindja came to America with a performance the immigration judge was unable to process. Her reason for coming to America is revealing of the international mythology surrounding the US as a 'humanitarian' country. Initially, Kassindja fled to Germany, but because she could not speak the language, she decided to move to an English-speaking country. When a friend of hers suggested she move to England, she replied, 'I don't know anything about Britain. I don't even know where it is' (Kassindja and Bashir, 1988, p. 144). But when asked to think of America, she wrote:

> [I]t was a good country from what I knew. I'd seen a lot of news reports at school about how America was always helping the needy, feeding hungry children, sending aid to refugees. I didn't know any Americans but they seemed like generous kindhearted people. My teachers at school ... said people believed in justice in America. (Kassindja and Bashir, 1988, p. 146).

Kassindja's sense of this media-produced 'America' is instantly destabilized when she reaches the US. After requesting political asylum, she is immediately taken to a back room at the airport's immigration office, where she is asked to strip naked, squat and cough (Kassindja and Bashir, 1988, p. 171).

Kassindja told the immigration officer she was from Togo, but the immigration officer did not believe her because she could not speak French nor correctly draw the Togo flag (she put a star in the wrong corner). The officer wrote in his report: 'Subject claims to be born in Togo. Subject has no knowledge of Togo (geography/language). Subject does not speak French. ... Subject does not know what the flag of Togo looks like or what the national colors are' (Kassindja and Bashir, 1988, p. 169). Though Kassindja was born in a French-speaking country, she did not speak French because her father sent her to an English-speaking school within walking distance across the border in Ghana. Also, French was not widely spoken outside the capital of Togo, where tribal languages were dominant. Kassindja's tribal affiliations were much stronger than her national affiliation, as she explained, 'I love my country and I am proud of being Togolese, but not in the same bone-deep, blood-thick way I am proud of being Tchamba-Koussountu' (Kassindja and Bashir, 1988, p. 9). What it meant to be from 'Togo' was itself a complex issue. In the late nineteenth century Germany invaded this part of West Africa and created 'Togoland', which was later invaded by the French and British during the First World War. The country was then divided, with the British taking the western part and adding it to Ghana, and the French taking the eastern part, which became Togo (Kassindja and Bashir, 1988, p. 8). Kassindja explained her complex feeling toward her country:

> Imagine what it was like for people of my father's generation to wake up one day in the same place their family had been living for generations and find themselves living in a country that didn't exist the day before. Or think what it must have been like to discover that the area just to the west of you, where some of your relatives live, is a different country now. The land didn't change, the people didn't change, but the country and its government did. (Kassindja and Bashir, 1988, p. 9)

For the immigration officers, however, the only reality was this colonial fiction of 'Togoland' (which 'didn't exist the day before') and so they were unable to see or accept the true identity of Kassindja. They even wrote down her name incorrectly as 'Kassinga', a misnomer that persisted in the media and the courts until the release of her own book. Surrounded by stereotypes of what it meant to be 'Togolese', Kassindja's own performance (her drawing of the flag, etc.) destabilized these stereotypes and thus weakened the colonial discourse that surrounded her. Kassindja's 'performance' ultimately weakened the neo-colonial rhetoric of the US as a country that is always 'helping the needy'. Instantly disillusioned, Kassindja portrays herself as a woman who was insulted, humiliated and threatened, first by the immigration officers and later by her own judge.

While in prison, Kassindja did everything in her power to get back home, terrified by her realization of what 'America' really meant. Labelled a 'Nigerian' by the immigration officers who believed she only wanted to come to the US to study, Kassindja was told she would be happy in prison because there were 'other Africans' there. Instead,

Kassindja twice wrote to the prison counsellor requesting to be sent home, even after her appeal trial began. She said, 'My legal team would be upset when they heard about what I've done, but I had to listen to my own heart. I knew they'd try to talk me out of it. ... They would try to convince me to stay for other people's sake' (Kassindja and Bashir, 1988, p. 5). Kassindja wrote,

> I needed to go home before I forgot my home, forgot where I came from, who I was, who my people were. My mother and father had disappeared, my father into the realm beyond life, my mother I know not where. Oh, I had to go home, before everything disappeared, before I lost everything and everybody I had ever cared about. I had to go home before I lost myself, too. (Kassindja and Bashir, 1988, p. 6)

Surrounded by who people *think* she is, whether Nigerian or women's rights activist, Kassindja's narrative resounds with an overwhelming homesickness, even after her release.

'The subaltern as female cannot be heard or read', Spivak once asserted (Spivak, 1988, p. 308). While I would agree with this statement on the surface – the patriarchal and colonial discourses surrounding and co-opting her are strong – I believe this lack of hearing is more revelatory of a fatal flaw in the colonial 'script' than a disability on the part of the subaltern. The question should be, why is the patriarchal order unable to hear the subaltern woman? It is interesting that Spivak places the 'subaltern' in the position of passive object in the structure of her very sentence. If, instead, we invert this sentence, we begin to see its true subject: 'The elite (colonial/patriarchal) subject cannot hear or read the female subaltern.'

Kassindja entered the US believing it would be a place that supported global humanitarian values. Her own attorney suggested, 'America is known around the world as a defender of liberty and a haven for the oppressed' (Kassindja and Bashir, 1988, p. 510). Kassindja's country had been colonized by the French, German and British, but it was the English language that would ultimately bring her to America, a language she had learned to help keep her father's business solvent. The power of the English language as an economic language, then, played a large role in the trajectory of Kassindja's experience. In this sense, the transnational power of the English language, along with the media-spread mythology of America's tolerant multiculturalism, brought Kassindja to America. The US, however, could only understand either the story of African nationalism (which would have her speak French and draw her own flag) or Muslim fundamentalism (which would have her mutilated). Caught between these two realms, Kassindja's own English was rendered incomprehensible to the judicial system. The only space it could allow for this woman, therefore, was incarceration. By erasing its own colonial past while celebrating the values of 'multiculturalism' and 'democracy', the US creates a vast blind spot in its own international vision. The lesson of Kassindja's experience can be applied to the academic realm as well. Minority 'texts' in the US need to be read for their colonial historicity rather than their multicultural difference. Whether 'reading' slave narratives, Native American films, Chicano/a murals projects, or African-American rap lyrics, the history of US colonization – internationally and domestically – can shed light on these reformulations of 'post-colonial' identity. Until then, the mythology of American 'tolerance' may continue to spread, drawing people like Kassindja into a conflicted colonial and patriarchal space. Kassindja's story, ironically, has since been aired on CNN, *60 Minutes* and *World News Tonight* – and now contributes to the mythology of this tolerance, bringing more women to a country that has become even more solidified against their entrance.

Works Cited

Ashcroft, Bill, Gareth Griffiths and Helen Tiffin, 1989. *The Empire Writes Back: Theory and Practice in Post-Colonial Literature*, London and New York: Routledge.

Bhabha, Homi, 1994. *The Location of Culture*, New York: Routledge.

BIA 1996. *Matter of Kassindja*, Interim Decision 3278. For a complete transcript, see <http://www.courttv.com/library/rights/mutilation.htmlKassindja>

BIA, 1996. *Matter of Kassinga,* Appeal Hearing A 73 479 695.

Cixous, Hélène, 1986. 'The Laugh of the Medusa', in *Critical Theory since 1965*, Hazard Adams and Leroy Searle (eds), Tallahassee: Florida State University Press.

Deleuze, Gilles and Félix Guattari, 1983. *Anti-Oedipus: Capitalism and Schizophrenia*, trans. Robert Hurley, Mark Seem and Helen R. Lane, Minneapolis: University of Minnesota Press.

Kassindja, Fauziya and Layli Miller Bashir, 1988. *Do They Hear You When You Cry*, New York: Delacorte Press.

Lewis, Anthony, 1997. 'Immigration Law Injustices are Mounting', *The Standard-Times*, New Bedford, MA, 2 March.

McClintock, Anne, 1993. 'The Angel of Progress: Pitfalls of the Term "Post-colonialism"', in *Colonial Discourse and Post-Colonial Theory: A Reader*, Patrick Williams and Laura Chrisman (eds), New York: Harvester Wheatsheaf, pp. 291–304.

Nietzsche, Friedrich Wilhelm, 1980. *The Portable Nietzsche*, trans. Walter Kaufmann, New York: Viking Press.

Parry, Benita, 1995. 'Problems in Current Theories of Colonial Discourse', in *The Post-Colonial Studies Reader*, Bill Ashcroft, Gareth Griffiths and Helen Tiffin (eds), London and New York: Routledge, pp. 36–44.

Roosevelt, Theodore, 1968. *On Race, Riots, Reds, Crime*, ed. Archibald Roosevelt, Metairie, Louisiana: Sons of Liberty.

Roosevelt, Theodore, 1998. *Selected Works of Theodore Roosevelt*, New York: New Bartleby Library.

Rushdie, Salman, 1991. *Imaginary Homelands: Essays and Criticism, 1981–1991*, London: Granta Books.

Said, Edward W., 1994, *Culture and Imperialism*, London: Vintage.

Sharpe, Jenny, 1995. 'Is the United States Postcolonial? Transnationalism, Immigration, and Race', *Diaspora: A Journal of Transnational Studies* 4 (Fall), pp. 181–97.

Spivak, Gayatri Chakravorty, 1988. 'Can the Subaltern Speak?', in Cary Nelson and Lawrence Grossberg (eds), *Marxism and the Interpretation of Culture*, Urbana: University of Illinois Press, pp. 271–313.

Spurr, David, 1993. *The Rhetoric of Empire: Colonial Discourse in Journalism, Travel Writing, and Imperial Administration*, Durham, N.C.: Duke University Press.

Stovall, Dennis. This quotation is taken from the press release for *Homeground*, Kathryn Trueblood and Linda Stovall (eds), the first American Literature Series title by the Before Columbus Foundation; see http://www.mpec.org/homegpr.html

Turner, Frederick Jackson, 1921. *The Frontier in American History*, New York: Henry Holt and Company.

3

Ethical Reading and Resistant Texts

Patricia Linton

Interest in ethnic and post-colonial literature – both inside the academy and out – renews questions about what it means to be a 'good' reader. The ideal readership for many contemporary ethnic and post-colonial texts is quite narrow, comprised of cultural insiders who are also familiar with the forms and discourses privileged in the traditional Euro-American canon. Most readers who take up an ethnic or post-colonial text, however, are in one respect or another not fully competent to comprehend it. In the case of prose fiction, enculturated ethnic readers who understand the referential world of the narrative may be distanced by the form of the contemporary novel, a genre inscribed with a complex of Western ideas concerning identity, authorship and ways of knowing. Eurocentric readers, on the other hand, often fail to understand either the core experiences or the epistemology and subjectivity represented in ethnic and post-colonial fiction.

Nevertheless, most readers make a good-faith effort to understand the world of the text. Peter Rabinowitz, in his study *Before Reading*, argues that the well-trained and well-intentioned reader aims to read as a member of the implied author's interpretative community (Rabinowitz, 1987, pp. 20–23). This is true, he believes, even when readers know that they do not share the author's worldview and that their construction of the author's intention may be mistaken in important respects. Rabinowitz suggests that an implied contract exists between writers and readers: writers try to provide the cues readers need to comprehend the text, and readers make an effort to become (at least initially) the reader anticipated by the text, to join the implied author's social/interpretative community at least as the first stage of their response to the text (Rabinowitz, 1987, pp. 23, 42–43). The argument that readers try to glean from the text their best approximation of the author's intention does not ignore the intricacies of the actual negotiations that take place in the reading process. Rabinowitz specifically rejects the idea that the authorial intention comprises the whole meaning of a text or that recovering the intended meaning is the only objective of interpretation (Rabinowitz, 1987, p. 29). Rather, his analysis supposes – and I think this is a particularly important observation for the reading of ethnic and post-colonial texts – that most reading begins with a certain openness and a willingness to be tutored by the text.

Whether it is in fact possible for readers to read as members of the authorial audience is a more complicated issue, particularly so in the case of ethnic, post-colonial and transnational texts – in any text in which alterity is an issue. Rabinowitz notes that much of what the reader needs to know in order to read as a member of the authorial audience must be acquired before the encounter with the text: '[L]iterary conventions are not in the text waiting to be uncovered, but in fact *precede* the text and make discovery possible in the first place' (Rabinowitz, 1987, p. 27). Readers who are members of a social/interpretative community develop habits of reading that reflect shared cultural and literary norms, habits that vary widely, not only on the basis of ethnicity or nationality but also on the basis of such factors as age, gender, class and education.

Thus, Native American novelist and critic Louis Owens analyses the 'dizzying' complexity of relationships between writers and readers of Native texts (Owens, 1992, p. 14). A Native novelist, Owens asserts, writes *for* the Native reader; nevertheless, a writer who seeks publication certainly anticipates a significant non-Native readership. From the perspective of the Native American community, the task the Native novelist undertakes is inherently counter-cultural: an oral, collective, ritual, non-linear narrative tradition must be rendered in a discourse developed to embody a wholly different cultural ideology.

> The Native American novelist works in a medium for which no close Indian prototype exists. The novelist must therefore rely upon story and myth but graft the thematic and structural principles found therein upon the 'foreign' (though infinitely flexible) and intensely egocentric genre of the written prose narrative, or novel. (Owens, 1992, p. 10)

The text becomes a 'richly hybridized dialogue' addressing cultural insiders and outsiders with different kinds and degrees of privilege. As Owens comments, 'The result of this exquisite balancing act is a matrix of incredible heteroglossia and linguistic torsions and an intensely political situation' (Owens, 1992, p. 15). While Owens suggests that the Native writer is attentive to the needs of different categories of readers, his analysis also implies that the positioning of the non-Native reader is particularly vexed.

Critically informed Eurocentric readers may ignore a 'local' context that excludes them, in favour of an overarching paradigm that seems to account adequately for the differences and disruptions in ethnic narratives. A brief example that makes the point is an incident that occurs in the 1990 novel *Mean Spirit*, by Native American poet and novelist Linda Hogan. The Osage tribe at the centre of this predominantly realistic novel shares with other North American tribes the cultural concept of 'medicine': objects or practices with extraordinary power, physical and spiritual. The concept first assumes strategic importance in the narrative as Joe Billy, a minister in two faiths, the Christian and the Osage, becomes increasing uncomfortable with his dual role. With his confidence in Western society and Western religion dying, Joe Billy spends many nights pacing and praying:

> Joe Billy prayed in his study, holding his father's bat medicine bundle in his hands. He felt it speaking to him. It was urgent, he knew, even though he didn't understand what was being said from inside the leather bag. Something was stirring in there. (Hogan, 1990, p. 137)

At first, the medicine bundle's 'speaking and stirring' poses a relatively modest challenge to Euro-American ideology because those terms can be taken on more than one level. The bundle contains a private (and therefore unspecified) collection of objects which have both cultural and personal significance; its 'speaking' can be interpreted as the emotional and intellectual pull of Joe Billy's heritage. But as the narrative continues, Billy's white wife, who is alien to the community and to Native American modes of thinking, observes its movement as well:

> She saw her husband asleep in the wooden chair. His head dropped forward, and in his hands he held a leather pouch. Inside it, Martha could see that something was moving. The sight of it bumping and turning in Joe Billy's hands startled her and she drew in such a frightened breath that Joe Billy woke and looked from her blue eyes to the moving bundle that he held.
> 'What's in there?' Martha asked.
> He blinked at her and all he could really say was, 'It's the older world, wanting out'. (Hogan, 1990, p. 138)

The fact that this phenomenon is witnessed and commented upon by Martha Billy – who, like the implied reader, is a cultural outsider – suggests that we are avoiding the novel's cultural ideology if we read the movement within the medicine bag as purely metaphorical: Martha actually sees the leather pouch bumping and turning in her husband's hands. Metaphor is not the Osage explanation for such an event. Metaphor offers the Euro-American reader a comfortable 'literary' account of an otherwise unaccountable event: it permits perplexed readers to acknowledge and deny at the same time. In other words, if Native American spiritual concepts are alien, it may be easier for readers enculturated in a different worldview to read 'as if' when the text says 'is'.

Such events in an ethnic narrative mark a boundary beyond which many, perhaps most, 'mainstream' readers cannot proceed. They have the potential to remind us of important differences that cannot be accommodated within a traditional Euro-American worldview. A similar incident occurs later in the novel when an Osage character named Michael Horse finds a painted and quilted medicine bag. As he picks it up, he finds it is moving: 'It bulged and struggled. He opened a corner of it to see what was moving inside the bag when a bat flew out' (Hogan, 1990, p. 241). While a sceptic might devise a 'rational' explanation for this incident (a bat managed to crawl into the closed bag just prior to the moment when Horse discovered it?), Michael Horse interprets it with a different logic: '[T]he bats had come out of the medicine. The medicines were coming alive' (Hogan, 1990, p. 241). Reading this statement as metaphor or magical realism misses the point: what counts as 'fact', what counts as 'logic', is culturally determined. The availability of such familiar literary conventions, however, permits a member of a different social/interpretative community to read across signs of difference, not so much suppressing them as failing to register them at all.

In a series of articles focusing on the relationship of the 'mainstream' reader to 'resistant texts', Doris Sommer places in question 'our unspoken assumption that books or their authors beg to be understood' (Sommer, 1994, p. 542). Not only, in her view, is the competency of the 'mainstream' reader dubious, so also is the willingness of the author to *admit* all readers to the authorial audience. Sommer argues that some ethnic and international texts 'neither assume nor welcome comprehension by the reader who would ... assimilate them' (Sommer, 1993, p. 150). That an ethnic or post-colonial writer hopes to be read by a broad or varied audience does not mean that he or she invites all readers to share the same degree of intimacy. 'Mainstream' readers, unaccustomed to being peripheral, may read themselves into narratives that aim to position them at the margins. To counter that impulse, the text positions cultural outsiders at a distance that no amount of good will or earnest scholarship will ultimately overcome.

Ironically, the 'good' reader represents more of a threat to the text that would resist assimilation than the naive or impatient reader does.

A reader may be 'good' technically and ethically. One kind of good reader is the reader accustomed to competence: experienced, skilful, critically informed. Sommer argues that readers whose skills have been honed by years of training and practice (particularly 'professional' readers) acquire a zest for the difficult text and a confidence in their own abilities that amounts to a sense of entitlement. Such readers assume that resistance is a strategy rather than a message and that challenging texts can be 'mastered'. Sommer articulates the extremes of this kind of will to know in tropes of conquest and rape:

> We take up an unyielding book to conquer it and to feel aggrandized, enriched by the appropriation and confident that our cunning is equal to the textual tease of what was, after all, a planned submission as the ultimate climax of reading. (Sommer, 1994, p. 528)

Even when the attempt to possess a text is less self-serving, a too enthusiastic embrace may do violence to the other represented in the text.

Sommer's emphasis on differential power and on the suspect will to 'master' a text shifts the focus from technical aspects of 'good' reading to its ethical dimension. Good reading can also be understood in terms of the attitude or intention with which the reader approaches the text. Broadly, readers may take either of two ethical positions analysed by Wayne Booth in his study of the ethics of reading: one emphasizes the avoidance of moral contamination, while the other advocates an embrace of the world with all its otherness, a stance often construed as a liberal openness, a desire to bridge differences through empathetic identification (Booth, 1988, pp. 485–87). But Sommer's argument suggests that the other side of openness is a refusal to be excluded. The assumption that empathic identification is desirable or even possible may co-exist with a certain arrogance, an unwillingness to acknowledge a world in which the reader's experience is marginalized or entirely irrelevant. At best, an earnest desire to connect may be dangerously naive, because it evades the recognition that if difference is never absolute, it may nonetheless be overwhelmingly important. Certain kinds of social difference are irreducible – precisely the point made in many ethnic and post-colonial texts.

Thus, according to Sommer, the most appropriate way for 'mainstream' readers to approach resistant texts is with modest goals of readerly competence: '[R]espect demands hearing silence and recognizing refusal without straining to get beyond them. Strategic silence may itself be the message' (Sommer, 1994, p. 537). Thus, 'mainstream' readers should be '(res)trained to stop at signs of resistance' (Sommer, 1993, p. 147), recognizing that as cultural outsiders, 'they are marked precisely as strangers, incapable of – or undesirable for – conspiratorial intimacy'(Sommer, 1993, p. 150). Other theorists issue similar cautions, sometimes in even harsher terms. María Lugones advises Anglo women to listen before attempting to engage in feminist dialogue with Latinas and African-American women across the gulf of linguistic and social distance:

> You need to learn to become unintrusive, unimportant, patient to the point of tears, while at the same time open to learning any possible lessons. You will have to come to terms with the sense of alienation, of not belonging, of having your world thoroughly disrupted, having it criticized and scrutinized from the point of view of those who have been harmed by it, having important concepts central to it dismissed, being viewed with mistrust. (Lugones, cited in Jaggar, 1983, p. 386).

In other words, Euro-American readers of ethnic or post-colonial texts must be prepared to have the differential power relations inscribed within the text altered, but not eliminated. The margin becomes the centre, and the centre the margin. Anglo readers will experience what marginalization means: invisibility, criticism, exclusion.

Native American and Canadian novelist Thomas King – whose remarkable 1993 novel *Green Grass, Running Water* will be my principal example here – asserts that non-Native readers are never offered more than 'limited and particular access to a Native world' (King, 1997, p. 246). Although he is aware that the bulk of his readership is not Native, King has made it clear that the 'insider' audience for his fiction consists of Native readers: 'I really don't care about the white audiences. They don't have an understanding of the intricacies of Native life, and I don't think they're much interested in it, quite frankly' (King, cited in Vizenor, 1994, p. 174). King affirms not only that his sense of a Native audience sustains his writing, but that he withholds information that might accommodate outsiders at their expense. Part of his responsibility to the Native community is to preserve silences, to avoid telling too much (Rooke, 1990, p. 73). As Sommer argues, 'The deadly serious object of the game is to stop us short' (Sommer, 1994, p. 547).

King's description of his own practice parallels Sommer's observation that strategic barriers in the text distance the normally privileged Euro-American reader. He comments:

> It does presuppose the white audience is going to be there. But it also reminds the Native audience that you're not telling too much, that you're not hanging out the laundry as it were. Native audiences know much of this and nothing else needs to be said. It's a tricky thing, because ... as you create those silences, in part you create them to place closure on those prying eyes that

are looking in. And those aren't Native eyes for the most part. But it also provides the Native community with that sense of being on the inside. (Rooke, 1990, p. 74)

King's comment makes it clear that silence or evasion in the text is deliberately crafted and that it is designed to preserve the boundary between the community of Native readers and others. That readers outside the Native community indeed feel marginalized by King's text is suggested by the following comment posted on the Internet in April 1998 by a reader who identified himself as Canadian. The reader says of *Green Grass, Running Water*:

Entertaining and funny, but slightly confusing. ... My only problem with the work lies in a feeling of being left out – I was somehow given the sense that I would understand the book more if I were Native, even though I am passably well versed in the mythologies the story deals with. Some of the understandings gained by the characters seem culturally specific, in a way, a feeling which I did not get from King's *Medicine River*' (http://www.amazon.com/exec/obidos/ASIN/).

One of the most striking and complex examples of this kind of reticence in *Green Grass, Running Water* is the novel's failure to clarify the ontological status of different clusters of characters. Indeed, not only are fundamental elements of Native American cosmology unexplained, the norms of narration in English are subtly altered in ways that challenge the expectations of conventional readers.

In *Green Grass, Running Water*, the narrative 'I' is the voice of a trickster, the companion or *alter ego* of Coyote, a traditional trickster figure in Native American myth and lore (King, 1993). The narration progresses on two levels that gradually converge. The 'inner' story space offers a narrative about a group of Canadian Blackfoot characters who are drawn back to their reservation for the annual Sun Dance. Intercut are conversations among six transcendent characters who are attempting both to tell a proper story, from the beginning, and to 'fix up the world' by intervening in the lives of the characters in the inner story. These transcendent figures include four Native elders (masquerading as Lone Ranger, Ishmael, Robinson Crusoe and Hawkeye, but actually avatars of First Woman, Changing Woman, Thought Woman and Old Woman) who have escaped from a government-run sanatorium in the United States, as well as the trickster Coyote, and the narrative 'I'.

The four elders are hundreds of years old, sometimes perceived as females, sometimes as male, capable of interacting both with humans in ordinary space/time and with Coyote in transcendent space/time.

Throughout their history superficial aspects of their identity have changed, altered whenever necessary for their survival. While their most ancient representations are the female archetypes of the Native American oral tradition, the four elders at some time in the past took the names and gender of well-known characters in the canon of Anglo-American narrative. Throughout the novel two threads of narrative are interlaced, both recounted by the narrative 'I', with commentary from Coyote. In one narrative line, Coyote and the narrator follow the successive efforts of the four elders to tell a proper origin story. Simultaneously, the elders are acting in the human sphere, travelling toward Canada from the hospital where they pass their time between interventions in the lives of ordinary humans.

Although the transcendent and the human characters have different ontological status, the perception that they share the same world is an important element of Native ideology. In *Grandmothers of the Light*, Paula Gunn Allen writes that for Native Americans myths are 'accounts of actual interchanges' involving transcendent beings (Allen, 1991, p.6). Such figures are not metaphors or representations of psychological realities, but share with humans the landscape of ordinary life:

> Though [myths] function on a number of levels of significance, as is the nature of all literature, they are factual accounts. They inform consciousness and direct awareness within as well as without, and they connect with deep levels of being, not because the figures they tell about are immaterial denizens of the shadowy world of the unconscious, but because the supernaturals live within the same environs that humans occupy, and interchanges with them are necessarily part of the fabric of human experience. (Allen, 1991, p. 7)

As the separate threads of plot finally intertwine, human characters engage in everyday conversation with the four elders, but do not 'hear' the origin stories told in the alternative narrative space. It is not clear that humans see or hear Coyote and 'I' at all. When Coyote speaks directly to an ordinary human, the response is typically mediated by one of the elders, although on one occasion Lionel Red Dog dimly perceives 'a yellow dog dancing in the rain' (King, 1993, p. 309). The different ontological status of the characters is reflected in the narrative by different structures of tense. Coyote and the narrative 'I' speak to each other in present tense. The narrator's accounts of the human characters are recorded in past tense. The activities of the four elders are sometimes past tense and sometimes present tense, depending on the context. When the elders interact with humans, the text records their speech and behaviour in past tense, like human activity. When the elders converse in the mythic realm, their speech is represented in present tense.

For example, in the following exchange, the human characters Charlie and Bursum (Charlie is Blackfoot, Bursum non-Native) are represented in the past tense; the transcendent characters Lone Ranger, Hawkeye, Ishmael and Robinson Crusoe are present in the phenomenal world, speaking with humans, and therefore their speech is also represented in past tense; Coyote speaks in the present tense and is apparently not perceived by humans:

> The movie was familiar. Charlie was sure he had seen it before. The old Indians stood transfixed in front of The Map, watching every movement on the screens.
> 'Boy,' said the Lone Ranger, 'look at those colors.'
> 'Yes,' said Hawkeye. 'Black and white are my favorites.'
> 'They could have made this movie in color,' Bursum explained. 'But the director wanted the brooding effect that you get with grainy black and white.'
> 'And the horses,' said Ishmael. 'Those are wonderful horses.'
> 'Look,' said Robinson Crusoe. 'Is that the president?'
> 'No,' said the Lone Ranger. 'That guy's too tall.'
> 'Are there any Coyotes in this picture?' says Coyote.
> 'I don't think so,' said the Lone Ranger. 'But we should keep looking, just to be safe.' (King, 1993, p. 351)

As in the passage from Linda Hogan's *Mean Spirit* cited above, in which a non-Native person observes the activity of supernatural forces in the ordinary world, it is significant that the non-Native Bursum converses with the elders: Lone Ranger and Hawkeye comment on the lack of colour in the videotape they are watching, and Bursum responds. But the status of Coyote in the phenomenal world is never entirely clear. Although there is no direct evidence that humans perceive Coyote, the elders later in the same scene suggest that under some circumstances his presence might be manifest. When Coyote becomes excited watching the film and begins to shout, he is cautioned by one of the elders: '"Not so loud", said the Lone Ranger. "You're going to scare these young boys"' (King, 1993, p. 355).

Meanwhile, the four old Indians also function in the transcendent realm where all things, including features of the physical world, are subjects whose consciousness is represented in the eternal present tense:

> Ho, ho, ho, ho, says that Big Muddy River. I suppose you want to get to the other side.
> That would be nice, says the Lone Ranger. We are trying to fix the world.
> Is that what we're doing? says Ishmael.
> Nobody said anything to me about that, says Robinson Crusoe.
> Well, says Hawkeye, I suppose somebody has to do it.

>   Okay, says that Big Muddy River, Hang on.
>   And right away the ground starts to shake and the trees start to dance and everything goes up and down and sideways.
>
>   'Earthquake! Earthquake!' yells Coyote.
>   'Calm down,' I says. (King, 1993, p. 458)

When Coyote and the narrative 'I' converse in transcendent space/time, their speech is represented in quotation marks. However, when the four elders converse in transcendent space/time, or in the narrator's accounts of their activities in this mythic realm, their dialogue is not represented in quotation marks. Nor, when Coyote inserts himself in those portions of the narrative dealing with the mythic activities of the old Indians, are his comments represented in quotation marks:

>   Okay, says those soldiers. Who shot Nasty Bumppo?
>   Not me, says Old Woman.
>   Not me, says Chingachgook.
>   Not me, says Coyote. (King, 1993, p. 438)

These intricate linguistic representations of unarticulated relationships are extraordinary examples of the novel's counter-appropriation of an imposed language and narrative form. The bantering tone of the dialogue between Coyote and the narrative 'I', reinforced by the rapid associational shifts from one thread of story to another, suggests the intimacy and improvisation of oral narrative. On the other hand, the shifting tenses and the variations in textual notation are rigorously patterned, even if their implications are never made specific. The novel uses the devices of written prose fiction, including metafiction, to acknowledge its unwritten origins: Coyote comments, 'All this floating imagery must mean something', to which the narrative 'I' responds, 'That's the way it happens in oral stories' (King, 1993, p. 391). The text both acknowledges and disrupts the linearity of its novelistic form by calling attention to it:

>   'Gha! Higayv:ligé:i,' said Robinson Crusoe.
>   'We've done that already,' said Ishmael.
>   'Have we?' said Robinson Crusoe.
>   'Yes,' said the Lone Ranger. 'Page twelve.'
>   'Oh.'
>   'See. Top of page twelve.'
>   'How embarrassing.' (King, 1993, pp. 257–58)

As the genuinely witty surface of the narrative propels the reader forward, there are constant reminders that in this text the conventional Eurocentric reader is positioned as the other. Occasional dialogue in the Cherokee language is untranslated and the section titles are printed in Cherokee calligraphy. Moreover, both in the narrative strand dealing with the efforts of the transcendent characters to tell a proper origin story and in the plot focusing on the human characters, the traditional narratives, social behaviour and insight of those outside the Native community are challenged.

As Laura E. Donaldson points out, King has conflated different versions of Native American origin stories in the tales told by the four old Indians (Donaldson, 1995). Although the elders disagree among themselves, their creation stories have in common the existence of something – water, an old woman, selected animals, particularly trickster figures – before the creation of earth. The failure to begin with a void or to stage the creation of a hierarchy of creatures with human males in the dominant position contradicts the biblical account likely to be familiar to most readers. However, as Donaldson makes clear, it is the narrative emphasis on the telling of multiple stories and the corollary idea that 'you can't tell it all by yourself' that constitute the most important discrepancies between Native and Western origin stories:

> This comedic bickering over the content of human beginnings serves a very important function since it suggests that the monotheist version of *creatio ex nihilo* – creation of the earth from nothing – achieves its singular and univocal status only by suppressing all other voices in this highly contested terrain. (Donaldson, 1995, p. 32)

As depicted in King's novel, the Judaeo-Christian god is a contrary Coyote dream that thinks it is in charge of the world but gets everything backward. Whereas Coyote is accustomed to mixed results and is engagingly nonchalant about his mistakes, the Christian god is petty and ill-mannered, shouting his objections to any origin stories but his own: 'What happened to my earth without form? ... What happened to my void? ... Where's my darkness?' (King, 1993, p. 37). The novel represents the Christian god's insistence on hierarchy in the form of a self-reflexive demand for appropriate textual notation:

> I am god, says that Dog Dream.
> 'Isn't that cute,' says Coyote. 'That Dog Dream is a contrary. That Dog Dream has everything backward.'
> But why am I a little god? shouts that god.
> 'Not so loud,' says Coyote. 'You're hurting my ears.'
> I don't want to be a little god, says that god. I want to be a big god!

> 'What a noise,' says Coyote. 'This dog has no manners.'
> Big one!
> 'Okay, okay,' says Coyote. 'Just stop shouting.'
> There, says that G O D. That's better. (King, 1993, pp. 2–3)

Thereafter, the text designates G O D's contributions to the debates about cosmology that occur in transcendent space/time with spaced capitals: 'Talking trees! Talking trees! says that G O D. What kind of a world is this?'(King, 1993, p. 41). Similarly, Jesus is self-absorbed and petulant, so concerned about hierarchy that he cannot acknowledge help from anyone, least of all from an Old Woman:

> Christian rules, says Young Man Walking on Water. And the first rule is that no one can help me. The second rule is that no one can tell me anything. Third, no one is allowed to be in two places at once. Except me. (King, 1993, p. 388)

This comic deflation of Western values and, by extension, the centrality of the Eurocentric worldview extends as well to the novel's depiction of human behaviour. In the thread of plot focusing on the Blackfoot characters assembling for the Sun Dance ritual, a running joke at the expense of Euro-Americans, whether from Canada or the United States, is the account of the Dead Dog Café. An ordinary diner has become a popular tourist destination on the basis of its dog meat cuisine (actually beef), shocking and titillating whites who believe that Native Americans have traditionally savoured dog meat. The proprietor of the café complements a menu of dog dishes – the daily special of Old Agency Puppy Stew plus 'Dog du Jour, Houndburgers, Puppy Potpourri, Hot Dogs, Saint Bernard Swiss Melts, with Doggie Doos and Deep-Fried Puppy Whatnots for appetizers' – with trophy photographs of Natives capturing dogs:

> She got Will Horse Capture over in Medicine River to make up a bunch of photographs like those you see in the hunting and fishing magazines where a couple of white guys are standing over an elephant or holding up a lion's head or stretching out a long stringer of fish or hoisting a brace of ducks in each hand. Only in these photographs, it was Indians and dogs. Latisha's favorite was a photograph of four Indians on their buffalo runners chasing down a herd of Great Danes. (King, 1993, p. 117)

White tourists from the United States and Canada are equally gullible; one initially suspicious Canadian who claims to have been with the Royal Canadian Mounted Police for 25 years accepts Latisha's assertion that eating dog is a treaty right: 'We raise them right on the reserve,'

Latisha explained. 'Feed them only horse meat and whole grain. No hormones or preservatives' (King, 1993, p. 144). In fact, Latisha prefers tourists from the US because they eat the more exotic and expensive dishes and buy the commemorative menus and postcards. Canadian tourists are tidy, quiet and financially conservative: they eat the daily special Puppy Stew.

The attitudes and behaviour of Euro-Americans are portrayed unflatteringly, and without humour, in accounts of the gathering for the annual Sun Dance. Two separate episodes recount the efforts of whites, one successful and one not, to 'steal' photographs of the ceremony itself – that is, to conceal photographs taken surreptitiously after the visitor has been informed that filming is forbidden. In the first instance, the photographer manages a sleight of hand that substitutes a blank roll for the exposed film. But when members of the tribe report the theft to the RCMP, they are told that nothing can be done because the man has not broken any laws. Like Christian rules, the secular laws of Western states defend Western values. In a country where taking forbidden photographs of artworks in a museum or committing a sacrilege in a church might carry civil penalties, a transgression of Native law does not.

Two other accounts are more subtle in representing both Euro-American desire for knowledge of Native culture and Native resistance of that will to know. In the first incident, Latisha remembers a conversation with a high school classmate who was seeking an explanation of the nature and meaning of the Sun Dance. The exchange calls attention to three features of Ann's inquiry: the aggressiveness of her questioning, her failure to permit what would be – from the Native perspective – appropriate turn-taking pauses, and her insistence upon Western analogues for Native experience. The passage suggests that, at least initially, Latisha is willing to attempt an explanation, but she is forestalled by Ann's single-minded focus on her own experience:

> 'We sit in pews and listen to the priest and then we receive communion, which is the body and blood of Christ,' Ann told her. 'What do you do?'
>   Latisha started to tell her about the women's society, but Ann jumped in and asked her if she had ever heard of the Catholic Women's League. ...
>   Latisha started again, remembering the women's lodge and then the men's lodge, the dancing, the giveaway, but Ann continued to hobble her with questions.
>   'Nine days seems a long time,' she said. 'What exactly do you do?'
>   Latisha stood there in the corridor of the school and worked her hands in her lap. Finally Ann said that it was probably a mystery, something you could never know but believed in anyway, like God and Jesus and the Holy Ghost.

Latisha wanted to tell Ann that that wasn't it, but in the end she said nothing. (King, 1993, pp. 409–10)

On one level, the conversation cannot proceed because Ann does not allow Latisha to speak – she 'jumps in' when Latisha begins to respond and 'hobbles' Latisha with more questions. More importantly, Ann cannot receive information except within the context of her own cultural experience: she immediately tries to align the Native women's society with the Catholic Women's League. Ultimately Ann gives her own explanation for Latisha's experience, filling in the blank of Latisha's silence with language drawn from her own religious training. Whatever the white girl's intentions – and there is no reason to assume that Ann is not sincere – it is clear that Latisha experiences this 'dialogue' as a form of aggression. While this exchange takes place between two teenagers, Latisha has, as an adult, learned to avoid such encounters altogether. In Sommer's terms, Ann is unable to track, or even to recognize, signs of difference. Like Ann, listeners and readers accustomed to privilege 'override restrictions they have never been taught to respect' (Sommer, 1994, p. 530).

A more poignant depiction of the limited entry permitted to cultural outsiders is the relationship between Eli Stands Alone and his wife Karen. In the present time of the novel Eli is a retired professor of literature, a widower who feels keenly the loss of what seems to have been a long and mutually satisfying marriage. Nevertheless, Eli could not share with his wife, and the novel does not articulate, the complexities of his relationship to his family and his tribal heritage, both represented in the annual gathering for the Sun Dance. While the novel makes clear the strength of the relationship between Eli and Karen, and the commitment of both partners, it also portrays the unbridgeable cultural difference between them. There is an element of exoticism in Karen's attraction to Eli. She 'liked the idea that Eli was Indian' and during their first night together, she calls him 'my Mystic Warrior' (King, 1993, pp. 181–82). She buys him books about Natives by people who are not Native – 'histories, autobiographies, memoirs of writers who had gone west or who had lived with a particular tribe, romances of one sort of another' (King, 1993, p. 180).

Only once do Eli and Karen attend the Sun Dance (a second trip planned 20 years after the first never takes place because Karen dies in an automobile accident). Nothing terrible happens; the text records Eli's discomfort but does not locate its source in his own relationship to his heritage or in Karen's: 'Eli started to follow her [into his mother's lodge]. But for a moment, for just an instant before he stepped across the threshold ... Eli had an overpowering urge to lower the flap, get into the De Soto, and drive back to Toronto' (King, 1993, p. 229). Karen's experience, however, is more defined: she feels welcomed, enthralled, entertained. She perceives the event as a moving anachronism, something from a film or from the past. Thereafter, Eli remains reluctant to return to the reservation with Karen, but the text deflects analysis of that reluctance in the same way Eli evades discussion of it with his wife:

> Karen was disappointed when they didn't go back the next year. Or the next. Each year, around May, Eli would get a letter from his mother. How was his health? How was Karen? Were there any grandchildren? Norma was fine. Camelot was fine. She was fine.
> 'Eli,' Karen asked, 'you're not embarrassed or something like that?'
> 'About what?'
> 'I don't know. Do you want to talk?'
> 'About what?'
> 'I don't know'. (King, 1993, p. 291)

Eli's silence, reinforced by the silence of the text, maintains a boundary between cultural insiders who do not need an explanation and cultural outsiders who should not seek one. It refuses to map Eli's internal landscape for the benefit of those for whom it is not home ground.

Green Grass, Running Water illustrates the paradoxical capacity of resistant texts to 'reach out to privileged readers in order to keep us at arm's length' (Sommer, 1994, p. 528). They require a readerly tact that recognizes boundaries and respects them. In Sommer's nice pun, they insist that readers accustomed to cultural and linguistic privilege be '(res)trained' (Sommer, 1993, p. 147). Good reading – skilful, ethical reading – is restrained by the recognition that culturally specific experience may have no equivalent outside its own context. A reader who, like Ann, supplies imprecise analogues in an effort to 'relate' to the text is both naive and dangerous in her earnest disregard for difference. Mature readers, on the other hand, should be disciplined to accept 'limited and particular access' to certain experiences represented in ethnic and post-colonial narratives (Rooke, 1990, p. 73). They should be trained to recognize rhetorical moves that distance and deflect the inquiring gaze. As in any other sensitive social interaction, the exercise of readerly 'tact' is an imperfect art, based on fine distinctions and a willingness to play by someone else's rules.

Works Cited

Allen, Paula Gunn, 1991. *Grandmothers of the Light: A Medicine Woman's Sourcebook*, Boston: Beacon Press.

Booth, Wayne, 1988. *The Company We Keep: An Ethics of Fiction*, Berkeley: University of California Press.

Donaldson, Laura E., 1995. 'Noah Meets Old Coyote, or Singing in the Rain: Intertextuality in Thomas King's *Green Grass, Running Water*', *Studies in American Indian Literatures*, vol. 7, no. 2 (Summer), pp. 27–43.

Hogan, Linda, 1990. *Mean Spirit*, New York: Ivy Books; Rpt. New York: Ballantine Books.

Jaggar, Alison M., 1983. *Feminist Politics and Human Nature*, Totowa, NJ: Rowan & Allanheld.

King, Thomas, 1993. *Green Grass, Running Water*, New York: Houghton Mifflin.

King, Thomas, 1997. 'Godzilla vs. Post-Colonial', in Ajay Heble, Donna Palmateer Penee and J. R. (Tim) Struthers (eds), *New Contexts of Canadian Criticism*, Peterborough, ON: Broadview Press, pp. 241–48.

Owens, Louis, 1992. *Other Destinies: Understanding the American Indian Novel*, Norman, OK: University of Oklahoma Press.

Rabinowitz, Peter, 1987. *Before Reading: Narrative Conventions and the Politics of Interpretation*, Ithaca: Cornell University Press.

Rooke, C., 1990. 'Interview with Tom King', *World Literature Written in English*, vol. 30, no. 2, pp. 62–76.

Sommer, Doris, 1993. 'Resistant Texts and Incompetent Readers', *Poetics Today*, vol. 15, no. 4 (March), pp. 141–53.

Sommer, Doris, 1994. 'Textual Conquests: On Readerly Competence and "Minority" Literature', *Modern Language Quarterly*, vol. 54, no. 1 (March), pp. 523–51.

Vizenor, Gerald, 1994. *Manifest Manners: Postindian Warriors of Survivance*, Hanover, NH: Wesleyan University and University Press of New England.

4

Fractures: Written Displacements in Canadian/US Literary Relations

Richard J. Lane

> The Canadian experience was a circumference with no centre, the American one a centre which was mistaken for the whole thing.
>
> Margaret Atwood, 1972

MINUS TIME – 1

There are two overriding contemporary views of America: the road (movie) and space (literally, and in terms of technology, that is, space exploration). Both views, or images, are consumed via television: at a distance. Does it matter if anyone is watching? Not at all, though even Baudrillard thinks there is something strange about the whole process:

> There is nothing more mysterious than a TV set left on in an empty room .... It is as if another planet is communicating with you. Suddenly the TV reveals itself for what it really is: a video of another world, ultimately addressed to no one at all, delivering its images indifferently, indifferent to its own messages. (Baudrillard, 1988, p. 50)

Sometimes it doesn't matter if *everyone* is watching TV; the result is no different from a lack of viewers, or so theorizes Catherine Bush in her novel *Minus Time*. Helen and Paul are in Florida to watch their mother, Barbara Urie, take off in the space shuttle; she will be the first Canadian astronaut. But Helen and Paul have decided to watch the launch incognito, instead of with the other space families who are being televised. After the launch they are in an archetypal American diner intersected by the video images of the modern world when it happens: the uncanny doubling of themselves –

Zooming toward the viewing stands, the TV camera began to pan: There was Nora Carter, Peter Carter's tanned and cheerful wife, and then – the ID flashed in yellow across the bottom of the screen: *Barbara Urie's family*.

For an instant, Helen could not quite believe what she was seeing: three people who –

Was that man, by some crazy chance, her father? After all, it had been so long since she had seen him. No. And yet this man looked so much like her father – at least her father as she remembered ... Beside him stood a young man and a young woman, who resembled him, just as she and Paul resembled David: Both had thick, sand brown hair and dark eyebrows. The young woman's hair was tied back with an elastic. All three of them stared upward, mouths partly open, heads craned back toward the sky. (Bush, 1995, pp. 11–12)

Disoriented by the uncanniness of NASA having a spare, 'identical' family to substitute in case of emergencies, Helen and Paul have to decide what to do and where to go. But they are in Florida, so when Helen asks if Paul wants to do anything else, his ironic reply invokes a Baudrillardian despair: 'What? Like Disney World? Space World? Like go to the beach?' (Bush, 1995, p. 13). Each of these ironic alternatives implies a hyper-reality, where 'the real' has been replaced by an intensified series of images and experiences that are both more real than the real and yet are somehow inherently childish, covering up the fact that there is nothing outside that is America: it is all contained within the theme park (and the beach is just an elongated theme park). Helen and Paul decide they need reality: reality is North. Reality is Canada. So they get into their car and enter instead, *the road movie*: 'Big transport trucks streamed long shadows in the pale winter sunlight, sweeping over their car, light, then dark, then light ... they had nearly two thousand miles to go before they would be home' (Bush, 1995, p. 17). Of course, their journey home is interrupted by televisions, a plethora of coin-operated televisions at a roadside restaurant; inside the restaurant they watch the space shuttle docking with the space station where their mother will try to break the record for staying up above Earth. The road movie continues as later they pass THE HAND OF GOD physically constructed by the side of the road, and the journey itself blurs into the smell of exhaust fumes and images of sleazy motels.

Road journeys provide both content and form for a significant number of American cultural texts. Russell Brown regards the binary opposition road/home as a significant way of defining the differences between American and English-Canadian fiction. He argues that 'road/home becomes one more in that long list of paradigmatic American/English-Canadian contrasting pairs, which includes terms such as southern/northern, revolutionary/evolutionary, individualized/communitarian, even male/female' (Brown, 1994, p. 25). That is not to say that texts from both nations don't contain elements of both sides of the oppositions, but that they are important structuring principles. For example, Barbara Urie's flight into space involves her in both the journey in the American space shuttle and then the perpetual journeying around the planet. Like Huck and Jim on the raft in *Huckleberry Finn*, Barbara and fellow astronaut Peter are orbiting earth in a perpetual journey where they take their home with them. Canadian literature usually constructs home as literally or metaphysically a more anchored place, even if at some stage it involves loss and dispersal: the location of home is more important than the journey (think of Malcolm Lowry's *October Ferry to Gabriola*; see Lane, 1996). An historical interpretation for this cultural difference is possible:

> American critics have also interpreted the recurrence of themes of flight, necessary exile from home, and the road as expressive of their country's founding experiences – most often pointing to an immigration that was a flight from European oppression and a western settlement characterized by a progressive rolling back of a frontier. (Brown, 1994, p. 26)

In *Minus Time*, Helen is deeply disturbed when her brother sets up home with a new girlfriend without telling her first; even more disturbing is the glimpse she has of these two architects' vision of the city, or home, of the future. Helen wants to protect and re-establish notions of home in Canada not for conservative reasons but on behalf of the cultural minorities who reject the American vision of home as one of perpetual travel. As Brown says: 'Canadian stories depict a road that leads back home' (Brown, 1994, p. 36).

IMAGE 1 – HOLLYWOOD NORTH

'Barbara could be anywhere, or nowhere, in a desert in Australia, a cave in New Mexico, a Los Angeles TV studio, even a studio blocks away in Toronto' (Bush, 1995, p. 276). Barbara could even be in Vancouver, that Canadian city which established itself firmly through the 1970s, 1980s and early 1990s as 'Hollywood North'. Stephen E. Miller notes how with the media world, 'in 1982 everything exploded':

> Eighteen projects were shot in the Lower Mainland, ranging from Fred Schepisi's *Iceman*, to local productions *Hello-Goodbye* and *The Deserter*. Notable for some real Vancouver content was a film about murdered Vancouver playmate Dorothy Stratten, Bob Fosse's creepy bio-pic *Star 80*, in which Vancouver played not only itself but also L.A. Since 1982, the industry has

never looked back: twenty-four film and TV projects in 1985, thirty in 1987, thirty-five in 1989, fifty-three in 1991, sixty-one in 1992 and seventy-three in 1993, thus spreading Vancouver incognito onto movie and television screens. (Miller, 1994, p. 284)

Later on in his essay Miller asks 'what does it all mean?' for Canadian identity, when most of the films shot in Vancouver (or Toronto for that matter) stand in for someplace else. What does it mean when an entire generation of young adults grows up watching *The X Files*, filmed in Vancouver, receiving and interpreting a specific, Canadian place in terms of a series of American images and locales? Is this a serious displacement of Canadian *or* American identity? Has one culture been dominated by the images of the other? Is this loss, or displacement, of identity a purely postmodern phenomenon? In which case, isn't postmodernism an inherently negative process? If we think of the media images of Vancouver or Toronto as being 'anywhere', then perhaps that is because such places are modern *and* postmodern cities; they have an openness *and* cultural specificity. Paul Delany argues that rather than reject the notion of universalism as totalitarian and oppressive, it can be viewed as in tension with cultural specificities:

> What is truly postmodern, I would argue, is the *simultaneous* existence of universalism and particularism as systems in conflict. The modern city has been the original site for a universalist praxis: the freedom to practice one's art, to enjoy religious or ethnic tolerance, and to buy and sell. Indeed, human rights in their classic sense were only available to the *citizen* – literally, the city-dweller – not to the mere *subject*. (Delany, 1994, p. 9)

Minus Time – 2

Helen's mother is now encircling the Earth; she has become like a god, all-seeing, all-knowing. Since she was a child, Helen has felt that her mother wants to occupy the role of the omniscient narrator; she asks Helen what she wants to be when she grows up, saying 'you can be anything you want'. But Helen knows that 'anything' is defined by her mother's vision of intellectual success. Helen responds to the question of aspiration at school with the word 'astronaut' – precisely what she *doesn't* want to be. It is no coincidence that as her mother becomes more successful, she unwittingly becomes more American; her elevation to a godlike position must come through a shared acceptance of 'vision', meaning technology, new frontiers, space exploration and absolute knowledge. Once her mother is in space, Helen can communicate with her by telephone, or by television:

They had been warned how it worked, how the picture would keep switching from camera to camera, room to room, although if you were in phone contact with one of the astronauts, the astronaut could choose to still it. There were also angles of vision they'd never see: the health-monitoring area, the astronaut's sleeping quarters. (Bush, 1995, pp. 41–42)

The lines of spoken and visual communication are *fractured*; there is the possibility of the two being aligned, but not only can the spoken be separated from the visual, the visual itself is ever-roaming, switching from location to location, perspective to perspective. The out-of-bounds areas, the health and sleeping places, are doubled in the novel with the reverse situation: Barbara can look down at the entire world, but she cannot see into the private spaces of Helen's own double-life. Helen's new, secret identity as an environmentalist or eco-protestor is transgressive, which, paradoxically, means that she enters a public space of protest to become out-of-bounds herself.

The live televisual feed from the space shuttle functions like a silent movie: there is more emphasis upon the spatiality of or within the shuttle and the tasks performed by its human inhabitants. The shuttle represents America: hermetically sealed, clean, bright and containing healthy, intelligent, fitness-seeking individuals. Like Baudrillard's crazed jogger ('The jogger commits suicide by running up and down the beach' [1988, p. 38]) the shuttle's inhabitants don't know when to stop: 'This entire society, including its active, productive part – everyone – is running straight ahead, because they have lost the formula for stopping' (Baudrillard, 1988, pp. 38–39). Helen interrupts her mother's narratives of technological progression to pause and think about the negative side of industrialized societies. From the poison dumped in the lake to the use of intensive 'farming' methods, *Minus Time* focuses on what is happening to the planet that Barbara seems so keen to leave behind. The environmental disaster to which Helen's father responds indicates that the differences between Canadian and US identity cannot be quite as simple as the opening chapter of the novel first suggests (although the fact that the chapter deals with stereotypes means that as readers we have to decode the inbuilt levels of postmodern awareness, even parody, within the chapter). In other words, the hegemonic force of both cultures *is* technology, although the awareness that technology is going wrong, and that it needs to be replaced with local alternatives, is far stronger in Canada.

Helen is at first disturbed by the cultural differences of eco-protestors that reject technology precisely because, like her mother, she cannot see them all at once. Helen occupies the intradiegetic perspective – she's not floating in the sky looking down on the characters in her story-world but is stuck with an internal, limited perspective – and this fracturing of her own personal vision unsettles her. She imagines, in a parodic way, the protestors: 'Cells of intense, hunched-shouldered activists gathered in small basement rooms, drinking Evian water and eating tofu burgers, planning this kind of speedy, anonymous action. The underground' (Bush, 1995, p. 65). The parody operates through laughter and seriousness: the 'underground' nature of eco-protesting means that these people are out of sight – they cannot be implicated in even the most simplistic form of surveillance and discipline, such as the Bertillon system used by the French police with the introduction of the criminal 'mug-shot'. And what if other *ethnic* groups were to join the protestors? What if other groups were to go underground, out of sight/site? It is surprising how quickly notions of community can shift from the acceptable to the unacceptable. Communities which provide rich visual spectacles for consumption by the cultural hegemony and/or media have an obvious 'place' in a multicultural society; but more combative notions of identity are quickly rejected, especially when individuals cannot be interpolated. A prime example of this problematic shift from the visible to the invisible (in terms of personal identity and affiliation) and a shift from the invisible to the visible (in terms of political protest) is Oka:

> Oka, who now does not know that word and the struggle for justice that took place? The words and images of the long summer have left an indelible impression on the minds of Canada and the world. Few events in recent history have been so divisive for the nation. For three months the stand-off between determined Mohawks and the Canadian government was in the headlines and the lead story on our television sets. It became a symbol and a rallying point for natives across Canada in their efforts to have long-standing issues brought to Canada's attention (Neel, 1991b, p. 132)

The Oka crisis arose most visibly from a land dispute over the expansion of a golf course; more fundamentally, the dispute was part of a wide-reaching mismanagement by the Canadian government of native land claims, sovereignty and demands for general cultural rights. In terms of a spectacular event, two images are significant here: the photograph of a Mohawk warrior used in David Neel's print 'Life on the 18th Hole' (Neel, 1991a) and the bruised and battered face of Mohawk Ronald Crosse, after being held in custody by the Sûreté du Québec. The visibility of Ronald Crosse's maltreatment had no effect in a Canadian court; the post-colonial struggles for rights and recognition were inscribed visibly upon the body but went unheeded. The image of an anonymous Mohawk warrior (or activist), used first on the cover of the *Globe and Mail*, is significant because it symbolizes a fear (on behalf of the cultural hegemony) of the simultaneous visibility and invisibility of Native resistance to injustice; David Neel, a Native artist, takes this image and reworks it in relation to the military force of the police as a way of reflecting upon such events in a more complex and ultimately positive way.

IMAGE 2 – THE BULLY

In an often quoted passage in Margaret Atwood's *Surfacing* (1979) an American offers to buy the (Canadian) land which belonged to the protagonist's father. One of the characters, David, reacts in an angry way, which the reader interprets ironically because he is the most 'Americanized' man in the novel. While the Canadian–American relationships in Atwood's fiction have been critically charted (see Colman, 1979 and Broege, 1981), David's response is fascinating in relation to fracturing and the image of America as the 'bully'. David starts by parodying the undercover way in which Americans are supposed to infiltrate Canada; he says that the American man isn't from a wildlife association, but the CIA; he continues the parody by theorizing that there is a forthcoming war between America and Canada because of a shortage of water in the States:

> [T]his country [Canada] is almost all water if you look at a map. So in a while, I give it ten years, they'll be up against the wall. They'll try to swing a deal with the government, get us to give them the water cheap or for nothing in exchange for more soapflakes or something, and the government will give in, they'll be a bunch of puppets as usual. But by that time the Nationalist Movement will be strong enough so they'll force the government to back down; riots or kidnappings or something. Then the Yank pigs will send in the Marines, they'll have to; people in New York and Chicago will be dropping like flies, industry will be stalled, there'll be a black market in water ... They'll come in through Quebec, it will have separated by then. (Atwood, 1979, p. 97)

David's hyperbolic, fantastic narrative, like a science fiction novel, is extrapolated from actual present-day facts, for example, the separatist movement in Quebec. While this situation is clearly unlikely, elements of it, and certainly tensions, have already arisen. The fracturing that occurs is not just that of a North American identity breaking down into its overall nationalist components, but also Canada breaking down into further autonomous fragments (the 'infiltration' by the CIA could be symbolic of the irrational and fundamentally racist fear of other internal ethnic groups 'turning' on the mainstream, like Oka). Still, there is the overriding sense that in the ensuing violence that David foresees it is America that bullies Canada into the situation in the first place.

In a talk on Canadian–American relations, Atwood argues that imperial, expansionist aggression is just as problematic in terms of new communications technologies as it is in any other field. Atwood rejects the notion that nationalist boundaries will be made redundant by technological progression: the bully can command the media as much as he or she commands the playground or the battlefield. Critics have long asked, in relation to such talks and more specifically Atwood's book *Survival*, whether Atwood is defining Canadians purely via the negative. Her response in *Second Words* is revealing:

> In a world where there seems to be increasingly less and less of more and more, it [survival] may be a more useful as well as a more ethical attitude towards the world than the American belief that there is always another horizon, a new frontier, that when you've used up what's in sight you only have to keep moving. (Atwood, 1982, p. 387)

Minus Time – 3

The world is geologically fractured in *Minus Time*; the American West, that site of a most beloved frontier, is being shattered and destroyed. Ironically, Hollywood is destroyed in an earthquake, affecting the movie and TV industries alike. All that is left is survival, viewed from above on a television across the continent and in another country:

> The helicopter flew in a little lower, faster ... over a street with cracks erupting in it, leading into a freeway littered with abandoned cars, people who stared upward violently, shaking their fists, the road rising like lips around a deep gash. Then the freeway crumpled and twisted, leaving a hole in the air, because the bridge underneath had collapsed. The earth had done all that, I thought. (Bush, 1995, p. 118)

The earthquake has destroyed not only people's homes, which is of concern in the novel primarily to Helen's father, but, perhaps more importantly from another perspective, *their cars and roads*! It is not clear whether the people in the scene are shaking their fists at the helicopter TV crew filming them, at the earthquake in general or at the loss of their road transport. The ambiguity is telling. Baudrillard regards the Californian freeways as the 'tissue' of the city, relating it to 'the power of pure open space' (Baudrillard, 1988, p. 125). Europe is about theatricality; in America, the only spectacle that matters is that of *road traffic*. *Minus Time* develops this notion technologically, but never moves entirely away from a Baudrillardian vision of the US, or the power of geological change. It is geology that connects Canada and America above all the political and aesthetic fractures. Laurie Ricou has theorized a cultural zone which is defined by the connections rather than divisions, between Canada and America: 'A regional literature and culture might be discovered where the boundary becomes so indeterminate – perhaps it must be discovered in an eco-region far too international to claim for one country' (Ricou, 1994, p. 49).

Ricou's is an extremely important essay in relation to Canadian/US literary relations, not just because of his questioning of artificially constructed boundaries and subsequent international law, but because of the form of his paper. He writes in a dialectical question-and-answer sequence or 'catechism', which is both a persistent questioning and instructional enterprise. Pedagogically, the result is an opening of ideas, and a residual notion that the questioning must continue long after the essay has ended. Ricou's geographically defined literary space is that of the Pacific Northwest, which 'has a long history, longer perhaps than any such comparable history in the other regions that look at one another – at themselves – across the Canada/US boundary' (Ricou, 1994, p. 51). The Pacific Northwest has cultural links among the First Nations peoples that precede European history, links which were themselves integrated with the natural habitat (and this is not a pastoral vision, just one which compares different technologies). What is this region to be called? Garreau calls it Ecotopia, which links up with the eco-protestors in *Minus Time*. Garreau's vision is primarily generated by, and in response to, the physicality of place:

> Fusion of ecological and utopian thinking is central to the culture I am discussing. Garreau's geography also raises a new problem of terminology and regional boundaries. To compare across political barriers in this region is first to be aware of the great power – emotional and imaginative, as well as climatic – of the barriers of rock, the coastal ranges, which run north/south. (Ricou, 1994, p. 53)

How does Ricou's literary-critical vision of the Pacific Northwest compare with the 'North East' landmass that would connect Toronto with other major North Eastern American cities? While it would be foolish to deny the environmental issues of the East, I would argue that semiotics is prevalent, rather than coastal mountain ranges. Of course the latter are also signifying systems in a structuralist or poststructuralist sense, and this gives a clue as to how an interpretative relationship can be constructed, via, once again, Baudrillard. At the beginning of *America*, Baudrillard meditates upon geological (and he says, hence, metaphysical) monumentality:

> Upturned relief patterns, sculpted out by wind, water, and ice, dragging you down into the whirlpool of time, into the remorseless eternity of slow-motion catastrophe. The very idea of the millions and hundreds of millions of years that were needed peacefully to ravage the surface of the earth here is a perverse one, since it brings with it an awareness of signs originating, long before man appeared, in a sort of pact of wear and erosion struck between the elements. Among this gigantic heap of signs – purely geological in essence – man will have had no significance. (Baudrillard, 1988, p. 3)

This is a semiological vision before and beyond man which nonetheless is neither Romantic nor idealized; instead, there is a fundamental erosion and collision of geological space and time that causes the fracturing of the elements that create a non-humanist/non-human sign-system: 'blocks of language suddenly rising high, then subjected to pitiless erosion, ancient sedimentations that owe their depth to wear (meaning is born out of the erosion of words, significations are born out of the erosion of signs)' (Baudrillard, 1988, p. 4; see also Milner, 1992). The East as a site of cultural 'centrality' needs to be re-read in relation to this geological semiology, just as 'Ecotopia' in the Pacific Northwest could be further theorized in relation to more ancient modes of generating signification.

FINAL IMAGE/IMAGE WITHOUT END – THE ABORIGINAL

Helen builds her alternative identity in *Minus Time* by acquiring a secret job and an apartment from an anthropologist who has gone to investigate the appearance of an Australian Aboriginal in a gas station:

> He walked further than he ever had before and he ends up at a gas station in the middle of the Australian outback. And no one knows what he's doing there or what he wants because they can't understand him. When they figure out he's never seen a gas station before, that he's never been in contact with the outside world, then things start moving very fast because this isn't supposed to happen any more. (Bush, 1995, p. 47)

This 'alien' Aboriginal is uncanny precisely because in contemporary, fractured, Western societies, every subject has become an anthropologist and every person has become an anthropological subject. What this means is that, hegemonic or heterogeneous, Canadian and US societies are composed of multiple ethnic identities which are cross-cultural as well as culture-specific; even the most obscure and/or private cultural activity can be fodder for a society of the spectacle, which may or may not gain some kind of epistemological and spiritual insight in the process of representing the Other. The aboriginal who appears out of non-anthropological, non-representational space (in terms of a Western power-knowledge) deeply disturbs the colonial, metaphysical project of *absolute knowledge*; instead, this figure is presented in *Minus Time* as someone who needs to be *learnt from*, not about. Homi Bhabha notes that: 'it is from those who have suffered the sentence of history – subjugation, domination, diaspora, displacement – that we learn our most enduring lessons for living and thinking' (Bhabha, 1994, p. 172).

This pedagogic effect is apparent also in terms of the theoretical models used to describe new or emerging literatures from the margins of society. Conceptual frameworks, such as literary theory, be it post-structuralist, postmodernist or ideological, are forced to engage not only with aesthetics, but also to go 'beyond the canonization of the 'idea' of aesthetics' (Bhabha, 1994, p. 172). Bhabha suggests that when culture is shown to be 'produced in the act of social survival' then the complexity of the post-colonial becomes apparent (Bhabha, 1994, pp. 172–73). In *Minus Time*, the fracturing of the nuclear family, spatially and visually – the latter through doubling, duplicity and distance – forces a re-reading of the critical strategies used to engage with the text. *Minus Time* situates itself in the struggle for North American identity primarily in terms of the image; its intertexts are therefore as diverse as Don Delillo's *White Noise* (1984), and Daniel Francis's *The Imaginary Indian: The Image of the Indian in Canadian Culture* (1992). The image of 'the mother' would also need exploration for a more detailed analysis of the novel (see Dunlop, 1998, for theoretical possibilities). *Minus Time* demands a critical strategy that not only thinks about the cultural fracturing of Canada under external and internal pressures, but one that theorizes it in terms of more complex notions of the image (something that much *thematic* new literatures criticism often fails to do). My bringing together, however minimally and provisionally, Baudrillard with critics such as Brown and Ricou is one suggestion. Perhaps for a closer reading of *Minus Time* it would be wise to bring together, say, Linda Hutcheon on the postmodern (1988), and Gilles Deleuze on the Movement Image (1986) and Time Image (1989). Bhabha argues that:

> Postcolonial critical discourses require forms of dialectical thinking that do not disavow or sublate the otherness (alterity) that constitutes the symbolic domain of psychic and social identifications. The incommensurability of cultural values and priorities that the postcolonial critic represents cannot

be accommodated within theories of cultural relativism or pluralism. (Bhabha, 1994, p. 173)

I am suggesting that a new theoretical paradigm is precisely the one which engages in a dialectic of indigenous critical specificities and theoretical models that can deal with the complexities of the representational, media processes that work continuously to simplify and reduce post-colonial cultures. If those theoretical models are drawn from 'elsewhere', then so be it; so long as they are placed in a productive relationship with the local then they will always make us aware that 'the local' is in itself a commodity represented and consumed within an international, visual domain.

Works Cited

Atwood, Margaret, 1972. *Survival: A Thematic Guide to Canadian Literature*, Toronto: Anansi.
Atwood, Margaret, 1979. *Surfacing*, London: Virago.
Atwood, Margaret, 1982. *Second Words: Selected Critical Prose*, Toronto: Anansi.
Baudrillard, Jean, 1988. *America*, London and New York: Verso.
Bhabha, Homi K., 1994. *The Location of Culture*, London: Routledge.
Broege, Valerie, 1981. 'Margaret Atwood's Americans and Canadians', *Essays on Canadian Writing*, **22** (Summer), pp. 111–35.
Brown, Russell, 1994. 'The Road Home: Meditations on a Theme', in Camille R. La Bossière (ed.), *Context North America: Canadian/U.S. Literary Relations*, Ottawa: University of Ottawa Press, pp. 23–48.
Bush, Catherine, 1995. *Minus Time*, London and New York: Serpent's Tail/High Risk.
Colman, S. J., 1979. 'Margaret Atwood, Lucien Goldmann's Pascal, and the Meaning of Canada', *University of Toronto Quarterly*, vol. 48, no. 3 (Spring), pp. 245–62.
Delany, Paul, 1994. 'Introduction: Vancouver as a Postmodern City', in Paul Delany (ed.), *Vancouver: Representing the Postmodern City*, Vancouver: Arsenal Pulp Press, pp. 1–24.
Deleuze, Gilles, 1986. *Cinema 1: The Movement Image*, London: The Athlone Press.
Deleuze, Gilles, 1989. *Cinema 2: The Time Image*, London: The Athlone Press.
Delillo, Don, 1984. *White Noise*, New York: Viking Penguin.
Dunlop, Rishma, 1998. 'Written on the Body', in Sharon Abbey and Andrea O'Reilly (eds), *Redefining Motherhood: Changing Identities and Patterns*, Toronto: Second Story Press, pp. 103–24.

Francis, Daniel, 1992. *The Imaginary Indian: The Image of the Indian in Canadian Culture*, Vancouver: Arsenal Pulp Press.

Hutcheon, Linda, 1988. *The Canadian Postmodern: A Study of Contemporary English-Canadian Fiction*, Toronto: Oxford University Press.

Lane, Richard, 1996. 'A Preface to Malcolm Lowry's *Last Notebook*', *Commonwealth: Essays and Studies*, vol. 18, no. 2 (Spring), pp. 29–35.

Lowry, Malcolm, 1971. *October Ferry to Gabriola*, London: Jonathan Cape.

Miller, Stephen E., 1994. 'The Grid: Living in Hollywood North', in Paul Delany (ed.), *Vancouver: Representing the Postmodern City*, Vancouver: Arsenal Pulp Press, pp. 282–94.

Milner, Clyde A., 1992. 'The View from Wisdom: Four Layers of History and Regional Identity', in William Cronon, George Miles and Jay Gitlin (eds), *Under An Open Sky: Rethinking America's Western Past*, London and New York: Norton, pp. 203–22.

Neel, David, 1991a. 'Life on the 18th Hole', *BC Studies*, no. 89 (Spring), pp. 132–39.

Neel, David, 1991b. 'Artist's Statement', *BC Studies*, no. 89 (Spring), p. 131.

Ricou, Laurie, 1994. 'Two Nations Own These Islands: Border and Region in Pacific-Northwest Writing', in Camille R. La Bossière (ed.), *Context North America: Canadian/U.S. Literary Relations*, Ottawa: University of Ottawa Press, pp. 49–62.

5

The Rhythm of Difference: Language and Silence in *The Chant of Jimmie Blacksmith* and *The Piano*

Marion Wynne-Davies

At the very end of Jane Campion's award-winning film, *The Piano* (1993), the disembodied voice of Ada McGrath recites three lines from Thomas Hood's nineteenth-century sonnet 'Silence':

> There is a silence where hath been no sound
> There is a silence where no sound may be,
> In the cold grave – under the deep, deep sea.
> (Hood, n.d., p. 306)

The accompanying image matches the dark gothic tone of the poem, for the screen displays Ada as she sees herself in a surreal dream, as a corpse floating above her piano in a gloomy subterranean world. This intense, almost metaphysical connection between Ada and her piano is made clear at the beginning of the film when, after being betrothed by her father to a man she has never seen (Stewart), Ada is stranded on the New Zealand coast with her daughter Flora and the piano. The marriage is doomed to failure as soon as Stewart decides to leave the instrument on the beach, and Ada is only able to retrieve it by entering into a sexual deal with another settler, Baines, in which he is allowed to touch her as she 'buys back' her piano, key by key. Ada, however, develops a relationship with Baines and, after a bloody sequence in which the jealous Stewart chops off one of her fingers, the two lovers leave the settlement together. Thus, while Ada may have evaded death in the film's formal narrative, choosing instead to fulfil the romantic and sexual ideal offered by her lover Baines, by concluding with a nightmare-vision Campion ensures that her heroine – and the audience – remain aware of the perilous attractions of suicide and the final grim silence of death. In this sense, the film's closing sequence, together with Ada's role as an elective mute, foreground Campion's political concerns: the subjection of women, their repression within Victorian society, and the silencing of the female voice. Indeed, *The Piano* was widely acclaimed as a 'feminist' film upon its release, as well as in subsequent film criticism; for example, Stella Bruzzi claims that,

> Ada's fierce independence is expressed through her repeated refusal to conform to the designated role of the pacified and distanced image of woman contained by the voyeuristic male gaze. In her muteness, her musicality and the expression of her sexual desire through touch, Ada represents the possibility of a radical alternative feminine and feminist mode of discourse. (Bruzzi, 1995, pp. 257–58)

Yet, as the quotation from Hood at the start of this chapter makes clear, the feminist agenda does not remain as clearly unproblematized as Bruzzi implies, an issue I intend to return to later. At this point, however, I wish to stress the importance of recognizing that while the film has a considerable investment in gender politics it is simultaneously and inextricably immersed within a colonialist discourse, so that the 'radical alternative' suggested by Bruzzi inevitably extends its remit into the fraught area of racial identity. Just as Stewart and the other conventional colonizers misunderstand Ada's expression through music, so the Maori speech is unintelligible to the white characters on screen (with the exception of Baines, whose linguistic flexibility and facial tattoos signify a desirable hybridity). Moreover, while Hira, the film's leading Maori character, is given some English dialogue, the Maori speech is mainly conveyed to a white audience through the use of subtitles, proffering an unsettling experience in which they/we both 'hear' and 'not hear' a considerable portion of the film's dialogue. The result of such doubling is to construct for the audience an uncomfortable self-consciousness for which race and gender are pertinent, as well as disquieting, aspects of identity both on and off screen.

It is precisely this layering of silence which Gayatri Spivak focuses upon in her path-breaking and much-quoted essay 'Can the Subaltern Speak?' in which she writes,

> Within the effaced itinerary of the subaltern subject, the track of sexual difference is doubly effaced. The question is not of female participation in insurgency, or the ground rules of the sexual division of labor, for both of which there is 'evidence'. It is, rather, that, both as object of colonialist historiography and as subject of insurgency, the ideological construction of

gender keeps the male dominant. If, in the context of colonial production, the subaltern has no history and cannot speak, the subaltern as female is even more deeply in shadow. (Spivak, 1993, pp. 82–83)

What Spivak is concerned with in this section of her critique is the way in which a subaltern woman's racial and gender identities reinforce her silence, and therefore her inability to claim an independent subjectivity constructed through language. If she is silenced by her race, she is simultaneously muted by her sex. In *The Piano*, by offering the audience a multiplicity of characters, Campion confronts several different aspects of this race/gender axis, shifting from the archetypal patriarch (Stewart), through the mute white woman (Ada), to the articulate otherness of the Maoris (Hira). Yet, the film was directed primarily at the 'Old World' and American markets where the linguistic domination of English (both as language and literary culture) and the late twentieth-century pro-feminist audience made *The Piano* immensely successful. The movie won Campion prizes at both Cannes and Hollywood, shifting easily from art house to popular cinema in the process. Given its obvious economic remit, the film's engagement with the more unsettling relationships between race and gender are at once radical and repressed. It is precisely this point of intersection that I wish to examine, moving on to explore how far *The Piano* allows the subaltern to speak, and in what way the racial elements of the film interact with its avowedly feminist agenda. Before excavating these various discourses, however, I would like to set up a comparison with another film/novel, which addresses the similar issues, but in a very different manner.

In 1978 Fred Schepisi directed and produced a film version of Thomas Keneally's novel, *The Chant of Jimmie Blacksmith* (1972), which was based on a real incident and Jimmie Blacksmith upon Jimmie Governor. The screenplay was written by Schepisi but remained close to Keneally's original, both focusing on the life of the Aboriginal Jimmie Blacksmith. The eponymous anti-hero is a half-caste who aspires to the nineteenth-century ideals of white colonialist culture – a wife, land ownership, and capital. His attempts to gain acceptance are perpetually and sometimes brutally thwarted until, at the narrative's climax, he murders the white Newby women and escapes into the bush. Jimmie and his brother Mort, whom he has implicated in the crime, are eventually killed, but Schepisi and Keneally both conclude with an uneasy combination of pity and resignation, of white justice and colonial guilt. There are, therefore, clear overlaps in terms of colonial commodification between *The Piano* and *The Chant of Jimmie Blacksmith*. For example, the musical substitute for the recognized language of the white patriarchal settler allows us to compare the experience of Ada's piano playing and her final poetic recitation with Jimmie's initiation chant and the Aboriginal music that accompanies that opening sequence in Schepisi's film. Both white woman and black man are silenced in terms of the white man's dominant codes: Ada's husband, Stewart, cannot appreciate her music any more than the Methodist minister, Mr Neville, can hear or understand Jimmie's chant. But the silencing of the subaltern's native speech is more harshly depicted in the works of the 1970s: Keneally translates and transcribes the Aboriginal songs, so that Jimmie's words may be understood by the white reader. After his initiation ceremony, Jimmie lies waiting for his genitals to heal, singing both to allay the pain and to keep the women of the tribe away:

> In the sting of our manhood,
> Mungara's daughters being few
> As hills beyond Marooka, river snake – scant hills,
> Mungara's daughters scant,
> Over Marooka we went singing,
> Stalking Widgarra under dusty suns,
> Came roaring at them from the moon
> Painting blood on Widgarra men with strokes of warclubs,
> Taking to us all the shrilling pee-wit women, daughters to Mungara,
> Wives unto the men of Emu Wren
> (Keneally, 1972, p. 4)

Some of the names ('Emu Wren') and syntax ('river snake – scant hills') suggest an Aboriginal language, but the overall impression is one of translation, albeit by a sympathetic humanitarian (see Griffiths, 1995, pp. 237–41). Indeed, Keneally's subsequent explication addresses a layered 'readership':

> He [Jimmie] sang it in monotone and with dissonances Mr Neville would have found strange. It was a fine song about an ancient raid. The woman-stealing it recounted had taken place during the English civil war, two and a half centuries previously. (Keneally, 1972, p. 4)

The first sentence appeals to an 'enlightened' readership, perhaps including Aborigines, and calls attention to the differences – equally valued – between the musical structures of the colonizer and the indigene. The account then takes on Jimmie's perception of the song being 'fine'. But then Keneally's authorial historiography asserts itself in describing the narrative events of the song as suggesting for the reader the parallel 'tribal' wars of seventeenth-century Australia and England. In providing this background information Keneally also suggests the comparison between the Tullam warriors of the past and the tribal leaders of Jimmie's present: 'Tribal elders, who cared for initiation teeth and knew where the soul-stones of each man were hidden and how the stones could be distinguished, lent out their wives to white men for a suck from a brandy bottle' (Keneally, 1972, p. 7).

Indeed, Jimmie himself begins to doubt the tribal values of the past and turns to the dominant culture of the white colonizers, embodied in the Nevilles. Yet Jimmie's chant has yet another signification, for it also predicts the murder sequence at the heart of the novel and film: Jimmie, Jackie Smolders and Mort will take up the tribal battle or 'ancient raid', and steal the lives of the white Newby women in a bloody attack which, for Jimmie, must be read as a perverted act of sexual fulfilment. The balance between white and black has shifted so that it hardly seems possible for Jimmie either to kill the Newby men or to rape their women, but his act of violence is replete with a combination of thwarted sexual desire and racial anger. For Keneally, therefore, the Aboriginal chant extends its signification beyond the basic translation into a dark portent which will ultimately bring about Jimmie's death and his final silencing. Not only is the subaltern denied his own language, but also any claim to linguistic independence serves merely to reinforce the absolute silence of extinction, individual, tribal and racial.

The primary, and perhaps inevitable, difference between *The Piano* and *The Chant of Jimmie Blacksmith* must be that Ada is, to a certain extent, free to choose between life and death, between articulate independence and muted repression, whereas Jimmie, whose desires for autonomous subjectivity are so deeply etched, can never be granted that freedom and must instead resign himself to the passive existence of a subaltern or suffer death as a consequence of revolt. The comic resolution of Campion's film and the tragic conclusion of Keneally's novel – and Schepisi's cinematic version – throw into sharp relief the inequalities of race and gender, as well as highlighting the differences between the cultural products of the 1970s and 1990s. In the remainder of this chapter I intend to look more specifically at the commodifications which recur in both 'texts' – language, sexual desire and violence – in order to explore the way in which Campion, Keneally and Schepisi explore the fraught relationships connecting and surrounding gender and race in a post-colonialist discourse.

Both Ada and Jimmie are 'muted'; they are silenced by patriarchal and colonial domination respectively. Yet, both narratives suggest a wide range of voices, none of which settles neatly into the expected dominant role. In *The Piano* Stewart is too nervous, too self-doubting, to assert a final authority over Ada: he violates her hand, but cannot rape her, he sells her piano but cannot stop her 'playing' even if it is only on a table-top carved to emulate the patterns of a keyboard. While he, as the representative of patriarchal ownership, should objectify her, it is she who strokes his body allowing the camera to play erotically over his flesh, instead of her body. Nor is Baines any more suited to the role of colonizer. With his facial *moko* (tattoos), his ability to converse with the indigenous Maoris, his illiteracy, his unkempt appearance and makeshift hut, Baines clearly represents a hybrid type, a white man who has become Maori-like through choice. Lynda Dyson argues that Baines as a character – and consequently the film as the macrocosmic version of his negotiations – represents the late twentieth-century New Zealand claims to white indigeneity; Baines is a *pakeha*. She explains that,

> 'Pakeha' is a Maori word, highly contested in translation, referring to those with European ancestry or, more generally, 'outsiders'. Increasingly, it is a term being used to stake out a white ethnic identity which can make claims to 'indigeneity' through the appropriation of traditional motifs and the claiming of spiritual attachment to the land ... [and] that post-colonial self-fashioning [uses] the ethnic category *pakeha* ... to avoid the connotations of supremacy that the word 'white' has acquired. (Dyson, 1995, pp. 268–69)

Viewed in this context, Baines, and subsequently Ada and Flora, may be seen as *pakeha*, the outsiders who have successfully laid claim to an indigenous ethnicity and who are receptive to the Maori identity and people they encounter. Indeed, the lovers are particularly idealized in comparison with Stewart's uptight, archetypal colonist and the narrow outlook of the Mission group, Aunt Morag, Nessie and the Reverend Campbell. The early white settlers of New Zealand are represented – and castigated – in terms of their land acquisition (Stewart) and their attempts at religious/moral conversion (the Mission), while present-day white New Zealanders are offered the possibility of identifying with the *pakeha* loyalties of Baines and Ada. The fact that the latter two characters are played by famous American 'stars' further contributes to the desirability of an association with them and all they represent, not only for a Southern hemisphere audience, but also for the US and European cinemagoers. Baines, therefore, who might initially appear as a radicalized alternative to the white patriarchal colonizer, begins to mutate into the acceptable (white) face of late twentieth-century post-colonial ethnicity, and it is important to remember that his *mokos* cannot give him a black face, any more than his fluency in the Maori tongue can offer a voice to the subaltern. As Gail Low comments in *White Skins/Black Masks*, 'The figure of the white man in native costume is an imaginary fantasy of the white man *as* native' (Low, 1996, p. 192).

Still, there are Maori actors and actresses in *The Piano* and they do speak in their own language on screen. When Stewart first meets Ada on the beach he is accompanied by a group of Maoris and by Baines, who together help him to transfer her belongings to the settlement inland. The Maoris speak to one another in their own tongue, but no subtitles are used unless there is direct reference to the whites on screen. For example, when Ada and Stewart argue about the transportation of the piano, one of the male Maoris stands behind Stewart parodying his every facial gesture. As the prospective husband becomes increasingly disquieted by the woman's mute, but stubborn pleas, the Maori jokes to the others and his words are translated for the audience via the subtitles, 'Old Dry Balls is getting touchy'. There is a ripple of laughter on the beach that is shared by the audience, which of course Stewart fails to understand. Thus, at one level we become complicit with the Maoris, understanding their humour and joining in their mockery of the sexual repression of Victorian patriarchy. The audience too becomes *pakeha*, acknowledging the open sexuality which an association with nature and the land may be seen to offer. Yet, are the subtitles and non-verbal gestures proof of the subaltern speaking? Does *The Piano* allow the indigene a full independent subjectivity? If so, it is not in these opening sequences, for the Maoris' words are translated *only* when they have a specific relevance to the white characters and, moreover, when that association reiterates a late twentieth-century post-colonial negotiation of ethnicity. The audience's ability to hear the indigene is limited in terms of content (about whites) and ideology (the censure of repressed Victorian male sexuality replicating a present-day white attitude). In other words, we only listen to the subaltern when we already agree with what he or she has to say. Even Hira, the most vocal and powerful of the Maoris depicted, remains a stereotyped figure. She is independent enough to offer Baines advice, suggesting that he reject the sanctions of colonialism in order to fulfil his natural sexual desires, and to look for a new partner, rather than wed in emulation of the formal and slightly ludicrous ceremony enacted by Stewart and Ada. Moreover, almost in a salute to political correctness, this scene is observed by a male homosexual Maori, whose desire for Baines is treated as an acceptable social gambit, even if it is finally repulsed. This interchange, therefore, offers a doubly idealized vision of the indigene, in that it calls upon the late twentieth-century *pakeha* to acknowledge their 'natural' sexual needs, as well as conjuring up the old Rousseau notion of the noble savage with his or her innocent and untainted participation in sexual activity. In the same way, the Maori children encourage Flora to rub herself erotically against the trees, an innocent game that is observed by Stewart who, with the baggage of his repressive ideology, interprets this act of 'consummating' a relationship with nature as 'dirty'. But, whether the romanticization belongs to the nineteenth or twentieth century, it makes little difference to the Maori women, since their sexuality is as thoroughly effaced as their language; they are, as Spivak points out, 'doubly effaced' (Spivak, 1993, p. 82).

Holly Hunter is presented, almost immediately, in the role of a desirable woman: the soft lighting of the first Scottish scenes, the fetishization of her petticoat and hoops on the beach, and Stewart's worried gaze at her photograph, all contribute to make her an object of sexual passion. The treatment of the Maori women could hardly be more different. The first two women focused upon by the camera do not speak, but sit either side of Ada and Flora, while the men determine the route they will follow to the settlement (the Maoris refuse to tramp through their burial ground, much to Stewart's irritation). One of the Maori women distracts Ada as the other steals her shawl, which is then worn with mock coquetry by the first woman. The white women are aware of what happens, but remain tense and silent, nervous of their new surroundings and the Maoris who sit next to them. As with the parody of Stewart on the beach, it might be possible to interpret the shawl-stealing scene as a complicity between Maori and *pakeha* audience, this time encoding a critique of the excessive and incommodious nature of European clothes (designed primarily to adorn), when worn in the wilderness. But the actress who wears the shawl cannot compete with, nor fully comment upon, Ada's sexual attractiveness, for she is, in the eyes of an American and European audience, unattractive due to her age and weight. The other Maori actress is younger and thinner and might possibly have offered a more powerful statement of indigenous sexuality should the camera have focused upon her, but the final frame of this sequence serves to efface, rather than affirm, the sexual identity of the female subaltern. This is further underlined when Hira's commentary upon Baines's desirability and his need for a 'wife' are followed by an immediate cut to Ada, eliding any possibility that Baines might find the Maori woman herself attractive. Although Tungia Baker, who plays Hira, would not comply with a Hollywood version of glamour, she is a strong attractive woman in her forties, and certainly outshines Harvey Keitel in the beauty stakes. But, Hira's role as a desexualized Maori woman is further stressed by the presence of the attractive young man Tahu who offers himself openly to Baines. In a film replete with otherness – in terms of race, gender, sexuality and even physical disabilities – it is only the subaltern woman who is denied the freedom of articulating a sexual identity and of asserting her own desirability.

The stereotypes called upon by Campion in *The Piano* are, to a certain extent, replicated in Keneally's and Schepisi's versions of *The Chant of Jimmie Blacksmith*. For example, the smiling Maori who parodies Stewart might be seen in the mocking easy laughter of Mort, Jimmie's brother.

When the two Aborigines work for a Scottish man called Lewis, '[He] mistrusted Morton, who had Dulcie's flippancy. As old Lewis stumped about with a yard-stick, breathing sinusitically through a soiled moustache, Mort would double with laughter, would sit down on a tree-stump and quiver at some quaintness in the man' (Keneally, 1972, p. 27). In both film and novel, however, the two brothers converse in English, Jimmie asking Mort to 'Give it a rest' and the latter replying that 'The whitey he made me' (Keneally, 1972, p. 28). Keneally's prose never allows Jimmie or his Aboriginal kin to speak in their own language, although he is clearly sympathetic to their social plight. Similarly, Schepisi allows the camera to dwell on the warm relationship between the two brothers and sets these images against the harsh brutality of the white farmers. Indeed, whereas Keneally maintains a bleak irony and comments wryly upon the ferocity of Scottish bookkeeping, Schepisi prefers to stress the violent and unjust repression of the indigenous Australian peoples by the white settlers. It is thus possible to situate both novel and film within the burgeoning social consciousness of the Australian liberalism during the 1970s (Griffiths, 1995, pp. 237–41). As Ania Loomba writes in response to Spivak's questioning of the subaltern's articulacy, 'Is objectivity possible, or are we merely ventriloquising our own concerns when we make the subaltern speak? Of course, to some extent, our investments in the past are inescapably coloured by our present-day commitments' (Loomba, 1998, p. 243).

With Keneally's novel in particular the concern that Jimmie merely ventriloquizes the concerns of the Australian liberal elite must be addressed, since the novel itself frequently imposes a double-voice, demanding that we hear the subaltern at exactly the same time as we hear the ironized voice of the white author. Of course, Keneally is supremely aware of the dangers of a post-colonial identification of the white intelligentsia with the repressed Aborigine and, almost as an answer to any possible criticism of his authorial self-awareness, consequently introduces the figure of McCreadie. Jimmie and Mort encounter the schoolmaster when on the run, and, perhaps to buy himself time or allay their fears, he shows them a newspaper cartoon:

> It was a caricature of two plump aborigines camped in a forest setting, feeding police bloodhounds with legs of mutton. One of the two aborigines was telling a satiated police-dog, 'Go back to yer boss an' tell 'im yer ain't seen nothing!' Both natives were smiling, and the one not bribing the bloodhounds was reading a newspaper which bannered the news: *Blacksmith Brothers still at large after two months*. (Keneally, 1972, p. 136)

In a magnificent leap of postmodernist verve Keneally offers us the image of the Blacksmith brothers reading the paper in which the Blacksmith brothers are pictured reading the paper, and this self-reflexive irony allows those same brothers to laugh, if briefly, and to value the intelligent skill of the man who made such a respite possible. McCreadie is able with a single gesture to question the dominant colonial ideology, to demonstrate that he is able to empathize with the Blacksmiths and their predicament, and to combine this wide-ranging perspicacity with humour and courage. Therefore it hardly comes as a surprise when, within the narrative, Jimmie decides to take McCreadie with them, although all three men become 'quickly disenchanted' since, as Keneally points out with authorial certainty, 'people are never passive mirrors' (Keneally, 1972, p. 139), which is, of course, precisely the point.

The voice inscribed in the cartoon purports to be the voice of the indigene, it mocks the futile authority of the white police and speaks in what is assumed to be the Aboriginal dialect – "im yer ain't'. Keneally's text, in which Mort points out to Mrs McCreadie that '"Three thousan' sure t'catch us in the end"' (Keneally, 1972, p. 138), thus takes on the role of both the authentic Aboriginal voice (the 'real' Blacksmith brothers speak) while at the same time affirming that no 'authentic' voice is possible (the words spoken by Jimmie and Mort are, after all, an integral part of the fictional text), and that all voices are 'ventriloquized', merely a further utterance of a subject position within the dominant ideology. Keneally towards the end of the novel further affirms this emphasis on the instability of post-colonial identity, where the homogeneity of the authorial voice is gradually eroded through a process of fragmentation and multiplicity. Consecutive narrative prose gives way to letters (seemingly unconnected to the story), to more newspaper excerpts and to historical records. When Jimmie is finally hanged the novel has already given up its claim to a single authentic voice, so that the silencing of the subaltern is lost within the polyphony of oppositional and mutually negating discourses. Yet Keneally never allows the post-colonial reader to escape the brooding unease that has accumulated throughout the novel. The subaltern's voice might be silenced within a postmodern disintegration of the metanarrative, but the sheer violence of Jimmie's crime and the crime against all Aborigines demands that the 'chant' be heard even though it has no one left to sing it.

Schepisi's film does not participate fully in the postmodern agenda, perhaps because of the differing historical allegiances of his genre. The 1970s were only just beginning to allow for experimental pastiche in popular cinema and as such *The Chant of Jimmie Blacksmith* shifts uneasily between a 1950s neo-realism and a 1960s mystic surrealism.

The latter's tonal qualities may be seen in the panning shots of the bush, the sky and the journeying figures which combine to offer the audience an almost spiritual communion with nature, thus participating in the same romanticized vision of the indigene portrayed in *The Piano*. In one of the few critiques of the earlier film, Brian McFarlane distinguishes these two elements in his comments upon the difference between director and author:

> Schepisi is in general more taken by the poetic possibilities of the story than Keneally, and this leads him, while retaining the same incidents, into a more obviously emotional, sometimes visually and aurally voluptuous, approach instead of the spare, ironic tone adopted by Keneally. (McFarlane, 1984, p. 160)

Yet, while McFarlane admires this mystical approach, he finds the quasi-realism of the film jarring. Indeed, McFarlane sees the most significant difference between the novel and film to be Schepisi's political commitment;

> Schepisi is passionately involved with the way the story embodies a harsh criticism of white injustice, its patronage and repression of another race, and this leads him to use the screen at certain key points as a platform. (McFarlane, 1984, p. 158)

While McFarlane believes that such investments are reductive to the artistic whole, there can be no doubt that the film leaves the audience as disquieted as does the novel. Take for example the two scenes that I have already examined in relation to the prose: the self-referential reading of the newspaper and the concluding implosion of the meta-narrative. While Schepisi retains the incident in which McCreadie shows the Blacksmith brothers the cartoon of themselves, the audience merely glimpses the image in the newspaper. Instead, the camera focuses on the individual faces of the group as they begin to laugh, but as the humour continues the camera shots move from the two black faces to the white couple and back again, thereby emphasizing the spatial distance between the races through image, even as the soundtrack continues to blend their voices. Moreover, the laughter continues too long and the audience, like Mort and the McCreadies, wait for Jimmie's reaction, wait for him to break the mutual, but precarious, moment of communion between races. The comic respite ends, as in the novel, when Jimmie decides to make McCreadie his hostage, but the fear and pain on the white faces underline the deep divisions that still exist between the colonizers and the Aborigines despite the brief illusion of shared understanding. The self-reflexive power of the cartoon sequence is lost as the film privileges political comment and the social recognition of a country still divided by its racial history.

The final sequences in Schepisi's film perpetuate the split from the novel already initiated by the rejection of the cartoon image: the metanarrative is sustained as Jimmie becomes increasingly victimized; he is shot, beaten and imprisoned, and as he is dragged from the convent where he has taken refuge, the camera adopts Jimmie's gaze, so that the audience too lies defenceless on the ground being attacked by the white soldiers and lynch-gang. Then, in a startling shift, Schepisi allows the camera's viewpoint to reside with Mr Hyberry, the hangman, so that the audience peers voyeuristically at Jimmie through the peephole in the cell door. The movement from victim to executioner echoes the earlier camera cuts from Blacksmiths to McCreadies, emphasizing an unhealable racial breach, while at the same time demanding that the audience acknowledge the victimization of the indigene and their own colonialist guilt. But finally, as the credits roll, the backdrop shifts to a green panoply of the Australian bush over which swoop white birds, the symbolism of which suggests – through a mystical commingling of tribal faith, Christian ideology, and the omnipotence of nature – the ultimate rebirth of Jimmie predicted by the initiation chant at the beginning of the film. Unlike the novel, which concludes with disruptive disintegration, the film offers the possibility of a spiritual/natural resolution that goes some way towards undercutting the political unease that Schepisi has already constructed. While McFarlane is right to suggest that the film version of *The Chant of Jimmie Blacksmith* 'offer[s] a harsh criticism of white injustice', at the same time it belongs to its mid-1970s cultural identity, in that a hopeful resolution becomes possible through the 'natural' merging of racial difference, almost akin to the *pakeha* idealization in *The Piano*.

Both films construct an audience for whom colonialist guilt is an inescapable aspect of their own culture's history, yet both offer the possibility, through character and symbolism, of a developing indigeneity. While the term '*pakeha*' is normally used to denote the appropriation of an ethnic identity in present-day New Zealand, this form of 'post-colonial self-fashioning' clearly extends its desirability beyond the margins of its national origins. During the last 30 years of the twentieth century, with the rapid development of post-colonial studies, dominant white groups have increasingly adopted the role of the *pakeha*. Both *The Piano* and Schepisi's *The Chant of Jimmie Blacksmith* rely for their effect precisely upon this need of a post-colonial audience, whether from Europe, the US or New Zealand/Australia, to identify, not with the repressive patriarchal forces embodied by Stewart and the Newbys, but with the indigene and the 'natural world' they occupy. As such, even the word '*pakeha*' is transformed from the Maori original into a term that reflects back to the white post-colonialist audience an idealized image of themselves. It is, therefore, Keneally's novel that offers its readership the most disturbing and searching image, for it openly proclaims that 'people are never passive mirrors'. Thus the only means of securing ascendancy is through violence and death, the ultimate breaking of the living 'mirror' of race and the final silencing of the subaltern's voice. For Keneally, in *The Chant of Jimmie Blacksmith*, the scars of racial conflict remain unhealed and the silencing of the indigene's voice is as utterly profound, and predictable, as the execution of Jimmie himself. Yet even in *The Piano* Campion cannot allow the camera to rest on the idealized vision of the *pakeha*-like Baines and Ada, but instead takes the audience beneath the waters to where piano and woman remain in muted stillness. The political import of the 'silence where there hath been no sound', of the merging of woman and nature in the 'cold grave', is, of course, feminist rather than post-colonial. But Campion, like Keneally, concludes with a dark reminder of women's silence and their continued repression within a dominant patriarchal ideology; a point which must have particular relevance for a female director in a predominantly male profession. Whatever the possibilities of change, either racial or gendered, that are initially proffered by the text and films discussed in this chapter, ultimately we are left with a choice of accepting the desirable, but hollow, identity of the *pakeha*, or of acknowledging that the final irony of the subaltern's voice is that it may only be heard at the moment of its negation, that the chant, like the piano, exists finally in 'a silence where no sound may be'.

Works Cited

Bruzzi, Stella, 1995. 'Tempestuous petticoats: costume and desire in *The Piano*', *Screen*, vol. 36, no. 3 (Autumn), pp. 257–58.
Campion, Jane and Kate Pullinger, 1994. *The Piano, a novel*, London: Bloomsbury.
Dyson, Lynda, 1995. 'The return of the repressed? Whiteness, femininity and colonialism in *The Piano*', *Screen*, vol. 36, no. 3 (Autumn), pp. 268–9.
Griffiths, Gareth, 1995. 'The Myth of Authenticity', in Bill Ashcroft, Gareth Griffiths and Helen Tiffin (eds), *The Post-Colonial Studies Reader*, London: Routledge, pp. 237–41.
Hood, Thomas, n.d. *The Poetical Works of Thomas Hood*, London: Frederick Warne and Co.
Keneally, Thomas, 1972. *The Chant of Jimmie Blacksmith*, Harmondsworth: Penguin Books, 1988.

Loomba, Ania, 1998. *Colonialism/post-colonialism*, London: Routledge.
Low, Gail Ching-Liang, 1996. *White Skins/Black Masks: Representation and Colonialism*, London: Routledge.
McFarlane, Brian, 1984. *Words and Images. Australian Novels into Film*, Melbourne: Heinemann Publishers Australia.
Spivak, Gayatri Chakravorty, 1993. 'Can the Subaltern Speak?', in Patrick Williams and Laura Chrisman (eds), *Colonial Discourse and Post-Colonial Theory: A Reader*, London: Harvester Wheatsheaf, pp. 66–111.

6

Locating and Celebrating Difference: Writing by South African and Aboriginal Women Writers

Gina Wisker

> Here they [women] are, returning, arriving over and again, because the unconscious is impregnable. They have wandered around in circles, confined to the narrow room in which they've been given a deadly brainwashing. You can incarcerate them, slow them down, get away with the old Apartheid routine, but for a time only. At the same time as they're taught their name, they can be taught that their territory is black: because you are Africa, you are black ... we have internalized this horror of the dark.
> (Cixous, 1981, pp. 247–48)

Women and women's bodies, notes Cixous, are consistently expressed as sites ripe for oppression or liberation. 'Otherized' triply because of gender, race and class, for black women silence and subordination is often a seemingly inescapable state. It would be naive to insist that the experiences of South African and Aboriginal women are identical, but there are similarities, both in that continued state of oppression and silence and in the power of articulation, through which arises expression of identity, a claiming of community and power.

The literary and feminist literary critical theories and practices of African-American women writers such as Toni Morrison, Alice Walker and bell hooks have provided both a stimulus and a framework in relation to which many emergent black women writers have developed their writing practices, and more particularly through which we can start to read their work. Distinctive feminist literary critical practices have, however, also grown up in Australia and South Africa and these too can influence reading of African-American texts. Through semi-fictionalized autobiographical forms South African and Aboriginal women write out against such colonization and silencing. They reinterpret labellings and constrictions, and reinvest relationships between land, community and individual. Aboriginal writers consistently stress land title, and the right to claim self as well as land, recognizing identity as formed and located in relation to cultural, geographical and historical context. South African writers, often in exile, also relate identity to the problematized constructed space of South Africa that so often, under apartheid, attempted to erase them.

The dangers of homogenizing the writing of black women writers are ever present when making critical comparisons between the writing of women from different locations. Indeed, the histories of many of our relationships with, and representations of, the people of previously colonized countries and their writings have suffered from such an accidental or deliberate erasure of their differences, their specificity and individual worth. But there are also many similarities and fascinating comparisons to be made, particularly between the writings of Aboriginal and black South African women. These arise, I would argue, from their very location in contested, colonially appropriated southern spaces and the vital interest in linking location and identity evident in their work. Land is important in the work of both groups of writers, because it relates to placing and locating identity in oneself and one's community:

> Aboriginality means to me that you come from the land. It's your land, Australia, the trees, the grass, the seas, the deserts, the rain forests, are all linked with ourself. It's something nobody can take away from you. (Whitlock and Carter, 1992, p. 99)

South African and Aboriginal women writers make a similarly powerful investment in the relationships between land and identity, and challenge the renaming and appropriating of their lands and identities by northern imperial invaders and settlers. Both South African and Aboriginal women, writing of identity and location, choose polemical, often semi-fictionalized autobiographical forms that utilize orally based structures and expressions. Such works articulate and embody their assertion of different readings, different interpretations, and different selves, challenging northern or Eurocentric imperatives of relationships with the land. Linked to this, there is another challenge, to postmodernism's denial of the subject. They assert a renewed recognition and expression of identity. Of Bessie Head, the South African writer, Craig Mackenzie notes that apartheid effectively prevented identification with African communities. But she became connected through her move across the border to Botswana: 'The sense of Botswana's almost uninterrupted African history had an immediate and profound influence on her, a victim of almost total deracination in the land of her birth' (Head, 1990, p. xvii).

The title of this chapter suggests several areas of argument that I wish to develop. Locating indicates relationships between people and their location – the place from which they speak – more than just context, and also a placing and naming. Historically, for both South African and, more particularly, for Aboriginal peoples, naming and labelling has been a dangerous, destructive act. It erased their land ownership rights and erased them along with it. Misnaming and renaming have taken difference as a first stage in relationships of hierarchy in which indigenous peoples are always subordinated, categorized and devalued in the terms of white European culture. I wish to indicate some of the difficulties in actually locating texts by South African and Aboriginal women writers, although this lessens with time as publishers seek to recuperate and publish lost texts, opening their categorization systems as well as their minds to the recognition of different kinds of writing which often evade canonical labels.

Semi-fictionalized Autobiography

> Why is it that just at the moment when so many of us who have been silenced begin to demand the right to name ourselves to act as subjects rather than objects of history, that just then the concept of subjecthood becomes problematical? ... Our nonbeing was the condition and being of the One, the center, the taken-for-granted ability of one small segment of the population to speak for all ... we need ... to develop an account of the world which treats our perspective not as subjugated or disrupted knowledge, but as primitive and constitutive of a different world. (Harstock, 1990, pp. 163, 171)

Aboriginal and South African women writers have in common their expression through semi-fictionalized autobiography, a form favoured by women writers, but often treated by postmodernist critics as critically dubious because of its assertion of a fixed subject position.

Autobiography is a form of testifying and in the hands of South African and Aboriginal women writers it enables not only the establishment of individual identity but an expression of the identity and experiences of a people, a community for whom the individual speaks. Both Aboriginal and South African women are recuperating versions of their past lives through the explorations and expressions of autobiography:

Telling our stories, using the 'self as subject', shows the intersection between the individual and the larger forces of our history. In telling our stories we attempt to understand both intellectually and emotionally. We each have a story to tell, in its uniqueness and commonalty, but also in its constructedness. In remembering in the present, we begin to realise that parts of our past are waiting to be reclaimed, re-visioned and told as we view the past through the lens of the present, weaving an inter-textual narrative. (Govinden, 1995, pp. 170–83)

Women writers in post-apartheid South Africa testify to a history of suffering and silencing, forming versions of a lived, shared history that can be communicated to others. The autobiographical project for both groups of women writers enables this kind of recognition, and expression of the self and the community in history, a reinscription of women's lives into the location from which they spring which has largely, historically, erased them at least in terms of their recognition by a wider audience. It would be a culturally arrogant mistake to assume that their stories have been unheard in a largely oral culture, clearly they have, but the time has come, they seem to say, through publication, to share their experiences with wider groups of readers. As they shape versions of their own lives they shape expressions of their shared histories, of experience. Critically, this is set against the postmodernist project that attempts to reject the expression of a constructed subject and subject position, aware of the constructedness of 'self' and 'reality'. In a time when self and reality need to be recognized and expressed, the postmodern project is clearly out of place. As André Brink puts it, 'it is too artificial, too controlled and then too conservative' (Brink, 1998, p. 18).

Autobiography enables the reclamation of voice, empowerment, and a choice over forms of representation by the writers themselves in the face of misrepresentation through the discourses of colonial power. Autobiography becomes a form that enables first steps to be made in establishing, sharing and expressing cultural identities.

Bessie Head and Zoë Wicomb use semi-fictionalized autobiographies. For them and the COSAW (Congress of South African Writers Collective) and Lesotho writing groups, forms of autobiography provide particularly authentic first person testimony of history and experiences otherwise rendered secondhand through other written versions, including journalism. As with the early slave narratives, testifying to one's experience has always had strength and authenticity for Black communities. When allied with the need to frame, control and make sense of experience rather than merely record it, and to construct an 'I' figure, a fictionalized version of the self, an awareness of the problematic, a constructed status of this authentic voice emerges. Bessie

Head and Zoë Wicomb's semi-fictionalized autobiographies are both authentic *and* constructed, interpreted; they represent the self and the community.

Noni Jabavu (1960; 1963) and Bessie Head (1969; 1974) led the way in South African fictionalized autobiography. Under apartheid, Black women's fiction was often banned. Miriam Tlali's *Muriel at the Metropolitan* (1975) reacted against oppression and subordination, and was banned. This was followed by *Amandla* (1980), and *Soweto Stories* (1989). Lauretta Ngcobo's *Cross of Gold* (1981) was banned in South Africa. Agnes Sam wrote *Jesus is Indian and Other Stories* (1989); Jayapraga Reddy, *On the Fringe of Dream-Time and Other Stories* (1987). Zoë Wicomb published her short story sequence/novel *You Can't Get Lost in Cape Town* (1987). All relate identity to location.

Cultural contexts affect, condition, encourage and prevent forms of reading as they do forms of writing. South Africa is in the exciting, challenging, often contradictory process of reinventing itself. Women's autobiographies are dialogues between an oppressive and silencing present and a resisting, culturally generated, self-creating individual voice.

The fictionalized autobiographical works of Bessie Head, Zoë Wicomb, Lauretta Ngcobo, Ellen Kuzwayo and women of the COSAW collective (*Like a House on Fire*, 1994 and Kendall, *Basali!*, 1995) represent different versions, from different South(ern) African contexts, of the wish to reconstruct, and represent the self in the face of silencing social, political and textual colonial master narratives. 'It is not the raw truth, the raw events of our embittered days of violence. Essentially writing is about the truth contemplated through the crucible of the imagination, and therefore truth becomes art' (Ngcobo, 1994, p. 2).

South African Ellen Kuzwayo (*Call Me Woman*, 1988) writes both as the individual 'I' and as a member of the collective community 'we'. Her autobiography 'puts aside the rhinoceros hide, to reveal a people with a delicate nervous balance like everyone else' (Head, 1990, p. 89):

> [O]ne feels as if a shadow history of South Africa has been written; there is a sense of triumph, of hope in this achievement and that one has read the true history of the land, a history that vibrates with human compassion and goodness. (Kuzwayo, in Head, 1990, p. 89)

The record of her life is a testament of suffering, and hope.

Autobiographical and semi-autobiographical works also belong to a long tradition of Aboriginal creative response:

The widespread use of biography and autobiography by Aboriginal writers can be linked to a cultural tradition in which verse or song would detail the lives of dreaming ancestors ... It remains to be seen, if this tradition was used to detail the lives of ordinary people ... It may have been so. (Narogin, 1985, p. 2)

Historically, Aboriginal women were subject to misrepresentation and sexual abuse: 'Black women were viewed by white males as being founts of insatiable libidinal desire' (Narogin, 1985, p. 18). Misunderstood and appropriated by white men, they were stolen, raped, owned, forced into servitude, abandoned, dehumanized on stations and throughout Australia while genocide wiped out Aboriginal people, reducing them in Queensland from 120,000 in the 1820s to less than 20,000 by the 1920s. Discourse is power. Dehumanizing language underwrote dehumanizing treatment. Aboriginal women, 'gins', 'stud gins', 'black velvet', were hunted, captured, mustered and kept for sexual and domestic chores on stations. Prostitutes and homestead girls were paid in bad drink and bad opium, then discarded. Venereal disease spread, starvation and exposure followed, the birth-rate fell, and kin alienation resulted, aided later by the mass removal of black children into adoption or into Mission upbringing, and the blurring of racial lines by mixed race relationships.

REPRESENTATION AND WRITING

Set against this history of disempowerment and translation, Aboriginal women write of their lives, and those of family and community to describe and so pass on the tenor of the everyday in these very different contexts. By doing so they dispel myths about Aboriginal peoples – for example, that they are always lazy and drunk – and tell the truth about racism and sexism. They also write of the difficulties of recognizing blackness and identity in a racist community.

Growing out of the oral tradition, many works are life stories, some co-authored, some semi-fictionalized. Autobiographies include Evonne Goolagong's *Evonne! On the Move* (1973), and work by Margaret Tucker, Theresa Clemens and Shirley C. Smith who, with the assistance of Bobbi Sykes, wrote *Mumshirl: An Autobiography* (1981). Marnie Kennedy's *Born a Half Caste* (1985), and Sally Morgan's *My Place* (1987), Glenyse Ward's *Wandering Girl* (1988), and Ruby Langford's *Don't Take Your Love to Town* (1988) followed. The very first novels, which have a great deal of autobiographical content, are Faith Bandler's *Wacvie* (1977), and Monica Clare's *Karobran* (1978). Recent works include Melissa

Lucashenko's *Steam Pigs* (1997), and Alexis Wright's *Plains of Promise* (1997).

Without partnership and cultural translation, Aboriginal women are now writing for themselves and their communities: 'A new phenomenon of contemporary Aboriginal writing is emerging whereby women writers have the double advantage of relating their history in literally black and white terms, and simultaneously transcending and cutting across cultural boundaries' (Huggins, 1987/8, p. 22). The scripting of oral story-telling and oral histories has its losses as well as its gains, and only the sensitive Aboriginal author can retain and build upon the cadences and the spiralling forms of the traditional modes of story and life tales. What can be lost in the written recording of oral history or oral literature is a 'different voice': 'Its rhythms, its spiral not linear chronology, its moods of non-verbal communication, its humour, and its withholding of information. Many of these things will be untranslatable to the printed page' (Ferrier, 1991, p. 135). Mudrooroo Narogin, among others, has questioned both the authenticity and the right of some Aboriginal writers to speak of their lives and those of their families, particularly if this involves white ghost writing, or the 'battler' genre, a largely white Australian mode.

Gillian Whitlock, collecting a variety of versions of autobiographical writings notes: 'The issue of who is authorised to speak, and who is not is complex and has attracted a good deal of critical attention of late, these debates draw our attention to the mechanics of the autobiographical text, the details of language, structure and point of view' (Whitlock, 1996, p. xvi). But, as Carole Ferrier argues, in a context where withholding of knowledge, and particularly that of the traditional elders, is seen as properly upholding cultural traditions, nonetheless speaking out is also empowering. Daisy, in Sally Morgan's *My Place* (1987), tells some parts of her history and withholds others, taking them to her grave.

> 'I got secrets, Sally. I don't want anyone to know.'
>
> 'Everything can't be a secret: You dunno what a secret is.'
>
> 'I don't like secrets. Not when thems the sort of secrets you could use to help your own people.'
>
> 'It wouldn't make no difference.'
>
> 'That's what everyone says. No one will talk, don't you see, Nan, someone's got to tell. Otherwise things will stay the same, they won't get any better.'
> (Morgan, 1987, p. 319)

Arthur, her uncle, says Daisy misunderstands history when she retains these secrets – so there is a tussle between telling to establish a history, and retaining to maintain the secret which is itself an act of power. This is a very different interpretation for readers whose Eurocentric or American-oriented reading practices always favour speaking out. Jan Labarlestier comments on this debate of empowerment and silence: 'Aboriginality has been constructed in dominant "white" discourses. In contemporary Australian society "Living black" and writing about it can be seen as a process of confrontation' (Labarlestier, 1991, p. 90). This confrontation some avoid.

The debate about the relative value of various forms of expression in the literary and Aboriginal community is highly politicized and problematic. 'Merely' recording black life has been a criticism levelled at Toni Morrison, who has seen herself as rising above this to produce fiction, creative, experimental, an art form, while fictionalizing itself might be a form of truth. Morrison addresses this problem in her essay 'The Site of Memory' (1987, p. 161), by arguing that her fictionalizing forms gain access to a deeper truth beyond the mere recording of facts. This recognition can inform our reading of both Aboriginal and South African women's fictionalized autobiographies, records of facts and experiences, individual and community, and fictional in their formats, constructing a speaking 'I', retelling tales which themselves grow from various cultural and myth genres.

Aboriginal women writers are aware of the disempowerment of remaining absent and silent, and of the reality of appropriation, of being misrepresented in any transaction which offers their works wider dissemination. Sally Morgan's *My Place* (1987) is a record of the lives of her family and her people, like Glenyse Ward's *Wandering Girl* (1988). The style of the latter is realistic, wryly humorous, a testimony to the ability to survive bigotry and racism, showing the survival tactics of this lively, outspoken, self-aware woman to speak out for others such as herself, brought up in a Mission away from her family then employed for basic wages in domestic labour. Unnamed in her work for Mrs Bigelow, Glenyse deliberately enjoys freedom, eating what she wishes in her employer's absence, and enters the dining room to present herself to guests, insisting that she has a name, much to her employer's embarrassment. She is speaking out and speaking back, and speaking for others also brought up in Missions away from their families, expected to be erased in the white households where they worked. Alexis Wright (1997) also speaks of the alienation of Mission upbringing.

My Place (1987) locates Sally Morgan and her family as Aboriginal people, their history and lifestyles devalued in a racist white society. Part of the book focuses on cultural identification. Sally's family hid their origins to escape abuse, and on realizing she was Aboriginal rather than Indian, Sally's identity confusions and locations clamour together.

No positive representations of Aboriginals aid her search for points of contact with her origins:

> The kids at school had also begun asking us what country we came from. This puzzled me because, up until then I'd thought we were the same as them. If we insisted that we came from Australia, they'd reply, 'Yeah, but what about ya parents, bet they didn't come from Australia.'
> One day I tackled mum about it as she washed the dishes.
> 'What do you mean, where do we come from?'
> 'I mean, what country, the kids at school want to know what country we come from. They reckon we're not Aussies. Are we Aussies, Mum?' (Morgan, 1987, p. 38)

Sally's artwork is the key to the expression of difference. It is laughed at at school, but clearly grows from an innately different way of seeing; one aligned with the Aboriginal forms in which Nan, her grandmother, draws in the sand. Nan's silences and anger indicate her own internalized response to everyday racism. One symbolic moment sees Nan hoarding Australian coins which are about to be devalued: a symbol of her precious hold on Aboriginal values which, ironically, the contemporary political world constantly denies and devalues like the coins. Nan's artwork and values, unknowingly inherited by Sally, enrich and unite the family (but are socially denied and devalued): 'Nan punched. She lifted up her arm and thumped her clenched fist hard on the kitchen table. "You bloody kids don't want me, you want a bloody white grandmother, I'm black. Do you hear, I'm black, black, black!"' (Morgan, 1987, p. 97). Sally and her sister find few positive representations with which to relate and friends disappear:

> 'Don't Abos feel close to the earth and all that stuff?'
> 'God, I don't know. All I know is none of my friends like them'. (Morgan, 1987, p. 98)

Nan and Arthur speak their stories to Sally and these, deriving from 'battler' genres recorded as part of her work, make it a semi-fictionalized community-linked autobiography, witty, ironic, and proud to identify with Aboriginal identity.

The writing of Faith Bandler, Glenyse Ward and Sally Morgan is based on particularly women-oriented forms, the diary and personal reminiscence, interwoven with the rhythms, patterns and cadences of traditional Aboriginal story-telling. Like Toni Morrison's recovery of lost periods of African-American history, they are speaking out powerfully against racism, and silence.

As black or 'coloured', mixed race women writing under apartheid, South Africans Bessie Head and Zoë Wicomb seek to explore their own histories, their identities, and to represent marginalized, silenced subjects. In so doing, they and other South African women writers choosing fictionalized autobiography as their form – Lauretta Ngcobo, COSAW, Ellen Kuzwayo and others – both creatively utilize and subvert the master narratives which would seek to subjugate their experience and prevent its expression.

Bessie Head

> If all my living experience could be summarised I would call it knowledge of evil, knowledge of its sources, of its true face and the misery and suffering it inflicts on human life ... What has driven me is a feeling that human destiny ought not to proceed along tragic lines, with every effort and every new-born civilisation throttling itself in destruction with wrong ideas and wrong ways of living. (Head, 1990, p. 63)

Head's own life story is fraught with the constrictions of the Immorality Act which, accompanied by the incarceration of her mother in a mental asylum for bearing a child from a relationship with a Zulu stable boy, inscribed on Bessie the horrors of apartheid. Her own silenced mother can be heard through her work which recuperates a lost past, like Alice Walker's *In Search of Our Mothers' Gardens* (1983). As Jayapraga Reddy comments of history in the written and oral expression transaction: 'Our writing tradition and culture can only be strongly built if we have a sense of the foundations on which we are building' (Reddy, 1994, p. 74). Head sought exile and a new life in Botswana, closer to African land, traditions and continuities. And it is through a creative relationship with the land, the Motabeng project of vegetable growing, that her protagonist, Elizabeth, moves on from her oppression-induced breakdown into health. Her work defies silence, working to recognize and express self.

In her letters, Bessie Head refuses the master narrative and literally recreates herself as a version of her mother, speaking for her. She creates an identity from this version of her mother in letters and narratives. Bessie spent her adolescence in an orphanage, married journalist Harold Head, had one son, Howard, divorced, and in 1964 left the restrictions of South Africa for neighbouring Botswana on an exit permit. When Botswana became independent in 1966, bureaucracy 'Otherized' South African refugees, denying Bessie citizenship. In 1979, her international literary reputation persuaded the authorities that she was worth claiming as a Botswanan writer. Citizenship enabled her to travel to conferences and sign books abroad. Head's early work appeared in *The New Africa*, with Lewis Nkosi and Eskia Mphahele. Her writing for *Drum* was more personal and 'apolitical' rather than the sensational journalism of her colleagues. She refused political activism and was sceptical about religion, although equating the idea of 'unholy places' with those that are clearly intolerant and oppressive – notably the South Africa of her youth.

In Botswana her writing flourished, but first she had to work through expressing and exploring her own breakdown, which took place in 1969. Of *A Question of Power* (1974), Bessie Head says:

> I had such an intensely personal and private dialogue that I can hardly place it in the context of the more social and outward-looking work I had done. It was a private philosophical journey to the source of evil. (Head, 1990, p. 69)

A Question of Power expresses the protagonist Elizabeth's restless struggle to find a sense of identity and belonging. Her daytime productive and creative work on the land with crops in the experimental utopian community of Motabeng contrasts with the engulfment she experiences in her waking nightmares, peopled by mythical figures – two awful men, Sello and Dan – warped, highly sexualized, oppressive versions of village men. Familiar, they turn terrifyingly into seductive, sexually perverse and patriarchal figures, products of her imaginative revolt against her own internalized sense of social and political, sexual and racial contradiction. Increasingly invading and disabling her days, their struggle for power almost destroys her.

Head transmutes the painful material of her alienation, isolation and mental breakdown in Botswana into Elizabeth's story in realistic/surrealistic detail both particular (one woman's breakdown) and representative of the effects of internalizing oppressions of race and gender under apartheid. Amidst his mother's breakdown, her son's normality and everyday demands help to restore her balance.

Startling events in the fictionalized autobiography parallel reality. Head pasted notices outside the Post Office in Serowe, accusing Sir Seretse Khama (Sello, in the book) of obscenity and cannibalism. This latter act helped to confirm her breakdown. Her hospital confinements led eventually to her stabilization, aided by writing of her experiences in *A Question of Power*, the novel *Maru* (1971) and, to a lesser extent, the works also featuring Serowe – *When Rain Clouds Gather* (1969) and *Serowe, Village of the Rain Winds* (1981). About her life, these also record the harshness of life in Southern Africa and the potential for utopian change. Racism and oppression have overwhelmed Elizabeth:

> In spite of her inability to like or to understand political ideologies, she had lived the back-breaking life of all black peoples in South Africa. It was like living with permanent nervous tension, because you did not know why white people there had to go out of their way to hate you or to loathe you ... there wasn't any life to the heart, just this vehement vicious struggle between two sets of people with different looks. (Head, 1974, p. 19)

and: 'I perceived the ease with which one could become evil and I associated evil in my mind with the acquisition of power' (Head, 1974, p. 77).

'She felt herself to be part of a soul drama, a new act of the eternal conflict between good and evil. She believed her strange birth and destiny to be part of a large pattern of things' (Stead Eilerson, 1995, p. 129). The narrative gives a controlling shape to what is initially perceived and experienced as pure evil:

> Her first drafts of *A Question of Power*, when she still called it *Summer Flowers*, were hardly to be distinguished from some of the descriptions of her own life she had given friends. She saw herself singled out for an incomprehensible assault of evil. She had come to the conclusions that it was necessary for the clearing of a lot of junk out of the soul. (Stead Eilerson, 1995, p. 149)

Bessie Head wrote through some of these feelings in *Maru* where Margaret the Masarwa or Bushman is ostracized by the village, considered the lowest of the low because of her racial origins. In 1969 this internalization of racism was tortuously real to Bessie. *Maru* was published in 1971.

Jolly and Attridge note of Boehmer's argument (1995), comparing autobiography and fiction, that:

> The unbearable reality of the apartheid world, she suggests, resists the novelistic imagination. There are some periods, it would seem, in which the task of imagining difference – temporally speaking and with regard to the other – is less possible than at other times. (Attridge and Jolly, 1998, p. 8)

It is important that we recognize in South African writing the ability to record detail and to document, and still to suggest that life could be other; thus harnessing both the realistic detail and the creative imaginative leap, positing another world.

LOCATION, GEOGRAPHY AND IDENTITY

South African women writers combine often dichotomous responses and forms to a creative imaginative end. They do this most particularly when investigating and embodying the shifting relationships between identity and self, and place and location. Miriam Tlali's characters in *Soweto Stories* (1989) seek homes in crowded rooms, are dominated by bed bugs in transit hotels, terrorized out of temporary apartments and find solace working in enclosed spaces. Zoë Wicomb's sense of place in *You Can't Get Lost in Cape Town* (1987) returns her to home and to the recognition of new versions of identity, based on memory and imaginative exploration, linked to Cape Town's exclusions and space regulations.

Basali!: Stories by and about Women in Lesotho (Kendall, 1995) collects semi-fictionalized autobiographies of women's lives in South Africa, Lesotho and Swaziland (the borderlands), evidencing the brutality of living under apartheid from which several authors escaped. 'Escape to Manzini' by Nomakhosi Mntuyedwa charts her escape, from Soweto, to a Swaziland convent. Hiding from South African cars at the border,

> We were alerted by the grind of gears that a vehicle of sorts was approaching us. It was coming from the South African side of the border. There was no place to hide. The alternative was to lie down flat in the veld and hope that our city clothes blended in well with the bush. Baba Mzimande had told us to dress plainly for the trip. (Mntuyedwa, in Kendall, 1995, p. 100)

Produced in writing seminars where they read Toni Morrison, Alice Walker and Ngugi wa Thiong'o and 'intrigued by the notion of creating a variant English as West Africa and African-American writers have done, which would be unique to Lesotho and therefore, in a sense, their own and not the colonisers' English' (Kendall, 1995, p. x), many tales are only tellable in multiple languages, 'a bridge, perhaps, between orature and literature' (Kendall, 1995, pp. xi–xii).

In the work of Miriam Tlali, Bessie Head, and Zoë Wicomb, imagery enabling exploration of the ideas of identity and hope for creative change in the future recurs as imagery of location, of the house and home space, and of journeying. The familiarity of spaces, the accommodation of difference in a place (usually outside apartheid South Africa) which allows you to expand and be yourself is a crucial stimulus to the writer, and nurtures engaged, imaginative works.

Spaces of Australia and Africa in colonial discourse and representation are figured as dangerous, different, to be renamed, and appropriated. J. M. Coetzee comments on this phenomenon in twentieth-century white South African poetry, arguing that:

> In all the poetry commemorating meetings with the silence and emptiness of Africa ... it is hard not to read a certain historical will to see as silent and

empty a land that has been, if not full of human figures, not empty of them either. (Coetzee, 1989, p. 101)

Emptying the spaces of indigenous people in order to fill them with your own people and with your own representations is a popular stance for the colonizer. Imperial and colonial texts reinscribed southern landscapes as if they were women: dangerous, rich, fertile, to be possessed. Renaming, insisting on the importance of location and identity is a shared cultural project for Aboriginal and South African women writers. It is through the identity and voice enabled by fictionalized autobiography that Aboriginal and South African women writers express their own versions of the relation between identity and location, celebrating difference.

Works Cited

Attridge, Derek and Rosemary Jolly (eds), 1998. *Writing South Africa,* Cambridge: Cambridge University Press.
Bandler, Faith, 1977. *Wacvie,* Adelaide: Rigby.
Boehmer, Elleke, 1995. *Colonial and Post-Colonial Literature,* Oxford: Oxford University Press.
Brink, André, 1998. 'Interrogating Silence', in Attridge and Jolly (eds), *Writing South Africa,* Cambridge: Cambridge University Press, pp. 14–29.
Cixous, Hélène, 1981. 'The Laugh of the Medusa', trans. Keith Cohen and Paula Cohen, in Elaine Marks and Isabelle de Courtivron (eds), *New French Feminisms, an Anthology,* New York: Schocken, pp. 245–64.
Clare, Monica, 1978. *Karobran: The Story of an Aboriginal Girl,* Sydney: APCOL.
Clemens, Theresa, Shirley S. Smith (Mumshirl) and Bobbi Sykes, 1981. *Mumshirl: An Autobiography with the Assistance of Bobbi Sykes,* Richmond: Heinemann Educational.
Coetzee, J. M., 1989. *White Writing: The culture of Letters in South Africa,* New Haven, CT: Yale University Press.
COSAW (Congress of South African Writers Collective), 1994. *Like a House on Fire: Contemporary Women's Writing from South Africa,* Johannesburg: COSAW Publishing.
Ferrier, Carole (ed.), 1985. 'Aboriginal Women's Narratives', in Carole Ferrier (ed.), *Gender, Politics and Fiction,* Brisbane: University of Queensland Press, pp. 200–219.
Ferrier, Carole, 1991. 'Resisting Authority', *Hecate,* vol. 16, no. 1–2, pp. 135ff.
Goolagong, Evonne, 1973. *Evonne! On the Move,* Sydney: Dutton.

Govinden, Betty, 1995. 'Learning Myself Anew', *Alternation*, vol. 2, no. 2, pp. 170–84.
Harstock, Nancy, 1990. 'Foucault on power: a theory for women?', in Joyce Nicholson (ed.), *Feminism/Post-Modernism*, New York: Routledge, pp. 163–71.
Head, Bessie, 1969. *When Rain Clouds Gather*, Oxford: Heinemann.
Head, Bessie, 1971. *Maru*, Oxford: Heinemann.
Head, Bessie, 1974. *A Question of Power*, Oxford: Heinemann.
Head, Bessie, 1981. *Serowe, Village of the Rain Winds*, Oxford: Heinemann.
Head, Bessie, 1990. *A Woman Alone, Autobiographical Writings*, ed. Craig Mackenzie, Oxford: Heinemann.
hooks, bell, 1982. *Ain't I A Woman: Black Women and Feminism*, London: Pluto Press, 1986.
Huggins, Jackie, 1987/8. 'Firing on the Mind: Aboriginal Women Domestic Servants in the Inter-War Years', *Hecate*, vol. 13, no. 2, pp. 5–23.
Jabavu, Noni, 1960. *Drawn in Colour*, London: John Murray.
Jabavu, Noni, 1963. *The Ochre People*, London: John Murray.
Kendall, K. Limakatso, 1995. *Basali!: Stories by and about women in Lesotho*, Durban: University of Natal Press.
Kennedy, Marnie, 1985. *Born a Half Caste*, Canberra: AIAS.
Kuzwayo, Ellen, 1988. *Call Me Woman*, London: The Women's Press.
Labarlestier, Jan, 1991. 'Through Their Own Eyes: An Interpretation of Aboriginal Women's Writing', in Gill Bottomley (ed.), *Intersections: Gender/ Class/ Culture/ Ethnicity*, London: Allen and Unwin, pp. 77–90.
Langford, Ruby, 1988. *Don't Take Your Love to Town*, Sydney: Penguin.
Lucashenko, Melissa, 1997. *Steam Pigs*, Brisbane: University of Queensland Press.
Morgan, Sally, 1987. *My Place*, Fremantle: Fremantle Arts Centre Press.
Morrison, Toni, 1987. *Beloved*, London: Chatto & Windus.
Narogin, Mudrooroo, 1985. Cited in J. Davis and B. Hodge (eds), *Aboriginal Writing Today*, Canberra: AIAS.
Ngcobo, Lauretta, 1981. *Cross of Gold*, London: Longman.
Ngcobo, Lauretta, 1994. Introduction to *Like a House on Fire: Contemporary Women's Writing from South Africa*, Johannesburg: COSAW Publishing, pp. 1–2.
Reddy, Jayapraga, 1987. *On the Fringe of Dream-time and Other Stories*, Johannesburg: Skotaville.
Reddy, Jayapraga, 1994. 'The Unbending Reed', in *Like a House on Fire: Contemporary Women's Writing from South Africa*, Johannesburg: COSAW Publishing, pp. 75–81.
Sam, Agnes, 1989. *Jesus is Indian and Other Stories*, Denmark: Dangaroo Press.

Smith, Shirley C. and Bobbi Sykes, 1981. *Mumshirl: An Autobiography*, Richmond, Victoria: Heinemann.
Stead Eilerson, Gillian, 1995. *Thunder Behind Her Ears*, Cape Town: David Philip.
Tlali, Miriam, 1975. *Muriel at the Metropolitan*, Johannesburg: Ravan.
Tlali, Miriam, 1980. *Amandla*, Johannesburg: Ravan.
Tlali, Miriam, 1989. *Soweto Stories*, London: Pandora.
Walker, Alice, 1983. *In Search of our Mothers' Gardens*, London: The Women's Press.
Ward, Glenyse, 1988. *Wandering Girl*, Broome: Magabala Books Aboriginal Corporation.
Whitlock, Gillian, 1996. *Disobedient Subjects*, Brisbane: University of Queensland Press.
Whitlock, Gillian E. and David Carter (eds), 1992. *Images of Australia*, Brisbane: University of Queensland Press.
Wicomb, Zoë, 1987. *You Can't Get Lost in Cape Town*, London: Virago.
Wright, Alexis, 1997. *Plains of Promise*, Brisbane: University of Queensland Press.

7

Coming in From the Margins: Gender in Contemporary Zimbabwean Writing

Pauline Dodgson

Eldred Jones has identified two significant developments in contemporary African writing. The first is 'the increasing importance of women writers and the consequent focus on women's situation in society' and the second is a literature of war that comes down on the side of the people against politicians and oppressors (Jones, 1996, pp. 1–2). Zimbabwean literature has now fallen in with these trends but what is interesting is how this has occurred.

Before independence in 1980, Zimbabwean writing in English was criticized for its lack of a common mission and for the individual stance that many writers took. Ranganai Zinyemba, using a quotation from the Zimbabwean writer Dambudzo Marechera's novella *The House of Hunger* (1978), referred to exiled black Rhodesian writers as 'the Jews of Africa', writers who had lived migrant lives outside Africa and who had become preoccupied with their own encounter with Europe (Zinyemba, 1987). Even those who wrote from within Zimbabwe, such as Charles Mungoshi, the author of the critically acclaimed novel *Waiting for the Rain*, appeared to be concerned with identifying a malaise in society rather than producing a nationalist literature to support the liberation struggle.

In the first few years after Independence in 1980 it was assumed that there would be a cultural renaissance in Zimbabwe with writers at the forefront, describing a heroic war against latter-day colonialism and praising the efforts of the new government to bring about national unity and put right the injustices of the past. However, writers who had published before Independence, with the exception of Marechera, published little in the early 1980s and, although new writers did emerge, their early work was slight or formulaic. Barbara Makhalisa's didactic

The Underdog and Other Stories, one of the few works written by a woman, was criticized for creating the stereotype of woman as victim (Gaidzanwa, 1985, pp. 80–81).

Marechera, the author of the pre-Independence postmodern fiction *The House of Hunger* and *Black Sunlight* (1980) was seen as a maverick writer, too influenced by Western culture to be authentically African. Although his multigenre work *Mindblast or The Definitive Buddy* was published in Zimbabwe in 1984, despite some anxiety on the part of his publisher College Press (Veit-Wild, 1992, p. 339), he was unable to get his manuscript *The Depths of Diamonds* published in Zimbabwe or Britain. College Press rejected it on the grounds that it was so erudite that it was 'unreadable' and that it contained 'four-letter words and lurid descriptions of sexual intercourse' (Caute, 1991, p. 108).

However, the influence of Marechera should not be underestimated. Flora Veit-Wild rightly points to how after his death at the age of 35 in 1987, he has become a cult figure, an inspiration for younger writers and a *poète maudit* in a country whose leaders frequently make public speeches condemning Western decadence (Veit-Wild, 1992, pp. 379–83). The outrageousness of Marechera's work and his refusal to adhere to any party line paved the way for other writers to adopt an oppositional and critical approach.

The publication of Tsitsi Dangarembga's *Nervous Conditions* and Chenjerai Hove's *Bones* in 1988 marked a departure in Zimbabwean literature. *Nervous Conditions* was Dangarembga's first novel. She had written a play, *She No Longer Weeps*, which had been published the previous year in Zimbabwe, but with *Nervous Conditions* Dangarembga reverted to the pre-Independence practice of Zimbabwean writers of publishing work with foreign publishers, in this case, the British-based Women's Press, allegedly because of failure to find a local publisher (Wilkinson, 1992, p. 197). *Bones* was Hove's first novel in English; he had previously published poetry in English and fiction in Shona.

What makes these works exceptional is that they both deal with issues of gender and challenge patriarchal institutions and practices – overtly in *Nervous Conditions*, through its critique of the power of the head of the extended family, the father of Nyasha and uncle of Tambu who is known by the kinship name of Babamukuru, and implicitly in *Bones* where Hove foregrounds women's resistance to traditional, colonial and nationalist oppression. *Bones* was welcomed in Southern Africa and Europe as a fresh beginning in Zimbabwean writing; *Nervous Conditions* received international acclaim but its reception in Zimbabwe, not surprisingly given its subject matter, was more mixed. However, it is *Nervous Conditions* which has become the one canonical Zimbabwean text and is now included in American and British women's studies and post-colonial courses, including the Open University's Third World Development course.

Comparison of *Bones* and *Nervous Conditions* reveals the contradictions in contemporary Zimbabwean writing but I do not want to make that comparison here. Rather I intend to analyse the male-authored *Bones* and a female-authored novel published six years later in 1994, Yvonne Vera's *Without a Name*. Vera, like Dangarembga, received part of her education outside Zimbabwe and studied modern literary theory at university in Toronto. Her book follows *Nervous Conditions* in engaging with modernity in its representation of a woman's desire for independence but it also uses a poetic language which is similar to the language of *Bones*. *Bones* and *Without a Name* recreate the suffering of rural women during the war of liberation but *Without a Name* also examines urban alienation and constantly shifting identities in a period of transition. My interpretations of these two novels are informed by my reading of *Nervous Conditions* which acts as a palimpsest for my text, putting pressure on my analysis of *Bones* and *Without a Name*.

Bones is, in many respects, a deliberately contradictory text. It is a war novel but, unlike most war novels, it is not centred upon the experiences of the guerrillas. It focuses on the farm workers whose history is an intrinsic part of the war but who are usually marginalized in narratives of the liberation struggle.

The central character Marita is a farm worker who goes in search of her son who has left home to become a guerrilla. It is with the representation of Marita that the contradictions begin. Marita is known for her story-telling ability. According to the Unknown Woman, 'Marita, she tells stories as easily as she breathes' (Hove, 1988, p. 80), yet Marita never directly tells her own story. We know the stories Marita told because those who have been influenced by her and cannot forget her tell us. Marita's words are mediated by the experiences of others, leaving us with fragments of her life; autobiography is displaced, not by biography, but by testimony that emerges from both individual and collective consciousness. Marita is, therefore, both absent and present in the text – absent in a material form (she is missing or dead in the novel's story time) and present in the memory and consciousness of others. The reader is, thus, denied what we might be tempted to see as the authenticity of her voice, the real presence behind the speaker which would erase any traces of other thoughts, other speech, other writing.

The absence of Marita allows Hove to use multiple viewpoints to tell multiple stories. Not only is the narrator likely to change from chapter to chapter but we also encounter shifting narration within each chapter. This can be seen in the second chapter, which begins with Janifa addressing the dead Marita. Then Janifa repeats the insulting words of the white farmer, Manyepo, and goes on to show how Marita answered Manyepo and how Marita's husband criticized her instead of supporting her. The next chapter is narrated by Marita's husband who is referred to simply as Murume (*murume*, Shona, man or husband). Murume addresses both Manyepo and Marita, developing, from a different narrative point of view, what we have already been told by Janifa.

In *Bones*, Hove constructs a house of fiction. In the manner of orature, story is built upon story and the final ending is delayed or denied. However, these multiple layers of fiction question fictionality itself as, in their testimony, each character strives to arrive at a version of the truth, however subjective, through the different stories they have been told. The Unknown Woman asks rhetorically, '[W]ho will tell me exactly what happened, the way things actually happened?' But then she concludes for herself, 'it does not matter too much because the little I should know, I know now' (Hove, 1988, p. 66).

Official historical records with their narrow orthodoxy can be supplemented or even subverted by fiction. The white farm-owner who might have been praised for his industriousness in colonial accounts has his own words used as evidence against him in the novel where the workers' replies, whether actually made to him or expressed to themselves, are recorded. His constant references to the workers as liars or idlers are undermined by their renaming of him as Manyepo (*manyepo*, Shona, liar), the only name by which he is known in the text and which he wrongly thinks is a respectable name, and by their repeated insistence that he profits from their labour.

When the government worker in independent Zimbabwe says that only important people can bury Marita, we understand that this is meant to ensure that part of Marita's story, the story of how she died, is hidden from public scrutiny and from history, that she becomes one of the 'disappeared'. However, this is challenged by the Unknown Woman when she, rightfully, claims that she should bury Marita because her story and Marita's are linked by their mutual oppression: 'Marita showed me all the burdens I have inside me' (Hove, 1988, p. 80).

In the rewriting of history as fiction, Hove moves away from linear time to what he has referred to as 'time recorded in memory' (Veit-Wild, 1993, p. 11). The seeming archaism of the language and the literal translation of Shona idiom into English, which has been discussed by Rino Zhuwarara (1996, pp. 42–43), is a consequence of this. Contemporary English, even contemporary Zimbabwean English, cannot adequately articulate past rural experience; the language used and the fusing of prose and poetry reveals the text's syncretism. Hove's use of time can be compared to the Caribbean writer Derek Walcott's rejection of history for myth or memory (Walcott, 1974, pp. 1–2).

Hove, like Walcott, goes beyond memory to re-enactment. In *Bones* there is a re-enactment and rethinking of how the remote past is understood in the recent past and in the present. The symbolism – bones, vultures, locusts – which forms part of the mythology and belief systems of the first *chimurenga*, the uprisings of 1896–97, have to be re-enacted as a means of interpreting their significance. In their re-enactment of Marita's life and their own lives, Janifa and the Unknown Woman employ the language of the ancestral spirits. This language is both diachronic, time-specific in its origins in the first *chimurenga*, and synchronic, part of a timeless pattern of omens and signs as available to the women on the margins of the second *chimurenga*, the 1970s war of liberation, as it was to the guerrillas who found it inspirational. The Cuban writer Alejo Carpentier's term *lo real maravilloso*, 'the marvellous in the real', seems appropriate here. Carpentier insisted that using the marvellous was not enough – the writer had to believe in the power of the supernatural (Williamson, 1987, p. 84). Janifa, the first and last story-teller in the novel, does have that belief:

> Then they will see footsteps of the bones of the woman rising early in the morning to urge all the villagers, all the cattle, the birds, the insects and the hills to rise with the rising bones, to sing with the singing bones. (Hove, 1988, p. 134)

Although the continuity between past and present is shown in *Bones*, the text also reveals an awareness of disruption, alienation, dis-ease and even rupture in pre-Independence and post-Independence Zimbabwe. This can most clearly be seen in the representation of the oppression and resistance of the women. From the beginning of the novel, Marita is seen in terms of difference. She is known for her outspokenness; it is Marita who tells Manyepo the truth when she criticizes his treatment of the farm workers. Her difference is also seen in her barrenness, which is condemned by the representatives of both colonialism and tradition. Manyepo advises her husband to find another woman who can bear him children because Manyepo wants more workers for the land. Whereas Marita's truth-telling is an act of conscious resistance, her barrenness provides her with a means of unconscious resistance. Her initial inability to have children means that she cannot reproduce existing social relations. The decision of the one child she does have to become a freedom fighter again breaks the chains of oppression.

However, both Marita's husband and Janifa's mother blame Marita for her infertility. Even after her death, her husband cannot forget the shame of having a wife who was childless for so many years: 'Do you not remember the days all the people came to try to take you away to a medicine-man to see why you could not nourish the seed I planted in you?' (Hove, 1988, p. 27), and Janifa remembers that her mother was afraid that Marita would pass on her infertility to her, 'How can you talk with such a woman unless you want to inherit her barrenness?' (Hove, 1988, p. 106).

The question of what Janifa does inherit from Marita is a crucial one. Liz Gunner points to the importance of cross-generational links between the women:

> What the text stresses is the continuity of strength and the links between the women of two generations, Marita and Janifa, and beyond them the historical figure of the defiant and inspirational Nehanda ... in Hove's text, made up as it is of voices locked in conversation, voices of the living and of the powerful dead in the form of the venerated Nehanda, the two women give strength to each other. (Gunner, 1991, p. 83)

Strength is clearly an important inheritance but so is pain. Marita does not want to pass her sorrow on to Janifa:

> The world is still large for you, too many unspoken words, too many unheard voices, so no need for me to fill your head with rags of stories. After all, you have your own dreams to carry you along. ... No, not to spill my own wounds into the heart of a young girl who needs to breed the plants of her own life for herself and for her people. (Hove, 1988, p. 9)

However, the 'rags of stories' are embedded in Janifa's memory and she cannot forget them; neither can she forget the stories she saw written on Marita's body:

> Marita, you told me sad stories of the wounds of your heart. Many wounds which no one can see. Wounds cut with big knives and machetes. I listened because I saw them. Now I have no one to listen to me. I have only the blood which I saw smeared on your black thighs. Thighs roughened with hard work in Manyepo's fields. A face stern, with stories found in the many cracks of the face. Did you not say every crack on the face of a farm worker is an endless story? (Hove, 1988, p. 112)

As in Toni Morrison's *Beloved* (1987), writing the body may finally be cathartic but what is actually written on the body tells stories of pain, mental and physical, rather than pleasure.

After she is raped by the man who also wanted to possess Marita, the cook Chisaga, Janifa suffers what appears to be a breakdown. She is isolated because she believes her own mother is complicit in her rape and because she does not have Marita to listen to her story. Janifa's alienation from her society is also a critique of that society. Like Marita, she does not fulfil her family's expectations by having children and, like Marita, she is subjected to the painful treatments of the herbalists. She repeatedly says that she wants to spit at her mother who does not deserve her respect; she argues against the traditional belief that eggs should be given to adults, not children, 'Eggs are good, Marita. Good things are good things. Those who have them always want to make rules so that others cannot get to the good things' (Hove, 1988, p. 117). Significantly, she also questions *roora* or bride price. Janifa's position is unequivocal:

> Mother says I must get married so that cattle can come to her house while she still has good teeth to eat them. But does she know that when cattle come to our home, I will not have the chance to eat them since I go the other way? What does it help to bring cattle that I do not eat myself? (Hove, 1988, p. 118)

According to Foucault, the speech of the mad is either excluded from discourse because it is believed that it is nonsense or it is said to have prophetic power, to contain divinely inspired hidden truths (Foucault, 1981, pp. 52–53). Janifa knows that her words have no currency within her society but she also knows that the truth she speaks comes from her own experience and Marita's. She has taken over Marita's role as truth-teller and in this role she tells us that there has been no change for the farm workers since Independence.

She also does not need divine inspiration to know that relationships between men and women have not changed. The ostensible reason that she gives for rejecting Marita's son when he comes to marry her and take her away from the 'house of ghosts' (Hove, 1988, p. 131) is that she does not want Marita to be remembered as the woman whose son married a madwoman but, throughout the novel, relationships between husbands and wives have been shown to be antagonistic. Moreover, although the young man may have changed during the war, she has the memory of the brutal words he spoke to her when he believed she had thrown away his letter. These words, in their violence, bear some resemblance to Chisaga's threat that is uttered before the rape, 'You make any noise and your body will be found in the dam after the dam has dried' (Hove, 1988, p. 110).

It is instructive to compare the representation of Janifa's illness with that of Nyasha's illness in *Nervous Conditions*. Whereas Nyasha, the anorexic, is silenced by the narrator Tambu who is able to tell herself, 'I was a much more sensible person than Nyasha because I knew what could or couldn't be done' (Dangarembga, 1988, p. 203), Janifa speaks until the end of the story. Her rejection of her mother is only possible because she has returned to the Imaginary where she is united with Marita:

> People here do not see the dreams which Marita left for me. They are good dreams which fall on me like the rains. All the time without seasons, dreams of rains, bones and footsteps falling from the height of a cliff, scattering to the earth while the boys in the field whistle and shout as if they have seen a vulture tearing away the flesh of a carcass. Bones in flower like flames of skeletons spread all over the place like a battlefield strewn with corpses of the freshly killed whose warm blood flows out of them like smoke from Manyepo's chimney. (Hove, 1988, p. 128)

Nyasha's condition improves with psychiatric help and drugs but Janifa, locked in a primitive madhouse, intends to free herself:

> I will take the broken chains with my own hands and say ... Do not worry yourselves, I have already moved them by myself. I have been removing them from my heart for many years, now my legs and hands are free because the mountains and rivers I saw with my own eyes could not fail to remove all the chains of this place ... . Then I will go without waiting for them to say go. (Hove, 1988, p. 135)

As the use of imagery in Janifa's semiotic language suggests, she retains a historical consciousness that derives from collective memory. Unlike Nyasha in *Nervous Conditions*, she has not been contaminated by the Englishness which Tambu's mother says the ancestors cannot be expected to stomach (Hove, 1988, p. 203). Does this mean that Hove's representation of the younger generation of Zimbabwean women is monolithic and traditional whereas Dangarembga's is progressive and multifaceted? I would argue strongly against this interpretation. Janifa's madness shows that she exists in a society which far from being monolithic contains divisions that can endanger psychic and physical health.

Between 1988, the year of *Bones* and *Nervous Conditions*, and 1994, the year *Without a Name* was published, a spate of novels appeared which, in different ways and with varying degrees of cynicism and criticism, depicted the struggle against settler rule. Notable among them are three novels which deal with the experiences of soldiers in the guerrilla army: I. V. Mazorodze's *Silent Journey from the East* (1989), Shimmer Chinodya's *Harvest of Thorns* (1989) and Charles Samupindi's

Pawns (1992). None of these works investigates issues of gender and, where they represent women, they do so in a fairly conventional manner.

Irene Staunton's collection of women's life stories in *Mothers of the Revolution* (1990) went some way towards redressing this imbalance but it is Yvonne Vera's work which powerfully inscribes women's experiences of desertion, rape, infanticide and incest. Since 1993, Vera has published three novels, a historical novel, *Nehanda* (1993) and two novels that represent the oppression of contemporary young Zimbabwean women, *Without a Name* (1994) and *Under the Tongue* (1996).

Like *Bones*, *Without a Name* depicts female suffering during the last years of the war. However, it represents the suffering of one woman, Mazvita, after she has been raped by a soldier, has left her rural lover, Nyenyedzi, been deserted by the man she lived with in Harari, Joel, and has killed her child. In story-time, Mazvita journeys from Harari to rural Mhondoro by bus with her dead child tied to her back. It is 1977, and the war is escalating. In analepsis, the details of Mazvita's past life are revealed in fragments. It may be possible to see Mazvita as one victim of the war representing other women who are also victims of the war but this is not an interpretation that the reader arrives at easily. If there is a collective history of female suffering and experience, and the novel's dedication 'for my mother and her mother' points to this as a possibility, then it departs radically from the nexus of Marita, Janifa and the Unknown Woman. Mazvita's experience is individual, as is her way of attempting to deal with pain. There is no network of support from family or women friends to prevent the tragedy.

Mazvita appears to seek security in anonymity; if she is to tell her story, then it has to be told to a stranger. After buying the apron in which she intends to wrap her dead child, Mazvita is 'not yet certain whether to confess or escape' (Vera, 1994, p. 10). She thinks momentarily about confessing to the woman who is selling the aprons:

> Some kinds of truths long for the indifferent face of a stranger, such truths love that face from the neck up, from the forehead down. There is little to remember in a face with which no intimacy has been shared, to which there is no kinship. There is nothing to lose between strangers, absolutely no risk of being contaminated by another's emotion; there are no histories shared, no promises made, no hope conjured and affirmed. Only faces offered, in improbable disguises, promising freedom. (Vera, 1994, pp. 10–11)

What is extraordinary about this is that it breaks the new orthodoxy in Zimbabwean and other post-colonial literatures, including womanist writing, which promotes the sharing of histories. A book such as *Mothers of the Revolution* follows *Bones* in implying that it is only through this sharing that different truths will be told about the past which will aid the process of reconciliation and healing (Staunton, 1990).

On her journey with the child, Mazvita is alone, and yet, this isolation is experienced as a bodily disintegration and splitting into different parts of the self. The text refers to this as a de-centring. Identity is no longer stable. Mazvita's wanderings dislocate her geographically. She tells Nyenyedzi that she cannot go back to her home in Mhondoro; 'The war is bad in Mhondoro. It is hard to close your eyes there and sleep. It is hard to be living. I left because I wanted to reach the city; I cannot return so quickly' (Vera, 1994, p. 23). She is also dislocated, both physically and psychologically, from *and* within her body which appears to have a separate existence from the self:

> Her neck had been broken. She felt a violent piercing like shattered glass, on her tongue where she carried fragments of her being. There was a lump growing on the side of her neck. A sagging grew with the lump, so that her body leaned to the left, following the heavy lump. She could no longer swallow even her saliva which settled in one huge lump in her throat. Whatever she swallowed moved to one side of her body. She had lost her centre, the centre in which her thoughts had found anchor. She was amazed at how quickly the past vanished. (Vera, 1994, p. 3)

It is the past, whether repressed or not, which has led to this predicament from which, as the narration keeps insisting, there is no recovery and yet Mazvita believes that she will be strengthened by remaining silent, not by bearing witness. After her rape:

> The silence was not a forgetting, but a beginning. She would grow from the silence he had brought to her. Her longing for growth was deep, and came from the parts of her body he had claimed for himself, which he had claimed against all her resistance and her tears. (Vera, 1994, p. 29)

It is tempting to see this as the silence endorsed by the French feminist Hélène Cixous and other feminist critics who have praised Dora, the subject of Freud's case history for refusing to continue treatment with Freud and, thus, challenging the power of the symbolic (Cixous, 1973). However, Mazvita believes that it is naming, that function of the symbolic, which binds a child to its mother; 'The child grew in silence with no name. Mazvita could not name the silence' (Vera, 1994, p. 75).

Moreover, journeying with the dead child, Mazvita attempts to bring about a rupture between the unity of mother and child in the Imaginary:

It was the constant nearness of her head to the child that made her frenzied and perplexed. There was not enough space between her and the child she bore on her back. If she could remove her head, and store it at a distance from the child she bore on her back, then she could begin. She would be two people. (Vera, 1994, p. 19)

Vera, in a recent talk, has explained how her work is inspired by everyday physical gestures. In this case, the commonplace image of a mother carrying a child is converted into the unthinkable – the child is dead (Vera, 1997). It can be argued that this quite self-evidently is what brings about the rupture but Mazvita is shown throughout the text as a woman who sees motherhood as a burden. One example is when she remembers how the apron seller addressed her:

Amai. She remembered that. *Amai.* She was indeed a mother. It was heavy to be a mother. It made one recognisable in the streets, even when one no longer recognised oneself. *Amai.* It was painful. *Amai.* The seller's voice followed her through the crowds, but it no longer referred to her. *Amai.* It referred to any woman who passed by, who carried a baby on her back, who was a potential mother. *Amai.* It had never referred to her, that *amai*, at least not specifically. (Vera, 1994, p. 40)

That the Shona word for mother, *amai*, is a form of address used to any woman makes Mazvita's horror at her pregnancy and denial of her motherhood 'unnatural', in her society. However, *Without a Name* always works with the notion that war has rendered both rural and urban society unnatural, and in unnatural times there is no solace to be found in nature or biology. When she is with her lover Nyenyedzi in Kadoma, she finds 'soft dying mushrooms' and always thinks of 'the spotless white mushrooms she had not found' (Vera, 1994, p. 8). In a reversal of the trope of the colonial rape of native land, Mazvita sees the land as being responsible for the soldier's violation of her; 'she thought of him not from inside her, but from outside. He had never been inside her. She connected him only to the land. It was the land that had come towards her .... The land had allowed the man to grow from itself into her body (Vera, 1994, p. 31). Mazvita tells Nyenyedzi, 'The land has forgotten us. Perhaps it dreams new dreams for itself' (Vera, 1994, p. 33). Her view is that 'the land had no fixed loyalties' (Vera, 1994, p. 34).

Carole Boyce Davies argues that one of the approaches of African feminist critics is to explore 'the idealization of women and motherhood in the Négritude vein – woman as supermother, symbol of Africa, earth as muse, how this supports or distorts the creation of a female mythos and how it conforms to the realities of women's lives (Boyce Davies,

1986, p. 15). A feminist critic analysing *Without a Name* would be forced to conclude that woman/mother/Africa is deconstructed in the text. Mazvita does not want to be symbolic or representative. Mazvita had left her home 'because it suited her to move forward' (Vera, 1994, p. 34). She leaves Nyenyedzi because 'She did not care for certainties, each moment would uncover its secret, but she would be there, ahead of that moment, far ahead' (Vera, 1994, p. 34). When she arrives in Harari, she believes that the city will fulfil her desires:

> She had faith in untried realities because she trusted her own power for change, for adaptation. She welcomed each day with a strong sense of her desire, of her ability to begin, of her belonging. Mazvita had a profound belief in her own reality, in the transformation new geographies promised and allowed, that Harari's particular strangeness released and encouraged. Mazvita recognised Harari as the limitless place in which to dream, and to escape. (Vera, 1994, p. 55)

What she finds in Harari is a society that does not know itself. The macabre experience she undergoes of carrying a dead child is mirrored in the reality of people's lives that they attempt to obscure through gruesome carnivals and lurid masquerades. Mazvita's bodily disintegration is matched by the peeling away of skin as people in a state of false consciousness literally attempt to buy white masks:

> Newspaper headings covered the dark alley, promised no freedom to the agitated people. But there were ample signs of the freedom the people had already claimed for themselves – empty shells of Ambi, green and red. The world promised a lighter skin, greater freedom. ... Freedom was any kind of opening through which one could squeeze. People fought to achieve gaps in their reality. The people danced in an enviable kind of self-mutilation .... The people had been efficient accomplices to the skinning of their faces, to the usual ritual of their disinheritance (Vera, 1994, pp. 26–27).

Vera's evocative description of the sexual promiscuity of city women departs from the stereotyping criticized by Gaidzanwa but it does reproduce images which associate women and sex with death and, although set in 1977, may, in a latent prolepsis, forewarn of the coming of AIDS:

> The carnival was barefaced and unbelievable, full of mimicry and death. The war was articulated in masks of dream and escape. It found expression in terror and courtship, in an excited sensuality, in figures speechless and dead. Guns soured the sky with black smoke. (Vera, 1994, p. 62)

Death appears to be omnipresent as reality, dream and fantasy all reveal a landscape of carnage. Journeys started may not be finished; 'It was not known what would happen to the body as it journeyed. A journey was not to be trusted. Only the promise to arrive could be resurrected and protected' (Vera, 1994, p. 77).

As in *Bones*, burial takes on ritual and symbolic significance. Caroline Rooney has described the three main women characters in *Bones* as Antigone figures: 'defying patriarchal laws and representatives of the state, they persist in their unanswered demands or appeals, to the point of death or incarceration' (Rooney, 1995, p. 121). Antigone, like the Unknown Woman, insisted on burying the dead. However, in *Without a Name*, burial is not a religious rite or an act of reconciliation or atonement. Instead burial takes on a more violent, confrontational meaning.

In one of the many retellings of the rape, Mazvita remembers that 'she thought only of being buried, of dying slowly after he had killed her' (Vera, 1994, p. 84). When she discovers after she has moved in with Joel that she is already pregnant by another man, 'She buried the child. She was submerged in her secrets, and she breathed hard, like drowning. She had died silently with the thoughts she kept to herself' (Vera, 1994, p. 73).

When Mazvita places the child in the apron, it is as if she is putting it in a shroud; 'The baby lay encased within the embroidered stitching. The baby was sown up there. She could not do much about the wild stitching though her heart rose against it' (Vera, 1994, p. 18). When Mazvita sings to the baby, 'The tune was familiar, but coarse, it seemed ground from between two violent stones. It was a tune for grinding corn, not for awakening tenderness' (Vera, 1994, p. 41). The song becomes a lament, a funeral oration which Mazvita believes is for herself as well as the child: 'She sang with the last breath in her body for she was certain there would be no life for her after this. It was not possible that she would be buried and then live. She had died a final death' (Vera, 1994, p. 42).

This song contrasts with the traditional *mbira* music which Mazvita hears on the bus and which acts as a semiotic language, replacing the child's *chora* sounds which she will now never hear. In language and imagery which is reminiscent of another transgressive novel, Kate Chopin's 1899 American text *The Awakening*, Vera allows Mazvita to experience a moment of *jouissance*:

> It fell in drops, the sound, into her cupped hands. She found the *mbira*. It was beneficent. The sound came to her in subduing waves, in a growing pitch, in laps of clear water. Water. She felt the water slow and effortless and

elegant. She breathed calmly, in the water. The *mbira* vibrated through the crowd, reached her with an intact rhythm, a profound tonality, a promise graceful and simple. She had awakened. (Vera, 1994, p. 69)

But perhaps it is the reader who is awakened by the text to Mazvita's plight as a woman who strives for independence and the fulfilment of her desires in a war-torn society. Given the opprobrium that the Zimbabwean press in the mid-1980s heaped upon women responsible for 'baby dumping' (the killing or abandoning of a child shortly after birth), Vera's invitation to the reader to identify empathetically with Mazvita puts pressure on the dominant and the powerful to listen to the stories of those at the margins.

In comparison to *Nervous Conditions*, the ending of *Without a Name*, which returns Mazvita to her origin and her past (whether in reality or fantasy is unclear), may seem nostalgic, even regressive, but it offers the possibility of a return, which may or may not be realized, to a time before the war and death. In the final chapter, Mazvita believes she hears her mother call her and she is at last able to release the baby from her back.

Bones, *Without a Name* and *Nervous Conditions* provide a way forward for Zimbabwean writing which is different from that envisaged at Independence in 1980. They have come from the margins to claim a place for Zimbabwean writing in newly emerging canon formations of post-colonial and women's writing. These texts co-exist with others that are more crudely written and often autobiographical but which also, in varying ways, challenge the official version of history.

Works Cited

Boyce Davies, Carol, 1986. 'Introduction: Feminist Consciousness And African Literary Criticism', in Carole Boyce Davies and Anne Adams Graves (eds), *Ngambika: Studies of Women in African Literature*, Trenton: Africa World Press, pp. 1–23.
Caute, David, 1991. 'Marechera in Black and White', in Preben Kaarsholm (ed.), *Cultural Struggle and Development in Southern Africa*, London: James Currey, pp. 95–111.
Chinodya, Shimmer, 1989. *Harvest of Thorns*, Harare: Baobab Books.
Chopin, Kate, 1899. *The Awakening*, London: The Women's Press, 1978.
Cixous, Hélène, 1973. *Portrait du soleil*, Paris: Denoel.
Dangarembga, Tsitsi, 1987. *She No Longer Weeps*, Harare: The College Press.
Dangarembga, Tsitsi, 1988. *Nervous Conditions*, London: The Women's Press.

Foucault, Michel, 1981. 'The Order of Discourse', in Robert Young (ed.), *Untying the Text: A Post-Structuralist Reader*, London: Routledge, pp. 48–78.

Gaidzanwa, Rudo, 1985. *Images of Women in Zimbabwean Literature*, Harare: The College Press.

Gunner, Liz, 1991. 'Power, Popular Consciousness, and the Fictions of War: Hove's *Bones* and Chinodya's *Harvest of Thorns*', *African Languages and Cultures*, vol. 4, no. 1, pp. 77–85.

Hove, Chenjerai, 1988. *Bones*, Harare: Baobab Books.

Jones, Eldred, 1996. 'New Trends and Generations', in Eldred Jones (ed.), *New Trends and Generations in African Literature*, London: James Currey, pp. 1–3.

Makhalisa, Barbara, 1984. *The Underdog and Other Stories*, Gweru: Mambo Press.

Marechera, Dambudzo, 1978. *The House of Hunger*, London: Heinemann.

Marechera, Dambudzo, 1980. *Black Sunlight*, London: Heinemann.

Marechera, Dambudzo, 1984. *Mindblast or The Definitive Buddy*, Harare: The College Press.

Mazorodze, I. V., 1989. *Silent Journey from the East*, Harare: Zimbabwe Publishing House.

Morrison, Toni, 1987. *Beloved*, New York: Plume Books.

Mungoshi, Charles, 1975. *Waiting for the Rain*, London: Heinemann.

Rooney, Caroline, 1995. 'Re-Possessions: Inheritance and Independence in Chenjerai Hove's *Bones* and Tsitsi Dangarembga's *Nervous Conditions*', in Abdulrazak Gurnah (ed.), *Essays on African Writing 2: Contemporary Literature*, London: Heinemann, pp. 119–43.

Samupindi, Charles, 1992. *Pawns*, Harare: Baobab Books.

Staunton, Irene (ed.), 1990. *Mothers of the Revolution*, Harare: Baobab Books.

Veit-Wild, Flora, 1992. *Dambudzo Marechera: A Source Book on His Life and Work*, London: Hans Zell Publishers.

Veit-Wild, Flora, 1993. '"Dances with Bones": Hove's Romanticized Africa', *Research in African Literatures*, vol. 24, no. 3, pp. 5–12.

Vera, Yvonne, 1993. *Nehanda*, Harare: Baobab Books.

Vera, Yvonne, 1994. *Without a Name*, Harare: Baobab Books

Vera, Yvonne, 1996. *Under the Tongue*, Harare: Baobab Books.

Vera, Yvonne, 1997. 'Imagining Zimbabwean Women's Lives', unpublished paper given at Britain–Zimbabwe Research Day, Oxford, June 1997.

Walcott, Derek, 1974. 'The Muse of History', in Orde Coombs (ed.), *Is Massa Day Dead?* New York: Anchor Press/Doubleday, pp. 1–27.

Wilkinson, Jane, 1992. *Talking with African Writers: Interviews with African Poets, Playwrights and Novelists*, London: James Currey.

Williamson, Edwin, 1987. 'Coming to Terms with Modernity: Magical Realism and the Historical Process in the Novels of Alejo Carpentier', in John King (ed.), *Modern Latin American Fiction: A Survey*, London: Faber, pp. 78–100.

Zhuwarara, R., 1996. 'Gender and Liberation: Chenjerai Hove's *Bones*', in Emmanuel Ngara (ed.), *New Writing from Southern Africa: Authors who have become prominent since 1980*, London: James Currey, pp. 29–44.

Zinyemba, Ranganai, 1987. '"The Jews of Africa": Aspects of Zimbabwean Fiction in English Before National Independence in 1980', a paper delivered at the University of Zimbabwe, April 1987.

8

The Memory of Slavery in Fred D'Aguiar's *Feeding the Ghosts*

Gail Low

> But it's the biggest of those shadows where the history of Europe meets the history of the Americas
>
> (Caryl Phillips)

> ... each has its own mystical sense of the relationship between blood, soil and seawater
>
> (Paul Gilroy, 1993a)

Slavery, as specifically British theme and subject matter, in fiction has only relatively recently emerged into prominence with Barry Unsworth's *Sacred Hunger*, Caryl Phillips's *Higher Ground*, *Cambridge*, *Crossing the River*, and *The Nature of Blood* and Fred D'Aguiar's *The Longest Memory* and *Feeding the Ghosts*. In their introduction to *The Discourse of Slavery: Aphra Behn to Toni Morrison*, Carl Plasa and Betty Ring argue that, in Britain, while racialized discourse has been explored 'in relation to colonialism, post-colonialism and imperialism', it has been less addressed in relation to slavery (Plasa and Ring, 1994, p. xiv). Likewise, Benedicte Ledent asserts that 'one can indeed say that slavery has rarely been tackled head-on' by an older generation of Caribbean novelists and that it is only with the 'new wave' black British novelists like Phillips and D'Aguiar that slavery becomes a 'fecund' site (Ledent, 1996, pp. 271, 273). This is not to say that slavery has entered the imagination only recently. Within the provenance of Caribbean and black British poetry, slavery has long been the site for an imaginative interrogation of questions of history and memory, culture, power and identity; coming to terms with the history of slavery is an abiding theme in Caribbean and black British poetry. Derek Walcott speaks poetry of the shards of traditions, 'a huge tribal vocabulary', that (re)combine to new creative potential despite the rupture of the middle passage and the histories of indentured labour. In his Nobel Prize speech, Walcott argues that 'deprived of their original language, the captured and indentured tribes create their own, accreting and secreting fragments of an old epic vocabulary ... an ecstatic rhythm in blood that cannot be subdued by slavery or indenture ...' (Donnell and Lawson Welsh, 1996, p. 507). Edward Brathwaite's collection of poems *The Arrivants* has been concerned to forge a distinctively Caribbean aesthetic; a language and mythology that reflects New World transatlantic connections and histories that have emerged from the history of slavery and from recovered African connections. More recently in *Slave Song*, David Dabydeen attempts to embody in sound and language not only the everyday violence of plantation life, but also the resistance and strengths of the slave communities. As Dabydeen puts it, 'what I wanted to show was the way of life that survived brilliantly and wickedly, mischievously and tragically, in spite of certain experiences of violence and brutality' (Donnell and Welsh Lawson, 1996, p. 417). Grace Nichols's *i is a long memoried woman* looks at the survival and endurance of slaves from the point of view of women, creating a web of kinship and mythology over time and space:

> Inerasable as my scars and fate
> I am here
> a woman ... with all my lives
> strung out like beads ...
> [I seek] the power to be what I am / a woman
> charting my own future / a woman
> holding my beads in my hand. (Nichols, 1983, p.79)

The scholarship of slavery has an even longer history, but with James Walvin's *Black Ivory*, Robin Blackburn's *The Making of New World Slavery* and Paul Gilroy's immensely influential *The Black Atlantic*, we have a more concerted attempt to link slavery to the history and processes of (Euro-American) modernity. Slavery becomes a counter-history of modernity, a history that has been erased and forgotten in the Enlightenment's narrative of rationality and progress. In his mammoth historical overview, Blackburn argues that the development of the 'slavery of the Americas' is associated with the 'processes' associated with modernity, such as 'the growth of instrumental rationality', the rise of the nation state, 'racialized perceptions of identity, the spread of market relations and wage labour, the development of administrative bureaucracies and modern tax systems, the birth of consumer societies' and the growth of the press and the rise of civil society (Blackburn, 1997, p. 4). Walvin's more popular account of British slavery remarks on the enormous changes to patterns of consumption, settlement development, and growth that emerged from the traffic in slaves, and asks, 'is it possible to consider the rise of nineteenth-century racial thinking without considering the legacy of slave empire, the growth of the slave colonies and their relationship to British prosperity and economic development?' (Walvin, 1993, p. 334). Gilroy's *The Black Atlantic* (1993) is also concerned with modernity's embeddedness in the history of slavery and its legacy of racial politics. Gilroy argues for an ethnohistorical approach to the narrative of the Enlightenment that is sensitive to its blind spots. In searching for an alternative discourse of cultural belonging, one that does not mystify blood and soil Gilroy's holds up the chronotope of the ship. The ship, used for its connections with the middle passage, enables an alternative vision of cross-cultural fertilizations, hybridities and diasporas. Gilroy's *Black Atlantic* charts the migrations, displacements, borrowings, 'affinities and affiliations' that link black intellectuals to the project of the Enlightenment; it also offers their specific contributions towards a theory and praxis of freedom and citizenship. The main motivation behind this paper is to explore Fred D'Aguiar's contributions to the contemporary discourse of slavery through a reading of *Feeding the Ghosts*. I want to examine his deliberate choice of a female protagonist to tell the story of the *Zong;* I aim also to explore his manipulation of a structuring pair of symbols to articulate the juxtaposition between connectedness/affective relations and severance/loss that shape the human tragedy of the middle passage. Such juxtaposition is of course vital to the way slavery has been imagined. I shall argue that in his choice of the sea as symbol, D'Aguiar echoes the work of Derek Walcott but refashions his meanings, entering into a dialogue with his predecessor and compatriot. In providing a reading of *Feeding the Ghosts*, I hope to use the novel as a means of opening up and exploring the specific way in which slavery is talked about and imagined and, consequently, also to reflect on its effects.

Feeding the Ghosts is based on the story of the murder of 131 Africans on board the slave ship *Zong* in 1781. The real ship was bound for Jamaica from the West Coast of Africa but ran into difficulties. Mortality rates were high on the journey but inflated outrageously by the captain's decision to throw sick (and allegedly dying) slaves overboard in order the claim insurance money. Luke Collingwood, the captain, is recorded as justifying his decision on the grounds of a scarce and diminishing water supply. He is also alleged to have said that if slaves died through illness or suicide on board the ship, the owners would have to bear the cost; but if they were thrown overboard or killed to safeguard a ship's safety, the insurers would have to underwrite the losses. There was some dissent on board the *Zong* at this course of action. It emerged that his first mate, a James Kelsall, had disagreed with his captain's decision to drown the sick and dying slaves but the drowning of slaves continued even after heavy rain began. The killing of slaves in this fashion was not new but the sheer numbers involved meant that the resulting court case became the subject of much attention. The initial trial found for the claimants but the case returned to the courts when the insurers refused to pay the required £30 compensation for each slave who died. At the second trial, the presiding judge, Lord Mansfield, agreed with the claimants that as slaves were mere property or goods, there was no 'impropriety' in the action: 'the case of the slaves was the same as if horses had been thrown overboard' (Walvin, 1993, p. 20); yet he also granted a new trial. But as both Walvin and Fryer note, no records of a subsequent trial exist and the efforts of anti-slavery campaigner Granville Sharp to prosecute the crew for murder failed. However, the case of the *Zong* galvanized abolitionist support and a parliamentary bill was passed in 1790 which ruled out insurance claims resulting from slave mortality through 'natural death or ill treatment, or against loss by throwing overboard of slaves on any account whatsoever' (Walvin, 1993, p. 20). The callousness and brutality of the *Zong* incident seems also to have motivated J. M. W. Turner to paint his famous portrait of a ship jettisoning her human cargo during a violent and turbulent storm entitled *Slavers throwing overboard the Dead and Dying*.

D'Aguiar's novel takes some poetic licence with known records of the real historical incident by telling the tale of the *Zong*'s tragedy through the eyes of a slave girl on board the ship. The main story of the incident is narrated in third person with Mintah, a Fetu slave girl, as focalizer; she is also given her own voice in the form of her written record of the events on board the *Zong*, and in a brief first-person narrative account of her life after the tragedy. The novel itself is divided into three main parts, and framed by a poetic prologue and an epilogue that links the necessary telling of tale to our narrative present. The first part of the novel belongs to Mintah, who is depicted as literate in the English language and used to the ways of Europeans from her life at a Danish Mission. Although Mintah serves as the main focalizer in the first and longest part of the novel, alternative perspectives are also given to add complexity and depth to the tragedy. For example, James Kelsall's ambivalence regarding his captain's actions and his refusal to deal with his former encounters with Mintah who had looked after him at the Danish Mission is also rendered sympathetically. But Mintah's anguish over her dispossession, uprooting and dehumanization, and the murder of her fellow slaves, forms the emotional centre of this first part; her attempts at resistance and insurrection also grant her an agency and dignity that is written out of official history. The second section is an account of the trial, over which Lord Mansfield presided, and is narrated in third-person voice. Here, the narrative voice is more distant and sits in judgement of the crewmen, judge and lawyers at the trial; there is little attempt to render them sympathetically (although the ambivalence of the first mate Kelsall and the conflicting loyalties of the cook's assistant are handled with some care). In this section, Mintah's written record of the incidents on board the *Zong* surface at the trial but is dismissed as incredible. In ruling against Mintah's record, her voice disappears from official history. The last section begins with Mintah's written account of the *Zong*, and continues, also in first person, with her life in Maryland and Jamaica, haunted by the memory of the *Zong*.

In retelling the tale of the *Zong* through Mintah, D'Aguiar seems to be suggesting that there are (extra)ordinary lives that have been silenced and erased from history. Unlike the slave narratives that appeared in abolitionist literature, and free men and women who have negotiated their own autobiographies in the wake of the abolitionist movement, Mintah's record cannot exist in this early period because 'it argued against the law concerning the status of Africans as stock' (D'Aguiar, 1998, p. 169). Barbara Bush, in her pioneering study on slave women, has written of the difficulty of recovering ordinary women's voices in Caribbean plantation society, and of having to 'generalise from specific examples due to the paucity of evidence and the absence of slave testimony' (Bush, 1990, p. 9). The historical records of the *Zong* case contest the status and significance of slaves, but this contestation appears as one conducted between men: Lord Mansfield (the judge), John Lee (the solicitor-general), Granville Sharp (the anti-slavery campaigner), Luke Collingwood and James Kelsall (the crewmen of the *Zong*), William Gregson and George Case (the owners of the ship), Gilbert (the insurers), the *Morning Chronicle* correspondent, and even Olaudah Equiano, who had alerted Granville Sharp to the *Zong* affair. The choice of Mintah is also bold in so far as it allows D'Aguiar to use the issue of Mintah's reproductive ability – her body – to explore slavery's severance of kinship and familial affiliations. The maternal is privileged in the choice of Mintah as the novel's central protagonist; the responsibility for the safety of her fellow slaves in the hold is marked as a nurturing burden. This makes her failure all the more poignant.

When we first encounter Mintah, she calls Kelsall's name in anger and is hauled out to the open deck to be interrogated. Made to entertain the sailors, she dances 'fertility, temporary death and eventual rebirth'. The ritual dance connects her with her home and with (generations of) other young women dancing to the sound of the drum beat in an African village. In Mintah's status as potential slave mother, we have a brutal contradiction of terms; her fertility dance, a cruel irony in the light of the drowning of slaves:

Mintah thought about her performance above deck not so long ago. She felt ashamed. What fertility gods? Her blood flowed for nothing. Her benediction to the gods was for what? None of it could save a single hair on the head of a child. She wanted her blood to run dry and for the intricate apparatus that she harboured inside to dislodge from its moorings and drift out of her; to expel it and never feel that particular pain again and never bleed for any god, for any dance. (D'Aguiar, 1998, p. 40)

Kin and family are obtained through the ties of blood and reproduction, and it is through Mintah's womanhood that the pain of slavery is felt. Her knowledge of European languages and customs means that others treat her as a translator and mediator of cultures; this role intensifies the responsibility she feels towards her fellow prisoners and her anguish at her inability to save them. In the third section of the novel, with her freedom, Mintah shapes 131 carvings out of wood; these shapes represent figures 'of some kind, man, woman or child reaching up out of the depths'. In a continuation of the maternal metaphor, they are the ghosts of the past but they are also her children, the progeny that her body refuses to bear:

The sea had taken my blood from me and my ability to bleed. Yet I was surrounded by my progeny. The figures came from me. My hands delivered them ... . From their shapes they appear to breathe like me. Each has a name, a likely age, and accordingly likes to be placed on the left or right side ... . The wood suggested its name and habits to me as I worked the grain to bring the shape to the surface. They named themselves through me. (D'Aguiar, 1998, pp. 210–11)

It is significant that D'Aguiar avoids the temptation to reify motherhood and childbearing into some kind of mystical feminine status; the maternal metaphor is powerful but it is not the only one that symbolizes familial belonging and affiliations. The novel is careful to balance the maternal and the reproductive with that of the traditional crafter or worker. The latter is represented as Mintah's inheritance from her father, who teaches her how to work with the grain of the wood and to shape it. In one sense, Mintah 'births' her wooden carvings at the end of the novel; but in another sense, she also crafts them, 'gouging chips from the birch in directions obedient to the flow of the grain' (D'Aguiar, 1998, p. 42). (Mintah's crafting is also linked to writing and the recording of her experiences on paper.) Woodwork is associated with her father, especially his approval when she exhibits her medium, and also with memories of her mother, home and village life. Wood is also associated with mud, earth and land and all four are the bases by which culture, kinsfolk and community are built upon. Mintah's longing for home is represented as a hunger for the depth and memory of connections that are expressed through wood and land. In her fantasy of escape from the *Zong* these become embodied – bodily – memories:

> First she wanted to feel soil, mud, stone, rock, clay, sand, loam, pebbles, boulders, grass. Then wood. ... There would be a path she could take and footsteps she would be able to retrace ... One with old roots and stones jutting above the ground to stub the toes against and holes to jolt the first careless foot stepping into them. ... Land would figure in her dreams like a lover or friend or parent ... . Everything she dreamed, all the shapes without a basis in the waking world that surrounded her, belonged deep in the soil. Wood worked by her hands had tried to find these shapes. Sleep was a descent into the ground. She moved underground like a root feeling its way along, but with more speed, and secreted herself among those shapes, curling around them and caressing them. But waking she often lost all that she had in her dreams. All that remained was a sensation, a flavour or smell or some pleasure she could not define. (D'Aguiar, 1998, p. 116)

I have included this long quotation to show the novel's method of creating a chain of associations that work by building upon each other. The reverberations of meaning around wood and land are layered one upon another, and coextensive with attributes of depth, belonging and connections. The novel's emphasis on creating poetic metanarrative forges a horizon of connections; events that happen in the different sections, spatial and temporal zones of the narration echo each other through imagery and a depth of meaning generated by their associations. D'Aguiar acknowledges such a technique in his 'The Last Essay About Slavery'. When describing his brand of contemporary novels about slavery, he speaks of eschewing realism, and of generating a poetic level: a 'deliberate reaching-up or elevation in the tone of the narration and a preponderance of suggestive imagery' (D'Aguiar, 1997, p. 143). Interestingly, in the passage above, D'Aguiar depicts the memory of previous cultural and familial connections as a bodily memory which surfaces as the symptoms of past life, and as such echoes the poetics of the novel. The notion of an embodied memory that will return to haunt the body is also a figure that is used in contemporary representations of slavery; slavery in this sense is both an artistic/mythic reservoir and memory of a trauma passed down through the generations. But first, I want to pause over the absent term that cancels out the connections made through wood/land; the opposite of the latter is the contrasting symbol of the sea.

In *Feeding the Ghosts*, the sea represents the dissolution of ties of kinship and culture in the middle passage; as the poetic prologue puts it, 'the sea is slavery'. The sea forms the companion symbol to the metaphoric associations of kinship, culture and community that coalesce around wood and land. Because the sea journey takes the Africans on board the slavers away from their homes, the sea represents a kind of death, a severing of all known forms of affective and cultural relations:

> love would be nowhere: behind them and impossible to recover; a flat line in the wake of the ship where the sky bowed down to the sea or the sea ascended to the sky. Love was lost somewhere in the very sea with its limitless capacity to swallow love, slaves, ships and memories. (D'Aguiar, 1998, p. 27)

But more than its metonymic association with transportation and uprooting, and the consequences that follow from those processes, the sea represents a far more symbolic impersonality. The slaves' passage across the waters is conceived of as a remorseless empty present, 'an in-between life' where 'time runs on the spot, neither backwards nor forwards' (D'Aguiar, 1998, p. 199). Cut off from civilization as they know it, and yet to arrive at a destination wherein they would 'be lost forever but not dead', the sea is a reminder that the impersonality of death awaits us all. The poetic prologue to the novel opens with such an image of the sea. The sea receives every body thrown into its waters with a soundless splash, 'each [body] opens a wound in this sea that heals over each body without the evidence of a scar' (D'Aguiar, 1998, p. 3). The sea consumes every morsel of the human body, 'swells the body to bursting point, tumbles it beyond the reach of horizons and gradually breaks fragments from that body with its nibbling, dissecting current' (D'Aguiar, 1998, p.4). Grinding their bones to dust and salt, the sea melts each body into nothingness and 'becomes them, becomes their memory'. But unlike the land that has a fixed geography and preserves the traces of bodily presence, and unlike wood that has a capacity for memory embedded in its knots and grain, the sea is ever-changing and endless; it 'destroys but does not remember'.

D'Aguiar's symbol of the sea owes much to Derek Walcott and it is possible to argue that *Feeding the Ghosts* uses Walcott's poetry as an intertext. The novel opens with Walcott's 'The Sea is History' as one of the two poems that function as an epigraph prefacing the narration proper. Some of the poetic language in the novel contains traces of Walcott's phrasing and extends his metaphors in poems such as 'Names' and 'The Sea is History' and 'The Schooner *Flight*'. For example, in 'Names', the narrator of the poem describes his emergence as one with 'no memory', 'no future', and with 'a different fix on the stars'. He searches for the 'moment / when the mind was halved by a horizon ... as a fishline sinks, the horizon sinks in memory'. D'Aguiar's horizon is a 'flat line in the wake of the ship' where sky and sea meet; his land is 'a geography of fixed points', 'fixed points in the mind' while his Africans come from cultures with a 'different fix on the stars'. Walcott's poet and sailor Shabine in *Flight*, dives into the depths of the Caribbean sea 'so choked with the dead' that they are part of the seascape; 'I saw them corals: brain, fire, sea fans, / dead-men's-fingers, and then, the deadmen. / I saw that the powdery sand was their bones / ground white from Senegal to San Salvador'. D'Aguiar's sea is also filled with the dead whose 'faces pressed in coral or sand and seaweed braided in their hair', whose bodies 'have their lives written on salt water'. Significantly, Walcott's sea in 'Names' is also a sea of impersonal erasure:

> Behind us all the sky folded,
> as history folds over a fishline,
> and the foam foreclosed
> with nothing in our hands
>
> but this stick
> to trace our names on the sand
> which the sea erased again, to our indifference

and in 'The Sea is History' Walcott refers to an ocean which 'kept turning back pages / looking for History'. In an important interview with J. P. White in 1990, Walcott argues that the sea is an important figure of island peoples' lives and functions as a structuring symbol in his poetry. For Walcott, the sea represents a kind of timelessness and immensity outside of human history:

> Nothing can be put down in the sea. You can't plant on it, you can't live on it, you can't walk on it. Therefore, the strength of the sea gives you an idea of time that makes history absurd. ... The sea is not elegiac .... The sea does not have anything on it that is a memento of man. (White, 1996, p. 159)

But while Walcott uses the symbol of the sea to invoke the creative and Adamic possibilities of Caribbean life, and the transcendence of art against a Eurocentric linear history narrative of progress and achievement, D'Aguiar's symbol of the sea is bleaker in its emphasis on the rubbing out of human life and affective ties. The sea has no memory even if bodies are transformed into coral and salt, even if the wind howling over the sea mimes the living breath and speech of the 'one hundred and thirty-one dissipated bodies'. In this reading of the seascape, the memory of the souls belongs to the living. This task of remembering is not a simply matter of choice. It is compulsive and undertaken by the survivors and their offspring who relive in ways that make sense of the trauma of death, dispersal and dispossession. In the prologue, the relation between the dead and living is conceived of as a haunting, the living 'will have to be a witness again' to the middle passage. Mintah's life after the *Zong* is dominated by the memory of the dead. She sees visions of the dead in the phosphorus glow above the water, shining with the life and love that 'they had to give but were robbed from giving'. The dead also return in the way in which her work in wood mimics the sea: 'the very element I sought to escape rose out of the wood shaped by me. Trees became waves. Waves sprouted roots, branches and leaves' (D'Aguiar, 1998, p. 207). Her 131 wooden carvings are unsettling sculptures, shapes that do not sit easily in normal domestic homes; they 'fill the eyes with unease' but they live with her in her wooden hut, 'like guests who will not leave and whom ... [she] eventually cannot bear to part with' (D'Aguiar, 1998, p. 209). In the epilogue to the tale, the narrator extends the theme of the past as a trauma that returns: the narrator's retelling of the story is one that is only temporarily laid to rest – knowledge is a burden; the past surfaces again and again in the present.

In 'The Last Essay About Slavery' D'Aguiar writes of trying to imagine 'a last poem, a last play, a last novel, a last song, about slavery' which would 'kill slavery off' – 'final acts of creativity' could 'somehow disqualify any future need to return to it' (D'Aguiar, 1997, p. 125). Yet he senses that such an act is not possible with the 'conflicts between races' and in the fracturing and scrambling of history that are a result of slave history. It is this belief, that one has to come to terms with a past in order to move on, that D'Aguiar shares with his fellow black British writer Caryl Phillips, who has in many ways been obsessively writing about slavery and the history of slavery since the 1980s. Phillips defends the return to slavery in similar terms, as an attempt to deal with how the past repeats itself in present relations; 'the root of our problem – of all those people, white and non-white, who live in Europe or the Americas – is to do with the forces that were engendered by the "peculiar institution"'. Dealing with the past is part of a process of 'understanding where we are or where we might be going' (Jaggi, 1994, p. 26). Interestingly, for D'Aguiar, even the past and present are shifting and should not be understood in terms of mere temporal linearity:

> the act of looking back not only acknowledges the present in the past, it admits too, the future in the past. The descendants of slaves are hurting because the present isn't working for them. They are shackled to the past by the failure of a present (the recent present), to examine that past in a way makes sense as rhetoric, as emblem, as art. (D'Aguiar, 1997, p. 142)

Every generation witnesses a compulsive need to revisit slavery in their own language and imagery; but rather than the past being laid to rest when it is told, each imagining 'feeds the need for a further act of retrieval. In fiction as in song, the story continues both to bring to life a past that might otherwise remain lost or distorted into shame, and to convert that past from pain to cure' (D'Aguiar, 1997, p. 138). D'Aguiar brings a self-reflexive quality to the debate about 'remembering' slavery; his essay exhibits an awareness that discoursing, telling stories, writing poetry about slavery creates a vast mythic reservoir or archive, 'an inexhaustible seam'. It corresponds in part to Stuart Hall's identification of the language of cultural identity and tradition as a hybrid point between authenticity and invention, essence and performance. Such a hybridity disrupts the linear flow of time as unidirectional; 'identities are the names we give to the different ways we are positioned by, and position ourselves within, the narratives of the past' (Hall, 1990, p. 225). It is at this point that I want to reintroduce Gilroy's *Black Atlantic*. There is much similarity in Phillips's, D'Aguiar's and Gilroy's attitudes towards the slave past and its reconstruction, especially in music. Phillips's conception of history as a redemptive act, his creation of a chorus of diasporic voices that 'repeat, mutate, and transform the motif of exile from kinsfolk in the original rupture of families under slavery' in *Crossing the River* can be read as an imaginative counterpart to Gilroy's *Black Atlantic* (Low, 1998, p. 139). D'Aguiar's examples of how the language and themes of slavery are reflected in popular contemporary music gesture towards Gilroy's more substantial analysis of black music as the quintessential expression of transatlantic mutated, hybrid artistic forms based on a common history. But it is in Gilroy's desire to formulate a language to address the commonality and the recurrent patterns of concerns in black diasporic cultures which is also not a reified notion of tribal memory and tradition, and it is his identification of slavery as a base matrix that I want to explore in connection to *Feeding the Ghosts*.

In his provocative last chapter, entitled 'Not a Story to Pass On: Living Memory and the Slave Sublime', Gilroy argues for the prominence of slavery in black diasporic intellectual and artistic life. Modernity for black intellectuals such as W. E. B. Du Bois, Frederick Douglass and Richard Wright was founded less on the 'dream of revolutionary transformation' of the European philosophical discourses of modernity but on the 'catastrophic rupture of the middle passage' and its legacy, 'the countercultural aspirations towards freedom, citizenship, and autonomy that developed after it among slaves and their descendants' (Gilroy, 1993b, p. 197). Gilroy wants to make a case for the distinctiveness of black expressive cultures that transfigures – even transcends – locality and time. Is there a strategic connection between the narratives of loss, exile, dispossession and journeying that recur in different musical and artistic forms? Are the 'love and loss' stories that populate black popular culture a way of transcoding 'other forms of yearning and mourning associated with histories of dispersal and exile and the remembrance of unspeakable terror' (Gilroy, 1993b, p. 201)? Gilroy introduces the idea of a displaced slave poetics that captures the notion of continuity amidst discontinuities ('changing same'). In a move that is reminiscent of Hall's disruption of linearity, Gilroy finds the distinctiveness of black expressive cultures in their memory of slavery, which is at once an 'ethnic tradition' (a tribal memory?) and also a strategy for creating, performing and renewing tradition/identity. In a highly contentious move, Gilroy reads the turn to death as the motif that links disparate forms across time:

> We will explore ... how the rapport with death emerges continually in the literature and expressive cultures of the Black Atlantic. It is integral, for example, to the narratives of loss, exile and journeying which, like particular elements of a musical performance, serve a mnemonic function: directing the consciousness of the group back to significant, nodal points in its common history and its social memory. The telling and retelling of these stories plays a special role, organising the consciousness of the 'racial' group socially and striking the important balance between inside and outside activity – the different practices, cognitive, habitual, and performative, that are required to invent, maintain and renew identity. They constituted the Black Atlantic as a non-traditional tradition, an irreducibly modern, ex-centric, unstable, and asymmetrical cultural ensemble that cannot be apprehended through the manichean logic of binary coding (Gilroy, 1993b, p. 198).

I do not want to deal with Gilroy's use of death and suffering as the key figure in a submerged slave poetics because others have dealt incisively with the problems associated with such an identification (see, for example, Chrisman, 1997). What I want to explore here is the isolation of slavery as the base matrix in the formulation of an ethnic or racialized tradition. In many ways, such a formulation invites comparison with the Jewish remembrance of the Holocaust, and Gilroy says as much in his comparison of the modern and the spiritual, exile and redemption, dispersal and connectedness in both groups. The link with the Holocaust is also one that is put to imaginative use in Caryl Phillips's *The Nature of Blood*. Alastair Pettinger in his review of *The Black Atlantic* suggests that Gilroy should have included a psychoanalytic approach to the issue of social memory, and argues that the term 'transgenerational haunting' would provide productive ways to explore how traumas of dispossession unconsciously repeat themselves across time in succeeding generations (Pettinger, 1998, p. 145). Jacqueline Rose's study of Jewish and South African narratives of the nation, *States of Fantasy*, from which the term is taken, argues that trans-generational hauntings are forms of remembrance which 'hover in the space between social and psychic history, forcing and making it impossible for the one who unconsciously carries them to make the link' (Rose, 1996, p. 6); they are the processes wherein 'one generation finds itself performing the unspoken and unconscious agendas of the one that went before' (Rose, 1996, p. 42). The powerful links between blood, land and national identity – the fantasies of identification – in Zionist rhetoric are the burdens of history, but one that 'unfolds [also] in the deepest recesses of the mind' (Rose, 1996, p. 6). Pettinger finds such that such a social memory of slavery would be more productive than 'all the talk of invented traditions'; seeing the past as mere 'cultural construct' means that the 'unconscious forces' go 'largely unacknowledged' (Pettinger, 1998, p. 45).

To link Pettinger's arguments with D'Aguiar, one could say that his work does engage with the idea of hidden depths of historical and psychic proportions in his use of the poetic metaphors of wood/land, and also in his manipulation of the sea as symbol. In the prologue to *Feeding the Ghosts*, the sea is an erasure of human life and memory, but it is also – paradoxically – an embodiment of history: the sea swallows up the slave dead and 'becomes their memory'. The phrase the 'sea is slavery' is extended with the suggestion that these 'bodies have their lives written on salt water'; the wind, the water and waves embody their charges, the 'sea current turns pages of memory' (D'Aguiar, 1998, p.4). Furthermore, the notion of the sea as a reservoir of the unconscious is developed with Mintah's creation of 131 wooden figurines; a result, she remarks, of a kind of haunting. As Mintah puts it, 'the shape of each piece is pulled from the sea of my mind and has been shaped by water, with water's contours' (D'Aguiar, 1998, p. 208). The process is not entirely within her conscious control; 'the very element I sought to escape rose out of wood shaped by me' (D'Aguiar, 1998, p. 207), she says. But here the difference with Pettinger's account occurs – Mintah shapes, gives form to the blocks of wood. She brings her skills to the manufacture of these sculptures. If the sea of the prologue, and its natural elements, become the live memory of the *Zong*'s murderous acts, it is the living that must bear witness to the crime – the living which fashions expression out of the traumatic memory of the past and (re)creates it. If one were to follow Pettinger's lead, that the traumatic effects of slavery recur in the present as a trans-generic haunting, we would deny any sense of creativity and agency to the writers and artists that shape our cultural imagination; slavery would in this version be reified as an unconscious 'tribal memory'. What is perhaps significant about both Gilroy and D'Aguiar's account is their sense that the accumulation of texts on the subject, their textual reverberation and their intertextual dialogue with each other, strives towards the structure of a mythic/cultural repository of symbols, discourses, language and memory which is outside any individual control. Such a mythic reservoir plays a formative part in organizing group consciousness and in this manner 'one cannot choose one's memories of a people any more than one can as an individual' (Pettinger, 1998, p. 145). The positing and return to slavery as a mythic ur-text, the shaping, reconfiguring – to use D'Aguiar's term – the 'nuancing' of slavery by each succeeding generation performs a distinctive transatlantic bonding of black diasporic identities.

I want to end this chapter by returning to the question of national identifications. I started with an assertion about the specifically black British contribution to the representation of slavery. But, in a sense, this is somewhat contradictory in so far as D'Aguiar, Gilroy and Phillips write of a transatlantic black diasporic community that moves beyond national boundaries. Partly because of the history of migration, and partly as a result of a long history of racism, the black community in Britain has had a long tradition of looking over the waters. As Gilroy argues in his earlier *There Ain't No Black in the Union Jack,* black Britain has always drawn 'inspiration from those developed by black populations' elsewhere, but particularly with regard to the 'culture and politics of black America and the Caribbean' (Gilroy, 1987, p. 154). Mike and Trevor Phillips in their collection of interviews that make up *Windrush* (1998) testify to the importance of these American connections: the Civil Rights campaigns (and the media attention it got), the Black Power movement, figures like Martin Luther King, Malcolm X and Stokeley Carmichael who visited, played a formative role in the creation of a black identity in Britain and in black politics generally. CARD (the Campaign Against Racial Discrimination) was formed in the aftermath of King's visit in 1965. Musical migrations across the Atlantic and back in popular culture is the bedrock of how young people make and remake themselves as part of a larger 'black' community. The movements of a younger generation of scholars and artists also reflect the Atlantic connections, with D'Aguiar and Phillips holding teaching positions and writing fellowships at American universities. The intellectual and imaginative debt can also be traced to the pioneering work done on slave narratives and African-American expressive cultures in the 1980s by a generation of intellectuals like Henry Louis Gates, Houston Baker, bell hooks, Hazel Carby and Toni Morrison. Morrison's *Beloved* is perhaps the most influential text in the contemporary American exploration of slavery, memory and trauma, but other writers such as Sherley Anne Williams and Charles Johnson have also made important contributions to imagining slavery and its legacy in black cultural life. The (re)turn to slavery in British novels reflects the wider black diasporic concerns and the formative role of African-American intellectual and cultural life in the production of a black aesthetics; but it must also mean a more integrative approach to history. This is to be particularly welcomed for it must also mean that Britain cannot simply displace slavery – its history and legacy – on to some other space and some other time.

Works Cited

Blackburn, Robin, 1997. *The Making of New World Slavery*, London: Verso.
Brathwaite, Edward, 1973. *The Arrivants, A New World Trilogy*, Oxford: Oxford University Press.
Bush, Barbara, 1990. *Slave Women in Caribbean Society 1650–1838*, Kingston: Heinemann; Bloomington and Indianapolis: Indiana University Press; London: James Currey.
Chrisman, Laura, 1997. 'Journeying to Death: Gilroy's *Black Atlantic*', *Race and Class*, vol. 39, no. 2, pp. 51–64.
D'Aguiar, Fred, 1995. *The Longest Memory*, London: Vintage.
D'Aguiar, Fred, 1997. 'The Last Essay About Slavery', in Sarah Dunant and Roy Porter (eds), *The Age of Anxiety*, London: Virago.
D'Aguiar, Fred, 1998. *Feeding the Ghosts*, London: Vintage.
Donnell, Alison and S. Lawson Welsh (eds), 1996. *The Routledge Reader in Caribbean Literature*, London: Routledge.
Fryer, P., 1984. *Staying Power: The History of Black People in Britain*, London: Pluto Press.
Gilroy, Paul, 1987. *There Ain't No Black in the Union Jack*, London: Hutchinson.
Gilroy, Paul, 1993a. *Small Acts*, London: Serpent's Tail.
Gilroy, Paul, 1993b. *The Black Atlantic: Modernity and Double Consciousness*, London: Verso.
Hall, Stuart, 1990. 'Cultural Identity and Diaspora', in Jonathan Rutherford (ed.), *Identity: Community, Culture, Difference*, London: Lawrence and Wishart.
Jaggi, Maya, 1994. 'Crossing the River: Caryl Phillips talks to Maya Jaggi', *Wasafiri*, vol. 20, pp. 25–29.
Ledent, Benedicte, 1996. 'Remembering Slavery: History as Roots in the Fiction of Caryl Phillips and Fred D'Aguiar', in Marc Delrez and Benedicte Ledent (eds), *The Contact and the Culmination*, Liège: University of Liège.

Low, Gail, 1998. '"A Chorus of Common Memory": Slavery and Redemption in Caryl Phillips's *Cambridge* and *Crossing the River*', *Research into African Literatures*, vol. 29, no. 4, pp. 122–39.

Nichols, Grace, 1983. *i is a long memoried woman*, London: Karnak.

Pettinger, Alastair, 1998. 'Enduring Fortresses – A Review of *The Black Atlantic* by Paul Gilroy', *Research in African Literature*, vol. 29, no. 4, pp. 142–47.

Phillips, Caryl, 1989. *Higher Ground*, London: Viking.

Phillips, Caryl, 1991. *Cambridge*, London: Picador.

Phillips, Caryl, 1993. *Crossing the River*, London: Picador.

Phillips, Caryl, 1997. *The Nature of Blood*, London: Faber & Faber.

Phillips, Mike and Trevor Phillips, 1998. *Windrush*, London: HarperCollins, 1998.

Plasa, Carl and Betty Ring (eds), 1994. *The Discourse of Slavery: Aphra Behn to Toni Morrison*, London: Routledge.

Rose, Jacqueline, 1996. *States of Fantasy*, Oxford: Clarendon.

Unsworth, Barry, 1992. *Sacred Hunger*, London: Penguin.

Walcott, Derek, 1993. *Poems: 1965–1980*, London: Jonathan Cape.

Walvin, James, 1993. *Black Ivory: A History of British Slavery*, London: Fontana.

White, J. P., 1996. 'An Interview with Derek Walcott', in William Baer (ed.), *Conversations with Derek Walcott*, University of Mississippi Press.

9

'Versioning' the Revolution: Gender and Politics in Merle Collins's *Angel*

Suzanne Scafe

In *Woman Version*, Evelyn O'Callaghan (1993) formulates a theory of writing by women from the Caribbean, using ideas from Dick Hebdige's study of Caribbean music *Cut 'n' Mix: Culture, Identity and Caribbean Music* (1987). The 'version' of her title refers to the practice, begun in Jamaica in the late 1960s, of producing 'new' music by rearranging the tracks of the original reggae song. On the whole, this was done in two ways: by foregrounding the drum and bass sections of the original track, usually called the 'dub' version, or by overlaying the track with a commentary or 'talk over' by a DJ, a practice known as 'toasting' (Johnson, 1986, pp. 398–402), which effects a celebration of the original even while creating a space for parody, political or social commentary, or a general updating of the lyrics. The isolation of the drum and bass could be said to represent a revoicing of the emphasis, in African music, on rhythm and percussion, particularly since the popularity of the musical form coincided with the rise of the Black Power movement in the Caribbean and in the production of African cultural expression.

This period also saw a rise in the popularity of story-telling artists such as Louise Bennett whose use of Jamaican creole and oral story-telling traditions in her written poetry first won the recognition of the literary world in the early 1960s and popularized the transformation of written poetic conventions in Caribbean poetry (Breiner, 1998, pp. 172–73). The 'dub version' can also be seen as a self-conscious affirmation of practices of oral story-telling, where each 'version' of the story changes with the telling, and more significance is attached to the newest 'version' than the form of its original conception. Hebdige links the production of 'dub' to the dynamic, mixed and overlapping cultural heritage of the Caribbean, evidenced in creole language forms such as 'Dread Talk', a term used by Caribbean linguist Velma Pollard to describe a linguistic code in which 'words have been subjected to a number of word-making processes drastic enough to give some words new sounds and others new meaning' (Pollard, 1991 p. 239).

The concern of O'Callaghan's work is less with the cultural context of 'dub', as I have outlined it, and more with its use as a means of defending the uniqueness of Caribbean women's writing. Her reference to 'dub' music provides a means of interrogating 'the whole notion of a hierarchical distinction between "original substantive creation" and the "version", a new form that has grown out of a process of altering, supplementing, breaking, echoing, mocking and playing with that original' (O'Callaghan, 1993, p. 10).

In this chapter I intend to use the principle of 'dubbing' in order to explore the ways in which the work of Caribbean writer Merle Collins uses and subverts the political theories central to Fanon's *The Wretched of the Earth*. My argument centres on the novel's representation of women in relation to two significant periods of decolonization in the Caribbean island of Grenada: the period immediately before and after the first post-colonial government of 'Leader' and the four-year period of the Marxist-Leninist government of Maurice Bishop. The use of 'dub' as a way of positing the relationship between the two texts allows an imaginative text by a Caribbean woman writer to be read as a critical challenge to a text which theorizes revolutionary decolonization. Her work reflects the insurrectionary politics of Fanon's essays but at the same time, in her own focus on the everyday experiences of a group of economically marginalized rural women, reveals as significant the absence of women in Fanon's work.

Better known as a poet, Collins wrote her first novel, *Angel*, in 1987 as a means of reflecting on the 'trauma' of events in 1983 when the Grenadian revolutionary government (the New Jewel Movement) of 1979 was brought to an abrupt end by an American military invasion. In an interview with Betty Wilson she describes her reasons for writing the novel:

> I think *Angel* also came at a period when I was looking at, looking back at, that whole period of Grenadian history and kind of looking behind headlines at the things that were happening .... *Angel* is definitely the product of 1983 and of the crash of October 1983 ... and about the whole of that trauma and my moving out and looking back at it all and feeling that, as so often happens the focus remains on the principal actors. (Wilson, 1993, p. 102)

The novel recounts the story of the growth to maturity of one of its main characters, Angel, born in and around 1951, during the early phase of decolonization in Grenada. Collins charts the same historical terrain as Fanon's work. By foregrounding the inhabitants of a tiny village, however, and their exclusion from the revolutionary process, and by representing in fine detail the lives of the community's women, Collins uncovers in Fanon's representation of the colonized subject women as the hidden other; in the imaginative spaces cleared by her work, the narrative recovers the voices of generations of women who witness but are silenced in the political process.

My interest in O'Callaghan's formulation is that it offers a way of theorizing Caribbean women writers within a framework located and defined by Caribbean cultural forms and practices. The use of 'dub' as a literary metaphor makes possible an intertextual approach, where a foregrounding of language, orality, culture and politics is both the function of the critical framework and a feature of the narratives under consideration. For the purpose of this chapter, however, I am emphasizing not the text's 'uniqueness' in relation to Fanon's 'master narrative' but the extent to which Collins's novel, in its reconnection with Fanon's theories of post-colonial liberation, disturbs, revises and extends some of the fundamental assumptions of his text.

Maria Helena Lima discusses Collins's use of an autobiographical subject, Angel, but characterizes the narrative not as autobiography or *Bildungsroman* but as *testimonio*, a form which represents a 'social model of self' shaped by the multiple and often conflicting discourses of the immediate community (Lima, 1993, p. 45). It is a form marked by its oral quality and 'by marginalization, oppression and struggle'. Collins's novel is dominated by her use of the creole form with its retention of some African words such as *kata* (headcloth). The narrative is expressed primarily in different forms of dialogue: as oral interactions, as letters, as songs and in the creole section headings which communicate directly with the reader. Her use of language is, Collins has said, a means of valorizing not only the culture and experiences of the women in her text, but their mode of expression (Wilson, 1993, p. 103). Significant historical moments in the island's recent history are represented from the different and shifting perspectives of the autobiographical subject and of other individuals from within a specific community; in this way the novel 'cuts' and 'remixes' the characters' subjective reconstructions of history in a fictional *testimonio*, with other narratives' privileging of historical 'fact', and of political theory.

Both texts are concerned with a representation of violence; in Fanon's text violence is one of the key tropes of historical progress and change. In his essay 'Concerning Violence', he argues that the only means by which a colonized subject can effectively overthrow the colonizer is through violence. Of the colonial regime, he writes:

> In capitalist countries a multitude of moral teachers, counsellors and 'bewilderers' separate the exploited from those in power. In the colonial countries on the contrary, the policemen and the soldier, by their immediate presence and their frequent and direct action, maintain contact with the native and advise him by means of rifle butts and napalm not to budge. (Fanon, 1961, p. 29)

'Decolonizing violence' – that is, the violent destruction of colonialism in all its forms by the colonized people – is not just a means of combating colonial violence, but of restoring to humanity the decolonized subject; it creates 'a new language and a new humanity'; it is, he argues, the 'veritable creation of new men'. Citing at length Cesaire's 'Les Armes miraculeuses (et les chiens taisaient)' with its poetic representation of decolonizing violence as a 'baptism', a cleansing and purging of evil, and a rebirth, he concludes:

> For the native, life can only spring up again out of the rotting corpse of the settler ... this violence ... invests their characters with positive and creative qualities. The practice of violence binds them together as a whole, since each individual forms a violent link in the great chain, a part of the great organism of violence which has surged upwards in reaction to the settler's violence in the beginning. (Fanon, 1961, p. 73)

The appeal of violence as a means of resistance is represented only in relation to a masculine subject whose physical freedom is constrained by colonial repression; and whose physical presence is literally diminished by colonial subjugation:

> The first thing which the native learns is to stay in his place, and not to go beyond certain limits. This is why the dreams of the native are always of muscular prowess; his dreams are of action and of aggression. I dream I am jumping, swimming, running, climbing; I dream that I burst out laughing, that I span a river in one stride, or that I am followed by a flood of motor cars which never catch up with me. (Fanon, 1961, p. 40)

Violent resistance is the means by which the incarcerated body of the colonial subject is set free; it also 'frees the native from his inferiority complex and from his despair and inaction; it makes him fearless and restores his self-respect' (Fanon, 1961, p. 74). Figures of combat and aggression are also used to describe the cultural product of decolonization and liberation movements; he writes of a 'fighting literature' (Fanon, 1961, p. 177) and of music that is expressive of a violent strength and energy.

The narrative of *Angel* is enclosed within the depictions of the anti-colonial violence which open the text and the bombing of the invading

American troops that herald the closing scenes. In the opening scene, the inhabitants of Hermitage watch with only partial comprehension as the most significant representation of colonial authority in their lives is being destroyed. The texture of the narrative, which immerses the reader in the minutiae of the villagers' lives without ever, as it were, lifting its head, emphasizes their exclusion and marginality. And in the opening scene of decolonizing violence it is Mano, a male member of the village who, unhampered by frightened and fretful children or the demands for care from the elders, is able, from his lookout in a distant tree, to tell the others that it is the *bukan* burning down and that the family owners, the de Lisles, might have been caught in the fire. Concealed within the more public, open expressions of jubilation are the women's more hesitant and private expressions of fear and unease. As Doodsie watches the burning described in the opening scene, her real focus is on the vulnerability of her dependent child, Angel. Even where one of the women expresses jubilation, she does so using metaphors of motherhood: 'All you hear dat? Ah sure is me basket o cocoa an dem dat bawling dey ... . No joke non, cocoa. Ah plant you, ah pick you, ah dance you, but you so damn ungrateful, you don even know you mudder ... You tink ah wounta ketch you?' (Collins, 1987, p. 3).

Ma Ettie, Doodsie's mother, waits back at the yard, fearful, hiding in her board house. Alone in the house, she utters a prayer: 'Lord, let this tribulation pass from us. Let not our enemies triumph over these your children, Lord. Take a thought to the life and salvation for the little children in that burning house' (Collins, 1987, p. 4). On the one hand, in its echo of the New Testament's 'Love thine enemies' her reaction demonstrates the power of colonial indoctrination through the agency of the church and the resulting inability of this character, as a colonized subject, to identify the agent of her own suffering and 'tribulation'. A clearer articulation of the extent to which Ma Ettie has been shaped by subservience, to the extent that she prioritizes the care and safety of those who dominate her, is illustrated in a later altercation with Regal, her son and a union organizer, who is one of Leader's strong men. She expresses horror at the violence inflicted on the animals on the de Lisle plantation: 'I hear all you cutting down people animal straight how dey stand up so in those people land ... you can't go into their land an destroy all the tings they work for' (Collins, 1987, p. 27).

Most of the women work, at some time or another as servants, caring for the children of the colonial middle classes; Ma Ettie herself had worked as a domestic servant for the de Lisle family and like all the other women was necessarily involved in the nurturing of those to whom she was also subservient. Her words express the doubleness of that experience; in the narrative they are used to represent the gendered character of colonial domination and, against a more uncompromising expression of truth in Fanon's text, a multiple, multilayered truth. To Regal, to Angel and other supporters of anti-colonial struggle, their unacceptability lies not just in the use of idioms rooted in a colonial and repressive past; enmeshed in both their overwhelming labour of maternal and familial care and in the narrow, grinding margins of unorganized labour their voices and experiences are discounted because they expose the limitations of the small spaces they inhabit.

Although, in the narrative, they do not belong to the early labour movements, and tend not to be part of the workforce of the large plantations, the work of the women is essential to the well-being of individual families; during the prolonged strike organized by Leader, and during Allan's period of absence as a migrant worker, Doodsie maintains the care of her family through the produce from her family's land. In all Collins's work these women are represented as the foundation of a fragile economy. In 'Gran', a short story from her collection *Rain Darling*, one of the characters says: 'Me mother well work a lot in she time already, yes. No wonder she could walk the streets of Grenada almost up to the end as if they belong to her. They belong to her in truth, yes. She work fixing road all over this country' (Collins, 1990, p. 54). In the midst of insurrectionary violence and the promise of a better future, one of the Hermitage women complains: 'Ah pickin nutmeg for the whole week an at the end of it ah could barely manage to buy the pound of saltfish' (Collins, 1987, p. 10). And after Leader installs the first independent government, Doodsie, in a letter to her friend, writes her own account of post-colonial history, with a firm assertion that things are 'changin' for the worse'. At the end of the novel, a generation on, she is still 'under the nutmeg' with her cutlass and 'heavy boots'. For these women, revolutionary change does not alter the structures of their dominance; and, through their dialogue and storytelling, the narrative insists on the importance not of the moment of anti-colonial victory but on the effect to which that victory is put in the long years that follow.

The narrative recuperates their discounted voices and, like the drum section of the dub, their voices form the more subtle though insistent anchor of the narrative's rhythm. The more strident section of the rhythm, the bass, is effected through the bold type section headings that counter Fanon's progressive representation of history and change. Against Fanon's conviction that the cycle of decolonizing and post-colonial violence will produce a cleansed and fully liberated nation, these creole fragments, which frame both the early depictions of violence and those of social and political change, represent history as cyclical and suggest a more compromised, even sceptical view of progress: 'Take win but you lose' (Collins, 1987, p. 18); 'Sometime you have to take de worse an call it de best' (Collins, 1987, p. 64); 'One day one day *congotè*' (Collins, 1987, p. 22).

The clearest instances of the novel's utilization of elements from Fanon's master narrative are in its representation of the political centre. Fanon's description of the anti-colonial 'leader', stresses the ostentation accompanying the early figureheads of the post-colonial governments. Fanon argues that the 'leader' of a newly decolonized nation state tends to have been part of a process of liberation through violence, fuelled in part by the envy and desire which characterizes the struggle of the native peasant. As 'leader', however, he uses his power and privilege to fulfil his desire to take the settler's place, which he does with the complicity of the national bourgeoisie, a 'company of profiteers', and at the expense of the peasants. Doodsie's letter inscribes her version of their anti-colonial hero, the vainglorious Leader, whose government, as the narrative shows, heralds a period of internecine violence, nepotism and political corruption: 'That man is the limit. He so like a show that he had the most biggest wedding possible. They say it had enough shampain to bathe in' (Collins, 1987, p. 17).

Both Angel's cautious and critical response to 'Black Nationalism' as a revolutionary political strategy and the novel's construction of the revolutionary government echo, revise and overlap elements not just of Fanon's political theory but of political statements made by the leader of Grenada's New Jewel Movement, Maurice Bishop, on whom the character Chief is based. In Fanon's text the role of the intellectual is as one of a 'highly conscious group ... armed with revolutionary principles', to contest the power of both the leader and the national bourgeoisie through whom he extends his power. He introduces his essay, 'On National Culture', an analysis of the means of contesting and progressing from what he describes as the 'bourgeois phase', with a quotation from Sekou Toure which identifies the key notes of Fanon's own argument:

> To take part in the African revolution it is not enough to write a revolutionary song; you must fashion the revolution with the people. And if you fashion it with the people the songs will come by themselves, and of themselves ... there is no place outside that fight for the artist or for the intellectual who is not himself concerned with the people. (Fanon, 1961, p. 166)

Collins's novel represents the connection of the intellectual and 'the people' in her portrayal of the political meetings of the revolutionary period. She uses a creole register both in the title of these scenes –

'Everybody puttin dey grain o salt!'; 'We runnin neck and neck wid you!' – and in the representation of the dialogue of all the characters. In this way the narrative effects a closing of the social and professional distance between the organizers, a government representative, the university-educated intellectual Angel, and the members of the literacy group who, in one instance, perform poetry which expresses their personal experience.

In an interview with Chris Searle conducted just nine weeks before his assassination, Maurice Bishop, invoking Fanon in his emphasis on the importance of unity between the government, the intellectual and 'the people', described his government's achievements:

> We have learned to develop a truly deep and abiding respect for the people of our country, particularly the working people, and have understood more and more their enormous creative power and ability to confront and solve their problems ... we have attempted to involve our people in the planning and running of the economy. (Searle, 1984a, pp. 9–10)

'Disunity' is figured as the 'enemy of the revolution' in all the texts to which I have referred. Searle writes: 'While the Grenada Revolution preserved its imperative unity, it was unassailable ... . When the breach in that fundamental unity came in October 1983 it [the US] struck out ... mercilessly' (Searle, 1984b, p. 2). In scenes such as those of Angel's arguments with staff members at the school where she teaches and with her own father, the narrative does reveal a more textured and discriminating representation of 'the people' than those of the political narratives cited above. However, specific representation of the kind of political disunity to which they refer is made in two distinct ways: through a domestic metaphor which recurs throughout the narrative and begins its closing section:

> High up the chicken-hawk circled ...
> 'Caw! caw! caw!' High up the chicken-hawk circled.
> Doodsie threw more corn. 'All you stay togedder!' she shouted ... .
> 'All you self too stupid,' she said to the fowls. 'Don run when they try to frighten you. Stay together an dey caan get none.' (Collins, 1987, p. 289)

and through the fragmentary quality of the closing sections which describe the scenes prior to the invasion, where 'disunity' is represented as the split of the Party from the people. As Angel's brother says: 'Any Party dat in Mars while people on earth is not no party we want to know about anyway!' (Collins, 1987, p. 270). Taken as a whole, however, I would suggest that the text articulates a representation of 'disunity' which is foregrounded along the lines of gender rather than political affiliation and reveals that it is this exclusion and discounting of the experiences of the older women that threatens social and political change and progress.

Using the theories of psychologist Carol Gilligan I am suggesting that the narrative reveals, through its revoicing of the older women's experiences, not only the double character of their oppression and exclusion but also the extent to which their voices can be read as a challenge to political slogans of unity, courage and bravery. A number of critics of Caribbean women writers have used the work of Gilligan and Nancy Chodorow in their studies of fictional texts; the appeal of their work, in its emphasis on the extent to which a woman's identity is developed within the context of relationships and connections with others, is that it serves as a useful critical methodology for interpreting Caribbean women's writing, so much of which is seen to focus on a loss of identity as result of separation, through migration, from mothers, families, a homeland and so on (see de Abruna, and Dunn and Morris, both in Nasta, 1991). In this chapter, however, my focus is on Gilligan's study *In A Different Voice* and its representations of a conflict between a feminine defined and practised 'ethic of care, nurturance and responsibility', and the more masculine assertion of a principle of 'right'. One of the examples Gilligan uses to illustrate this principle is an interview with a woman doctor, Nan, who, describing her motivation for becoming a doctor, says: 'When I first applied to medical school, my feeling was that I was a person who was concerned with other people and being able to care for them in some way or another.' And in response to another question, she continues: 'By yourself there is little sense to things. It is the sound of one hand clapping, the sound of one man or woman, there is something lacking' (Gilligan, 1982, p. 160).

In her discussion of morality and ethics, Gilligan suggests that for men truth and fairness are absolute, as are notions of equality, which depend upon an articulation of individual 'rights' around which concepts of justice and fairness are developed. Her own emphasis, however, is on the need for each principle to be modified by the other; absolute principles of right need to be modified by less absolute principles of care and tolerance; at the same time, the principle of care has to include the care and responsibility for the properly defined and safeguarded 'self':

> While an ethic of justice proceeds from the premise of equality – that everyone should be treated the same – an ethic of care rests on the premise of non-violence – that no one should be hurt. In the representation of maturity, both perspectives converge in the realization that just as inequality adversely affects both parties in the unequal relationship, so too violence is destructive for everyone involved. (Gilligan, 1982, p. 174)

'One han caan clap!' is in fact a subtitle of one of the sections of the novel which describes Hermitage on the night of the hurricane, when everyone has to shelter in the 'wall house' newly built by Doodsie and Allan. There are other numerous examples of the ways in which this small community protect each other, and it is almost a cliche to identify these instances as expressions of care, connectedness and collective responsibility. Their responsibility extends beyond the communal 'yard'; women who have migrated, such as Ezra, who pays for Angel's operation and medical care in America after she has lost her eye during the invasion, continue the same tradition of care. In the novel's representation of community, its emphasis on collectivism and care as a gendered function is made more emphatic through its contrasting representation of the men such as Regal who, after a violent betrayal by Leader, migrates and simply disappears for a while before making a sudden reappearance.

The narrative's many other instances of the women's commitment to the care of others, however, leave the women exposed, vulnerable and compromised as individuals. Ma Ettie cared for her children, Doodsie, Regal and her others almost single-handedly; Allan's sister Christalene – to his disgust – cares for her five children on her own. Because of her commitment to her role as a mother, Doodsie makes the decision to tolerate her husband's affairs and even, as she confides to Angel, to help support his twins born, during their marriage, to another woman. In an angry exchange Angel, echoing Doodsie's own words in an earlier conversation, reminds her that her status in the house is like that of a servant, to which she replies:

> If ah did take on a servant work without the wedding ring, Angel, ah still might end up gettin no money and youall might still have been there without the respectability. Bad as it is, ah manage to give youall an education. So climb down ... You jus passin ... you have to swallow vinegar and pretend it honey. (Collins, 1987, p. 190)

The rhythmic refrains of the women: 'Swallow vinegar an pretend it honey', 'Tek night an mek day', are illustrative of the extent to which their identities seem only to be defined in discourses of caring and responsibility for others, and of self-sacrifice. The particular knowledge, which their words reflect, is formed by their experiences as women; because they are each dependent on the other they know that dependency necessitates tolerance of difference and compromise. Interpreted in relation to political action, however, they express a lack of commitment to or belief in the 'right' of an individual to personal freedom, or to individual agency in the political and social development of a non-dependent society.

Because a colonial system of government denies the right of a people to self-government, and therefore infantilizes its subjects, creating a culture of dependence, the claim of the 'right' of the individual to equality, justice and fairness has no tradition or authority of the kind evidenced in developed capitalist economies. There are a number of examples in the novel, which illustrate the ease with which the characters' claim to the right of equality is surrendered in favour of an acceptance of hierarchical, paternalistic structures.

To the comment: 'People like you an me so, the harder we work in people kitchen and in people lan, the more we kill weself out and bring riches, the poorer we get while we sweat goin in other people pocket', Ma Ettie responds: 'Chile doh hurt you head. Is de way life is. Look at the fingers on you hand. God make them all different length. We can't all be the same in this worl. It mus have high and low' (Collins, 1987, p. 28). The scene identified here is one of the narrative's many domestic scenes which mirror the broader social and political complex of relations of power and powerlessness, and of dominance and resistance. Doodsie too has learnt to diminish herself, to conceal her aspirations for herself within her ambitions for her children. As the novel progresses and she witnesses the seemingly inevitable cycle of failure evidenced in the collapse of the revolutionary 'Party', she retreats back into the philosophy of her mother, Ma Ettie: 'Look at the fingers of you han, chile. Some long, some short. You can't change the Lord world!' (Collins, 1987, p. 286). In contrast is Angel's insistence on political freedom and equality as a right, even after the Party's collapse. Angel's coming of age is used to represent the island's coming of age, and, in the initial success of the revolution, its awareness of its need for real independence. Her personal identity, however, her developing sense of self and the right to that self, is not fully expressed in the narrative. Its hesitance or inability to clearly define her individual identity is an expression of the ways in which the personal identity of the individual, its autobiographical subject, is bound by the national identity of the post-colonial state. The state, Grenada, is, at the end of the novel, a neo-colonial dependency; the invasion by the Americans is accepted, even welcomed by a large number of its inhabitants.

For Fanon, the way forward in the cycle of violence, the inevitable by-product of a struggle for liberation, can only be figured in global terms, through the political alliance of the colonizer and colonized; the result of this alliance is a restoration of human values which reintroduce 'mankind into the world': 'What it expects from those who for centuries have kept it in slavery is that they will help it to rehabilitate mankind, and make man victorious everywhere, once and for all' (Fanon, 1961, p. 84). In his text humanity is the *product* of the exorcising violence of decolonization and of the total loyalty and commitment to a clearly defined set of revolutionary principles.

Collins's novel disturbs the completeness of Fanon's political vision, 'dubbing' into it the complexities of gender. One of the first successful exponents 'dub' poetry in Jamaica, Oku Onuru defines the 'dub' of his work as the process of inserting 'but more fi put in' the rhythms and linguistic features of a creole language and cultural expression:

> Dub poetry simply mean to take out and to put in, but more fi put in more than anything else. We take out the little isms, the little English ism and the little highfalutin business and ... dub in the rootsical, yard, basic rhythm. ... [T]hat is what dub poetry mean. (Morris, 1997, p. 66)

The novel *Angel* represents a 'version' of post-colonial freedom and independence which reveals as central to its project a problematic but necessary recognition of the distinct, contradictory, but interconnected principles of right, fairness and equality with those of tolerance, conciliation, care for others. Framed by images of circling, by her mother's voice and Doodsie's own return to Grenada some 30 years before, its closing scene enacts a kind of epiphany where, as Angel looks again at the land around her parents' house, she sees in the power and beauty of the landscape its potential for renewal and regeneration. In Angel's reconnection with Grenada and with her family's land is represented the narrative's own revoicing, recuperation and reconnection with the more difficult and perhaps dangerous, in its tendency towards regression, knowledge of the mothers.

Works Cited

Breiner, Laurence, 1998. *An Introduction to West Indian Poetry*, Cambridge: Cambridge University Press.
Collins, Merle, 1987. *Angel*, London: The Women's Press.
Collins, Merle, 1990. *Rain Darling*, London: The Women's Press.
Fanon, Frantz, 1961. *The Wretched of the Earth*, London: Penguin, 1990.
Gilligan, Carol, 1982. *In A Different Voice: Psychological Theory and Women's Development*, Cambridge, MA: Harvard University Press.
Hebdige, Dick, 1987. *Cut 'n' Mix: Culture, Identity and Caribbean Music*, London: Methuen.
Johnson, Linton Kwesi, 1986. 'Jamaican Rebel Music', *Race and Class*, vol. xvii, no. 4, pp. 397–412.

Lima, Maria Helena, 'Forms of Autobiography in the Fiction of Michelle Cliff and Merle Collins', *Ariel*, vol. 24, no. 1, pp. 35–58.

Morris, Mervyn, 1997. 'A Note on Dub Poetry', *Wasifiri*, vol. 26 (Autumn), pp. 66–69.

Nasta, Susheila (ed.), 1991. *Motherlands: Black Women's Writing from Africa, the Caribbean and South Asia*, London: The Women's Press.

O'Callaghan, Evelyn, 1993. *Woman Version: Theoretical Approaches to West Indian Fiction by Women*, Basingstoke: Macmillan.

Pollard, Velma, 1991. 'Mothertongue Voices in the Writing of Olive Senior and Lorna Goodison', in Susheila Nasta (ed.), *Motherland: Black Women's Writing from Africa, the Caribbean and South Asia*, London: The Women's Press, pp. 238–53.

Searle, Chris, 1984a. 'Maurice Bishop on Destabilisation: An Interview', *Race and Class*, vol. xxv, no. 3, pp. 1–13.

Searle, Chris, 1984b. 'Grenada: Diary of an Invasion', *Race and Class*, vol. xxv, no. 3, pp. 15–28.

Wilson, Betty, 1993. 'An Interview with Merle Collins', *Callalou*, vol. 16, no. 1 (Winter), pp. 94–107.

10

Erupting Funk: The Political Style of Toni Morrison's *Tar Baby* and *The Bluest Eye*

Alan Rice

As with many writers from a wide range of communities a close attention to Toni Morrison's style helps uncover her radical politics and poetics. One of the most influential and radical Morrison critics has been Susan Willis, who in her excellent study of African-American women novelists, *Specifying* (1987), discusses the concept of 'funk' at length, though with very little information about musical style. Her materialist feminist approach ably shows how Morrison indicts the hegemonic forces of capitalist America for making many African Americans ashamed of their vernacular culture and anxious to disown it. As internally colonized subjects, the predicament of African Americans can be linked to the position of other colonized peoples who are encouraged to disown their vernacular culture as a means to make headway within the majority culture. Morrison's foregrounding of vernacular modes is a 'funky', decidedly political response to demands for conformity to Anglo-American modes. As Stelamaris Coser says of such gestures by African-American women writers, 'Rooted in culture and community [they are] an attempt to counter the version of truth and facts presented by the colonizer of yesterday and today with the view from the dominated' (Coser, 1994, p. 16). I hope to show how a critical paradigm mindful of vernacular black aesthetics in a post-colonial context enhances Willis's critique and that, far from aestheticizing a materialist paradigm, such a methodology contributes to strengthening a materialist reading of Morrison's work; in effect, that Morrison's concern to write a vernacular form itself comes from a political imperative.

The very history of the word 'funk' attests to the political nature of language and the way in which African-American peoples have reconstructed language literally from the verbal detritus of their former 'masters'. 'Funk' was at one point African-American slang for a bad smell before becoming a term used to describe the particular soul quality in black music (Major, 1971, pp. 56, 70). Amiri Baraka notes the political nature of the African-American adoption of this term when he talks about jazz musicians' concept of the term in the late 1950s:

> In jazz, people started talking about funk and the white man had always said: the negro has a characteristic smell, but then the negro takes that and turns the term round, so that if you don't have that characteristic smell, that funk then the music, or what you are is not valuable. The very tools the white man gave the negro are suddenly used against him. (Harris, 1985, p. 33)

I will return later to the way such language use and inversion is also part of the jazz aesthetic Morrison uses by virtue of its sounding of a Signifyin(g) discourse, but for now it is sufficient to know that 'funk' is not presently confined to a musical signification, and many African Americans, including Toni Morrison, use it to indicate a particular lower-class and radical African-American attitude to the world. Thus, as Willis points out, when Morrison uses images of 'funkiness' she is envisioning an alternative social milieu. Willis's idea that 'funk' erupts in order to project a different reality to the black bourgeois world seems to me very astute, if a little close to an essentialism which undermines the force of her argument. She examines how Morrison uses 'eruptions of funk' to posit an alternative to the alienation many African Americans encounter when they move north, away from the wellspring of their culture. She assesses the problem thus: 'The problem at the center of Toni Morrison's writing is how to maintain an Afro-American cultural heritage once the relationship to the black rural South has been stretched thin over distance and generations' (Willis, 1984, p. 264).

The 'eruptions of funk' literally juxtapose an alternate reality to that 'bourgeoisification' which encourages African Americans to forget their cultural roots. Right from her early fiction, Morrison poses this dialectical struggle, foregrounding the importance of class in African-American culture in the process. The character of Geraldine in *The Bluest Eye* (1970) is portrayed as a typical bourgeois African American. In counterpoint to her desire for refinement and moderation is the alternate mode of 'funkiness'. Morrison says middle-class blacks learn,

> the rest of the lesson begun in those soft houses with porch swings and pots of bleeding heart: how to behave. The careful development of thrift, patience, high morals and good manners. In short how to get rid of the funkiness. The dreadful funkiness of passion, the funkiness of nature, the funkiness of the wide range of human emotions.

Wherever it erupts, this Funk, they wipe it away; where it crusts, they dissolve; wherever it drips, flowers, or clings, they find it and fight it until it dies. They fight this battle all the way to the grave. The laughter that is a little too loud; the enunciation a little too round, the gesture a little too generous. They hold their behind in for fear of a sway too free; when they wear their lipstick, they never cover the entire mouth for fear of lips too thick, and they worry, worry, worry about the edges of their hair. (Morrison, 1970, p. 78)

In the first paragraph, the repetition of 'funkiness' ironically builds up a wonderful rhythm of, or riff on, the very 'funkiness' that Geraldine is striving to deny. In this context riff means the repetition of lexical phrases analogous to the background phrases repeated as a 'foundation' in many types of jazz solo (Berliner, 1995, p. 300). The free-flowing riff on 'funkiness' and the attempt to suppress it is continued in the second paragraph by an involved passage that uses repetitions of words and phrases ('worry, worry, worry'), assonance to connect the gestures which highlight 'funkiness' ('loud', 'round', 'generous'), and parallelisms ('wherever', 'where', 'wherever'), to build up a musical rhythm which in itself shows a funkiness just beneath the surface of even the most uptight bourgeois African American. The rhythmic style here exemplifies a funkiness at the level of style which complements and serves to enhance the theme of Geraldine's entrapment within a working-class cultural milieu from which she hoped her light skin would save her.

Morrison's riff on funkiness here is given added power by the force of the word in the black vernacular which Baraka exemplified by his anecdote about the musicians' theorizing on 'funk' which I quoted earlier. Its resonances, though, stretch throughout the African-American community, and its power to range over a whole welter of African-American experiences from physical appearance through fashion to musical style could justify the appellation 'mascon word' to the term 'funk'. The concept of mascon words was developed by Stephen Henderson in his seminal analysis *Understanding the New Black Poetry* (1973) and can, I believe, be extended to other African-American artistic practices. A mascon word is one that carries '*a massive concentration of Black experiential energy*' (Henderson, 1973, p. 44). 'Funk' is such a word as it carries 'an inordinate charge of emotional and psychological weight, so that wherever ... [it is used it sets] all kinds of bells ringing, all kinds of synapses singing, on all kinds of levels' (Henderson, 1973, p. 44). Morrison, by her riffing on the word, brings the reader's attention to a phrase she discusses as key to an understanding of black reality. She does this elsewhere in her work by riffs on such concepts as naming in *Song of Solomon* (Morrison, 1978, pp. 17–18) and cannibalism or the jungle in *Beloved* (Morrison, 1988, pp. 198–99). As Henderson is quick to point out though, the repetition of mascon words or phrases is paralleled in jazz history, where repeated boogie-woogie or blues phrases have similar charges of emotional and psychological weight (Henderson, 1973, p. 45).

Morrison, then, in using such mascon words is adapting a technique developed in the musical culture that she utilizes. The riffing on a mascon word like 'funk' is analogous to a jazz form at a stylistic level. Willis surprisingly all but ignores this, preferring to concentrate on the implications of the passage for Morrison's major themes. However, it is by the very foregrounding of Morrison's stylistic riffing and use of the concept of mascon words that the vernacular aesthetic helps the critic to underpin Willis's critique, showing how the passage's rhythmic nature and literal worrying around a key concept in the culture (as in the way blues men or jazz musicians slur or slide on a phrase or end line they want to foreground) emphasizes the very funkiness that middle-class blacks seek to deny. Thus even from such a cursory look at the mechanics of this short passage we can see how the alternative mode is not just present at a thematic level, but also at a stylistic level.

'Eruptions of funk', then, not only pose an alternative social world through their thematic undermining of African-American middle-class (and even light-skinned) values, but also provide an alternative discourse through which this world can best be imagined. Of course this is not the only occasion in Morrison's work where such eruptions occur. In *Jazz*, Alice Manfred's fear of such eruptions of funk is even more blatantly related to the 'playing of lowdown stuff' and again the style of the passage mirrors its jazzy theme (Morrison, 1992, p. 57). Morrison uses specifically African-American stylistic devices to create this alternative world. In doing so, she is engaged in a radical restructuring of the traditionally Anglo-American novel form, in effect 'colouring' the language with the timbre of a jazz-inflected mode. African American writers like Toni Morrison resist being confined by the language of the oppressive white culture and seek to create from its ashes a musically inflected language of their own. In her headlong rush to materialize Morrison's radical gesture Willis does her a disservice by ignoring the wonderful use of riffing that makes the passage (and others in Morrison's oeuvre) work so well. Morrison's jazz-inflected language has brought a literal funkiness to the Anglocentric form of the novel through its use of such extended riffing passages.

Willis's partial sighting of the vernacular mode is valuable, though her painting of it as merely a nostalgic mode always harking back to a Southern past undermines the vernacular's wilful doubleness which envisions a modernist urban future at the same time as it invokes a southern rural idyll. There is radical possibility in the 'funkiness' too and the riff's energy points to this. For instance, as the vernacular and, in particular, jazz hearkens back to a pre-modern rural past, it simultaneously, through its syncopation and polyrhythms, responds effectively to a contemporaneous modernist cityscape as is exemplified most aptly in Morrison's novel *Jazz* (1992). Willis's 'eruptions of funk' should, then, not merely be seen as the nostalgic interventions of a primal folk culture fighting a rearguard action against a bourgeois ideology beholden to Anglocentric modes of behaviour, but as vital emancipatory tools for the modern African American in his/her desire for voice in a cityscape.

Another concept which is most important to the vernacular (and indeed to jazz) is Signifyin(g). Morrison, along with many other black writers, uses this technique to create passages which posit a different reality from that which the dominant Anglocentric culture is used to hearing. This Signifyin(g) mode is outlined in Henry Louis Gates, Jr.'s *The Signifying Monkey* (1988). He uses the specific term 'Signifyin(g)' to foreground instances where 'the absent (g) is the figure for the Signifyin(g) black difference' (Gates, 1988, p. 46), but other critics talk of Signifyin' or 'sigging'. Gates shows how the mode is a retention from an African past which valued smart talking and moralistic story-telling above other communicative modes. When retained in the African-American community in long oral narratives known as 'toasts' and in verbal jousts such as the 'dozens', this Signifyin(g) mode developed into a core oral technique in African-American culture. Geneva Smitherman defines it thus:

> the verbal art of insult in which a speaker humorously puts down, talks about, needles – that is signifies on – the listener. Sometimes signifyin (also siggin) is done to make a point, sometimes it's just for fun. ... [it is] characterized by exploitation of the unexpected and quick verbal surprises. (Smitherman, 1985, pp. 118–19)

Morrison's use of it, then, should not surprise us, as it is a core African-American verbal and musical praxis. The work of cultural theorists such as Henry Louis Gates, Jr. and Ingrid Monson detail its use in a jazz context. Gates's description of a Signifyin(g) mode in jazz highlights the centrality of the praxis in jazz composition and improvisation. For in the jam session and in performance, jazz players take a tune, a previous performance of it, or one of their colleagues' just completed solos and respond by using the raw material and transforming it into a new composition on the spot. Such Signifyin(g) has been a constant of jazz history from Louis Armstrong's willed use of spirituals in the 1920s to Charles Mingus's use of a gospel mode in the 1950s, to the radical revision of popular Broadway tunes by the free jazz players of the 1960s and 1970s.

For instance, Ingrid Monson in her discussion of John Coltrane's legendary recordings of the Rodgers and Hammerstein tune 'My Favourite Things' (1960), follows on from Gates's discussion of the tune (Gates, 1988, p. 105). She outlines the methods by which 'a sentimental, optimistic lyric is transformed into a more brooding, improvisational exploration' (Monson, 1994, p. 298). Coltrane's performance often lasted 20 minutes or more as he remade the tune in his own image. As Monson goes on to say: 'In the core of "My Favourite Things" the transformation of the tune simultaneously communicates the resemblance between the two versions and the vast difference of the Coltrane version' (Monson, 1994, p. 305).

Coltrane uses the seemingly predictable pop tune for his own artistic practices, creating a whole new meaning for the tune through irony, parody and even burlesque, until it becomes secondary to his flagrant revision of it. Such Signifyin(g) practices were brought across the Atlantic by Africans and informed many of their early cultural practices. Thus, in slave times, the 'cakewalk' burlesqued the seeming high seriousness of Southern plantation life. As Stearns notes, '[They] take off the high manners of the white folk in the big house, but their masters who gathered round to watch the fun missed the point' (Stearns, 1956, p. 116). Such irony and parody, such doubleness, of appearing to do one thing while doing another, are 'central and expected means of aesthetic expression in the African American tradition' (Monson, 1994, p. 303) and can be traced throughout the history of the jazz form, including in Louis Armstrong's playing of 'All of Me' in 1931 (Armstrong 1983). Marshall Stearns comments on this performance:

> given the most banal of tunes to record and with impressive consistency, he transformed them into something else, something intensely appealing. ... He makes fun of the tune, sharing with his listener his insight into the silliness of the whole expression and at the same time, he improvises with such gusto and imagination that a tawdry ballad emerges as a thing of beauty. (Stearns, 1956, p. 318)

Morrison's use of a Signifyin(g) mode is wide-ranging and can be seen in all the novels. In *Tar Baby* (1981), for instance, the 'waste' riff is key to an understanding of the novel as an intervention in the debate around the exploitation of resources by multinational companies. It is, however, merely the centrepiece of a Signifyin(g) rebuke from Morrison to an exploitative and ecologically damaging capitalist system. Here, and throughout the novel, the inversion and exaggeration which exemplify Signifyin(g) are used not in intra-communal contestation but as a marker of inter-communal contestation between Anglo-American and African-American value systems. The 'waste' passage is connected to a whole series of other passages which link a critique of the European and American waste of resources in the colonial and neo-colonial world to the impoverishment and exploitation of African peoples throughout the diaspora. As Evelyn Hawthorne states succinctly, '*Tar Baby* is a contemporary re-visioning of racial history' (Hawthorne, 1988, p. 100). Valerian, the retired candy manufacturer, is used by Morrison as symptomatic of the exploitation such re-visioning of racial history exposes and in a passage of great emotive force she indicts him for his crimes against African and working-class peoples. He has just dismissed his servants for thieving apples, a product that would not even have entered the local economy without his intervention (Hawthorne, 1988, p. 102). Morrison indicts him through Son's perception of his calm manner after he has sacked the servants:

> Son's mouth went dry as he watched Valerian chewing a piece of ham, his head-of-a-coin profile content, approving even of the flavour in his mouth although he had been able to dismiss with a flutter of the fingers the people whose sugar and cocoa had allowed him to grow old in regal comfort; although he had taken the sugar and cocoa and paid for it as though it had no value, as though the cutting of cane and picking of beans was child's play and had no value; but he turned it into candy, the invention of which really was child's play, and sold it to other children and made a fortune in order to move near, but not in the midst of, the jungle where the sugar came from and build a palace with more of their labor and then hire them to do more of the work he was not capable of and pay them again according to some scale of value that would outrage Satan himself. (Morrison, 1981, pp. 203–204)

Son strips away colonialism's illusory mask here, showing how the matter-of-fact, seemingly commonsense nature of progress and capitalism is based on the stealing of resources and the selling back of these as finished goods either to those stolen from originally, or to the children of those whose labour power had been utilized to produce them. Hence, Valerian's designation of his servants as thieves is seen to be a function not of some abstract philosophical notion of right and wrong but of his power in an exploitative relationship where their thieving is in fact a justifiable response to years in which their labour power and other resources have been stolen by greedy colonial exploiters like Valerian. It is a modern version of the African-American myth in which the slave, when accused of stealing his master's chicken that he has eaten, replies that he has merely been improving the master's most important human resource by feeding it sufficiently. Such decoding of the reality lurking beneath the illusory is a dynamic intervention in the discourse of colonialism, only with a voice often marginalized, that of the exploited and dispossessed. Such a siren voice destabilizes and dialogizes language within the colonial linguistic economy. This becomes even clearer as the passage continues:

> and when those people wanted a little of what he wanted, some apples for their Christmas, and took some, he dismissed them with a flutter of the fingers, because they were thieves, and nobody knew thieves and thievery better than he did and he probably thought he was a law-abiding man, they all did, and they all always did, because they had not the dignity of wild animals who did not eat where they defecated, but they could defecate over a whole people and come there to live and defecate some more by tearing up the land and that is why they loved property so, because they had killed it soiled it defecated on it and they loved more than anything the places where they shit. Would fight and kill to own the cesspools they made, and although they called it architecture it was in fact elaborately built toilets, decorated toilets, toilets surrounded with and by business and enterprise in order to have something to do between defecations since waste was the order of the day and the ordering principle of the universe. And especially the Americans who were the worst because they were new at the business of defecation spent their whole lives bathing bathing bathing washing away the stench of the cesspools as though pure soap had anything to do with purity. (Morrison, 1981, p. 204)

After Morrison has elaborated on theft so that it reaches its logical conclusion – that the whites are the thieves in the colonial context – the passage gets even more breathless and animated, linking such thievery to the laying waste of the resources of the colonized world. She uses riffs on lexical items like 'defecation' and 'toilets' to emphasize the link between such scatological terms and the whites who are used to blaming the Africans for a lack of hygiene. Such inversion is a Signifyin(g) response which means that white Americans in this vision cannot ever be clean because of the dirt they have created in other cultures. No amount of 'bathing' can wash away the stench they cause. The criticism in this section of the novel is one strand of an avowedly political and polemical theme; however, Morrison uses the full resources of the jazz aesthetic to create an insistent, riffing and Signifyin(g) stylistic response that helps to make the charge stick.

The dysfunctionality of Valerian's family is a product of their colonizing status and is shown most clearly by his wife Margaret's abuse of their son. This is linked to Valerian's involvement in the sugar trade by Margaret's use of a language of satisfying ingestion to describe her torture of Michael:

> Nothing serious though. No throwing across the room, or out of the window. No scalding, no fist work. Just a delicious pin-stab in sweet creamy flesh. That was her word, 'delicious'. 'I knew it was wrong, knew it was bad. But something about it was delicious too.' She was telling him, saying it aloud at the dinner table after everyone had gone. His knees were trembling and he'd had to sit down again. ... She was serene standing there saying it, and he agreed with that, thought it could be, must be, true – that it was delicious, for at that moment it would have been delicious to him too if he could have picked up the carving knife lying on the platter next to the carcass of the goose and slashed into her lovely Valentine face. Delicious. Conclusive and delicious. (Morrison, 1981, pp. 233–34)

'Delicious' is repeated and debated (or in Bakhtin's language, 'dialogized') by Morrison in this passage so that its provenance escapes this section of the novel, becoming not merely a word concomitant with Margaret's individual pathology but to a whole culture that steals delicious goods (like sugar) from the Third World to underpin a market economy whose destructive nature eventually distorts and undermines the lives of those who colonize as much as it does the colonized peoples. Her 'pin-stab in sweet creamy flesh' shows a greedy invasion and expropriation of her son's body equivalent to the invasion and exploitation of colonial resources by her husband, and Valerian's 'delicious' anticipated response of violent revenge stresses the simmering violence that exists in a family made dysfunctional by their central position in the colonial economy. The riffing on 'delicious' here is Morrison's Signifyin(g) retort to a worldview which sees market and colonial relationships continuing as natural and unproblematic whilst apparently satisfying common human needs. She figures them as being as abusive as violence against an innocent child, and at the same time shows how the powerful are undermined by this abuse of their power, and she does this by reworking a lexical term. Such an inversion is quintessentially a Signifyin(g) gesture by Morrison, albeit a subtle and complex one.

It is not only to the Caribbean islands that the tentacles of the world capitalist system, as exemplified by sugar production, reach. In her first novel, *The Bluest Eye* (1970), Morrison shows how the consumption of finished goods is as much dictated by the forces of racial exploitation and capitalism as the production of raw materials. This is best illustrated when the main protagonist, Pecola, whose desire to have blue eyes is the central concern of the text, buys candy from Mr Yacobowski. As so often in her novels, Morrison illustrates the ramifications of the commercial transaction at the level of style. Mr Yacobowski looks at the black girl with 'glazed separateness' (Morrison, 1970, p. 47), yet his look is strong enough to be a controlling look, for it is this look which undermines Pecola's humanity:

> She does not know what keeps his glance suspended. Perhaps because he is grown, or a man, and she a little girl. But she has seen interest, disgust, even anger in grown male eyes. Yet this vacuum is not new to her. It has an edge; somewhere in the bottom lid is the distaste. She has seen it lurking in the eyes of all white people. So. The distaste must be for her, her blackness. All things in her are flux and anticipation. But her blackness is static and dread. And it is the blackness that accounts for, that creates, the vacuum edged with distaste in white eyes. (Morrison, 1970, p. 48)

Madonne M. Miner appositely discusses Mr Yacobowski's look in terms of gender politics, seeing it as another instance of a male denying presence to a female which 'parallels previously described rape scenes' (Miner, 1985, p. 185). However, it achieves more than this. As in so much of Morrison's prose style it is the repetition and dialogization of words that create meaning here. 'Distaste' and 'blackness' are repeated here to stress Pecola's entrapment in a white dominated world that does not allow her to fulfil her human potential. In the bottom lid of Mr Yacobowski's eyes is a distaste that constructs her blackness as her all-important signifier. The constant linking of the two lexical terms here as riff and counter-riff means that their difference in meaning is elided so that the blackness for which Yacobowski has distaste becomes that which *creates* the distaste. For Yacobowski, who in the final part of the paragraph becomes representative of white folk, distaste and blackness become interchangeable and an inevitable function of the dominant white gaze.

On leaving the shop Pecola strives to overcome the shame and anger caused by the encounter with the racist shopkeeper by eating the candy which he has sold her. To literally taste sweetness is an antidote to the 'distaste' of the transaction. Barbara Hill Rigney rather excessively sees this passage as an assumption of cannibalistic power as Pecola symbolically eats those who have dominion over her. In eating the Mary Janes (candy with wrappers showing a perfect white girl) they become a symbol of the white body and Rigney comments that in a rare moment of autonomy in the text Pecola 'perhaps enacts a primitive rite of passage, a cannibal feast as she gorges herself on the body of the enemy in order to assume its power' (Rigney, 1991, p. 85).

Such an interpretation ignores the troubled history of candy and its major component, sugar, which Susan Willis so brilliantly foregrounds in her analysis of *The Bluest Eye*. Willis's discussion uses Sidney Mintz's scholarship to show how sugar production oils the wheels of both the systems of slavery and capitalism meaning that sugar became 'a substitute for real food' and an 'opiate of the working class under capitalism' (Willis, 1987, pp. 177–78). Far from being a liberating gesture, the eating of candy here shows how Pecola is entrapped by Anglo-American value systems in a capitalist economy. A close look at the style of the passage that describes Pecola gorging on the Mary Janes shows how Willis's reading is more pertinent:

> Each pale yellow wrapper has a picture on it a picture of a little Mary Jane, for whom the candy is named. Smiling white face. Blonde hair in gentle disarray, blue eyes looking out of a world of clean comfort. The eyes are petulant mischievous. To Pecola they are simply pretty. She eats the candy, and its sweetness is good. To eat the candy is somehow to eat the eyes, eat Mary Jane. Love Mary Jane. Be Mary Jane.
>   Three Pennies had brought her nine lovely orgasms with Mary Jane. Lovely Mary Jane for whom a candy is named. (Morrison, 1970, p. 49)

The language of the passage with its simple sentences and imperative clauses resembles not one of Morrison's spectacular anti-capitalist or anti-colonial passages, which she would surely have used had she meant the eating of the candy to be a liberating gesture, coming from the assumption of cannibalistic power, but that of the reading primer, the 'Janet and John book' which frames the novel. As Inger-Ann Softing contends, 'here the language of the narrative significantly adopts the rigid and lifeless style of the pre-text' (Softing, 1995, p. 87). So Rigney's assertion of the potential radicalism of the cannibalistic feast at the level of theme is shown to be wrongheaded because the passage is couched in the language which Morrison uses to show the working of Anglo-American hegemony. Willis's astute reading of the passage as a negative one, then, is buttressed by paying close attention to Morrison's stylistic praxis. Other clues to the negative interpretation of the eating of the candy come earlier in the passage as Pecola surveys the sweets. The narrator notes, 'A peal of anticipation unsettles her stomach' (Morrison, 1970, p. 47). The peal here is figured as negative and literally unsettling. Moreover, as Shelly Wong notes, 'the peal' anticipates the 'high yellow' character Maureen Peal who represents the closest a black girl can get to a white appearance and who will unsettle Pecola later by screaming insults at her (Wong, 1990, p. 479). Thus Morrison's introduction of an unsettling 'peal' is merely the coda to the human Peal to come. Such a subtle pattern of call and recall (O'Meally, 1988, p. 198) links this passage about eating sweets to the later passage about Pecola's perceived ugliness in a world which values light-colouring above all else. Such connections show the all-pervasive nature of a racist hegemony that stretches from commerce (the general store) to education (the school playground).

Morrison shows that African Americans are not totally dominated by an oppressive culture through the set-piece confrontations of other of her characters. For instance, Claudia attempts a move toward autonomy from the white standards of beauty that oppress and constrict Pecola by her destruction of white dolls. This allows her the satisfaction of destroying these key icons of Anglo-American standards of beauty. As Softing contends, 'Claudia is the only character in this novel who consciously makes an attempt at deconstructing the ideology of the dominant society' (Softing, 1995, p. 90). Her dismemberment of a doll is an act of demystification which foregrounds the fact that an object of veneration is nothing more than a squalid consumer item:

> I had only one desire: to dismember it. To see of what it was made, to discover the dearness, to find the beauty, the desirability that had escaped me, but apparently only me. ... I could not love it. But I could examine it to see what it was that all the world said was loveable. Break off the tiny fingers, bend the flat feet, loosen the hair, twist the head around, and the thing made one sound – a sound they said was the sweet and plaintive cry 'Mama,' but which sounded to me like the bleat of a dying lamb, or, more precisely, our icebox door opening on rusty hinges in July. Remove the cold and stupid eyeball, it would bleat still, 'Ahhhhhh,' take off the head, shake out the sawdust, crack the back against the brass bed rail, it would bleat still. The gauze back would split, and I could see the disk with six holes, the secret of the sound. A mere metal roundness. (Morrison, 1970, p. 23)

Claudia's dismemberment of the doll is her way of discovering the falsity of Western values of beauty. Her recognition of its sounds as mere bleatings indicate that her growing awareness of the object's falsity is a discovery made through the rupture of its sound; the way the sound does not signify what the world has told her it does. The signifier literally gets detached from the signified so that the cry of 'Mama' the world hears is just a bleating lamb or a rusty hinge. Such signification means that the doll is not merely negatively dismembered, it is used, once destroyed, to illustrate the hollow nature of Anglo-American social and cultural hegemony. As Softing describes it, the destruction of the doll deconstructs the white cultural myth and this is synonymous with 'the text's act of undressing the inadequacy of the pre-text (the primer)' (Softing, 1995, p. 90). So Claudia is indulging in the same kind of uncovering as Morrison herself, showing how stylistic praxis is mirrored within the narrative itself. It is telling that Morrison shows Claudia's discovery of the truth about the doll through sound, as such demystification is at the heart of a jazz praxis which similarly takes Western pop tunes and dissects them before making a new tune from them rather than merely reproducing them as written. The demystification of the popular tune is here paralleled by the demystification of the popular icon and Morrison's final comment on it – 'A mere metal roundness' – stresses the pathetic nature of the object that enthrals. Its falseness and inauthenticity is contrasted almost immediately by the blues songs which Claudia's mother sings on a lonesome Sunday:

> She would sing about hard times, bad times, some-body-done-gone-and-left-me times. But her voice was so sweet and her singing eyes so melty I found myself longing for those hard times, yearning to be grown without 'a thin di-i-me to my name'. I looked forward to the delicious time when 'my man' would leave me, when I would 'hate to see the evening sun go down ... ' cause then I would know 'my man has left this town'. Misery colored by the greens and blues in my mother's voice took all of the grief out of the words and left me with a conviction that pain was not only endurable, it was sweet. (Morrison, 1970, p. 27)

Here blues lyrics are embedded in the text to show how African Americans have coped with the constrictions that the hegemony of Anglo-American values have imposed on them; how misery caused by the resultant racism and poverty has been turned on its head by the blues impulse which makes an art out of suffering that elevates African Americans beyond the conditions that undermine their humanity. As Ralph Ellison has said, 'the blues ... are an art form and thus a transcendence of those conditions created within the Negro community by the denial of social justice' (Ellison, 1972, p. 257). In the novel, the 'mere metal roundness' which bleats out of the prized white doll is contrasted to the human quality of voice which has the power to make pain seem sweet. It is such human voices from the vernacular culture of black America that Morrison seeks to foreground through her use of a musical mode. As I have shown in examples from these different Morrison texts, the mode is most successfully employed, not at the expense of or as a diversion from her political agenda, but as integral to her radical project and at its service. As George Lipsitz has said, such literature 'combines the subjectivity and objectivity that employs the insights and passions of myth and folklore in the service of revising history' (quoted in Coser, 1994, p. 15). Or to be more specific, her radical jazz-inflected style, coming from the core African-American culture, is integral to her theme of the importance of African-American autonomy from Anglo American hegemony and to the revisioning of majority narratives that seek to deny such autonomy.

Works Cited

Armstrong, Louise 1983. *Greatest Hits*, LP, CBS.
Bakhtin, Mikhail M., 1981. *The Dialogic Imagination*, Austin: University of Texas Press.
Berliner, Paul, 1995. *Thinking in Jazz*, Chicago: Chicago University Press.
Coltrane, John, 1960. *My Favourite Things*, LP, Atlantic.
Coser, Stelamaris, 1994. *Bridging the Americas: The Literature of Paule Marshall, Toni Morrison and Gayl Jones*, Philadelphia: Temple University Press.
Ellison, Ralph, 1972. *Shadow and Act*, New York: Vantage.
Gates, Henry Louis, Jr., 1988. *The Signifying Monkey: A Theory of Literary Criticism*, New York: Oxford University Press.
Harris, William J., 1985. *The Poetry and Poetics of Amiri Baraka: The Jazz Aesthetic*, Columbia: University of Missouri Press.
Hawthorne, Evelyn, 1988. 'On Gaining the Double-Vision: *Tar Baby* as Diasporean Novel', *Black American Literature Forum*, vol. 22, pp. 97–107.
Henderson, Stephen, 1973. *Understanding the New Black Poetry*, New York: Morrow.
Major, Clarence (ed.), 1971. *Black Slang: A Dictionary of Afro-American Talk*, London: Routledge, Kegan and Paul.
Miner, Madonne M., 1985. 'Lady No Longer Sings the Blues: Rape, Madness and Silence in *The Bluest Eye*', in Marjorie Pryse and Hortense J. Spillers (eds), *Conjuring: Black Women, Fiction and Literary Tradition*, Bloomington: Indiana University Press, pp. 176–91.
Mintz, Sidney, 1986. *Sweetness and Power: The Place of Sugar in Modern History*, Harmondsworth: Penguin.
Monson, Ingrid, 1994. 'Doubleness and Jazz Improvisation: Irony, Parody and Ethnomusicology', *Critical Inquiry*, vol. 20, pp. 283–313.
Morrison, Toni, 1970. *The Bluest Eye*, London: Triad Granada.
Morrison, Toni, 1978. *Song of Solomon*, New York: Signet.
Morrison, Toni, 1981. *Tar Baby*, London: Triad Grafton.
Morrison, Toni, 1988. *Beloved*, New York: Plume.
Morrison, Toni, 1992. *Jazz*, London: Chatto and Windus.
O'Meally, Ralph, 1988. 'The Black Sermon: Tradition and Art', *Callaloo*, vol. 11, pp. 198–200.
Rigney, Barbara Hill, 1991. *The Voices of Toni Morrison*, Columbus: Ohio State University Press.
Smitherman, Geneva, 1985. *Talkin and Testifyin*, Detroit: Wayne State University Press.

Softing, Inger-Ann, 1995. 'Carnival and Black American Music as Counterculture in Toni Morrison's *The Bluest Eye* and *Jazz*', *American Studies in Scandinavia*, vol. 27, pp. 81–102.

Stearns, Marshall, 1956. *The Story of Jazz*, Oxford: Oxford University Press.

Willis, Susan, 1984. 'Eruptions of Funk: Historicizing Toni Morrison', in Henry Louis Gates, Jr. (ed.), *Black Literature and Literary Theory*, New York: Methuen, pp. 263–80.

Willis, Susan, 1987, *Specifying: Black Women Writing the American Experience*, London: Routledge.

Wong, Shelley, 1990. 'Transgression as Poesis in *The Bluest Eye*', *Callaloo*, vol. 13, pp. 471–81.

11

Afro-Hispanic Literature and Feminist Theories: Thinking Ethics

Rosemary Geisdorfer Feal

> When we write about the experiences of a group to which we do not belong, we should think about the ethics of our action, considering whether or not our work will be used to reinforce and perpetuate domination.
> (bell hooks, 1981, pp. 43)

> Often, feminist concerns are seen as a divisive, white importation that further fragments an already divided and embattled race, as trivial mind games unworthy of response while black people everywhere confront massive economic and social problems. I don't deny feminism's potential for divisiveness, but the concerns of women are neither trivial nor petty. ... Feminist theory, like black aesthetics, offers us not only the possibility of changing one's *reading* of the world, but of changing the world itself.
> (Sherley Anne Williams, 1990, pp. 68–69)

I

When I first began thinking about feminist criticism as it may be applied to the literatures produced by writers of African descent in the Spanish-speaking Americas, I worked under the belief that it was possible, by means of this analytic vehicle, to contest prevailing liberal humanistic approaches to the texts in question. At the same time, I questioned the feasibility of this type of contestation within North American university settings, which have been quick to accommodate a range of academic feminisms and render them innocuous (Feal, 1991a). I thus realized that I was seeking out an ethic by which to perform resistance or oppositional criticism, yet, paradoxically, of the kind that would not compel us to renounce absolutely the new 'master's tools' (Audre Lorde's term) fashioned by some strains of feminist criticism within the academy. If Lorde is right, so long as these are in fact tools of mastery of one sort or another, they will never dismantle the master's house. Instead, they will be employed to modify the 'mainhouse' or build an annex to it (Lorde, 1983). This chapter will survey the critical house of Afro-Hispanic studies and feminism, and will address the pressing question of the reception and interpretation of these texts in North American academic institutions in view of theories of race and gender in a post-colonial studies context. I want to ask how we can formulate accountable critical practices that pay attention to issues of marginality and domination as they concern Afro-Hispanic literary historiographies. The appeal that bell hooks has sounded implies that the ethics of our actions should engage us not in the apologetic 'confessional mode' that often paves the way for fresh hegemonic transgression, but rather should inspire us to account for what we do and how we do it.

The call for feminist interventions in (the race for) theory with respect to the field of Afro-Hispanism has elicited both positive responses as well as considerable resistance. Given that feminist studies examine 'women's experience as it has been constructed and described for women and by women in a gendered world' (*Liberal Learning*, 1991, p. 8), it would seem incontrovertible that the experience of women of African descent in the Americas as represented through literature should warrant sustained attention, as Sherley Anne Williams's words suggest. But the edification of what the intellectual community recognizes as the discipline of Afro-Hispanic studies has taken place on heavily contested territories. Those (mostly male) scholars who accomplished the first-stage labours ventured out to recover the textual artifacts of Afro-Hispanic peoples that had been ignored, undervalued, misappropriated, or lost, at least to North American Hispanists. Richard Jackson characterized Afro-Hispanism as an underdeveloped area in 1965, and he performed what we might call field work as he gathered materials with which to fashion a canon. It is tempting to depict Richard Jackson as pioneer, archaeologist, anthropologist, and 'father of the discipline', as so many scholars have in fact done. It would be more tempting to draw parallels between Jackson's labours and the feats of a conquistador, explorer, hunter, or chronicler, but that sounds a colonialist note that would certainly ring false in Jackson's case. Richard Jackson has worked with a strong sense of community and has been generous in crediting others for their contributions to the field of Afro-Hispanism (Jackson, 1989). Still, Jackson's approach reminds us that within the United States certain groups have construed a 'Latin America' within a dependency model when they depict the countries that make up the

Caribbean, Central and South America as politically and economically 'underdeveloped areas'. Most who write about Afro-Hispanic literature would be displeased to find themselves included in groups who view the 'Third World' as a monolithic block of 'underdevelopment' ripe for our interventions of all sorts. It is therefore crucial that we contemplate the trajectories that brought certain texts to the critical arena by noting the significance of a work in its country of origin and by elucidating how it got its place in the canon. Post-colonial strategies figure largely as viable methods to achieve this aim, especially as we revise and expand the work initiated by scholars such as Jackson.

It is noteworthy that Richard Jackson and other critics who first spoke of 'Afro-Hispanic literature' as a corpus have also taken great pains to discuss the specificity of the subjects they study. The construction of what we call 'Afro-Hispanic literature' has a solid place within the context of the United States, which of course has an African-American literary tradition of its own. Those North American scholars who first began to write about Afro-Hispanic literature therefore needed to distinguish it not only from the Europeanized Latin American texts so widely embraced throughout international markets, but also from the North American works by writers of African ancestry. This is not to claim that critics have ignored ties and tensions among the so-called mainstream literatures of Latin America, the literatures of North American blacks, and works in the Afro-Hispanic or Afro-Latin American traditions. To the contrary: many recent trends in the field as Richard Jackson discerns them point exactly in this direction. But even in establishing this cohesive and generalizing rubric of 'Afro-Hispanism', its scholars have been particularly sensitive to local historical issues and to the specific experiences of Africans in the Spanish-speaking Americas, which accounts for the literary histories focused on Afro-Colombian literature, on the slave narratives of Cuba, on the literature of the Esmeraldas province of Ecuador, and so forth. Why, then, has the 'theory' question, and, particularly, the 'feminist theory' question, been such a problematic one for a field that has theorized itself into recognized existence and has positioned itself with caution and self-scrutiny? And why are feminist approaches to this literature sometimes viewed as divisive or as undesirable 'foreign imports?' A bit of history may shed some light on the issue.

The current publishing vehicle that gives definition, unity and sustenance to the field of Afro-Hispanic studies from within the United States is the *Afro-Hispanic Review*, founded in 1982. The editorial board is composed primarily of scholars based in North America, along with Afro-Hispanic creative writers who either live in their countries of origin or have settled in other nations. The stated functions of the *Afro-*

Hispanic Review aim to correct the narrow presentation of Afro-Hispanic culture in academic programmes in North America by introducing neglected Afro-Hispanic works, authors and themes; encouraging curricular modifications that reflect a greater appreciation of the contributions of the diverse constituent groups to Hispanic civilization; sensitizing more students and other sectors of the public to the active, rich and interdisciplinary content of Afro-Hispanic literature; and providing a publishing outlet for scholars in the humanities and social sciences who work in Afro-Hispanic studies (see Smart, 1989). The explicit goals of the journal, and the story of its founding as Ian Smart tells it, reaffirms my contention that the field of 'Afro-Hispanic studies' should be viewed as a joint creation of those working from different sites, which we might choose to designate as 'the inside' and 'the outside' if we conceive of these terms in some strict essentialist fashion related to specific ethnicities and nationalities. The commitment, passion and vision of the pioneers such as Stanley Cyrus, Ian Smart, Miriam DeCosta-Willis, Henry Richards and Marvin Lewis have reshaped the boundaries of 'inside' and 'outside', thus producing – or reflecting, depending how we look at it – a complex network of positionalities and identity politics. The constituents of Afro-Hispanism cannot make claims to separatist or 'pure' practices when they/we already represent the diversity that typifies the stratified field that we study, for Spanish America as a whole is 'neither black nor white', neither 'Spanish' nor 'indigenous', neither 'African' nor 'European' (Degler, 1971; see Feal, 1995). A post-colonial framework can help to decipher these tensions and to provide an intelligible system for their analysis.

The shifting paradigms in the field of Afro-Hispanism respond to several factors. In the first instance, we may now speak comfortably of a large and diverse canon of writers whose works both reflect and produce (hi)stories of people of African descent in the Spanish-speaking regions of Central and South American and the Caribbean, a canon that has been solidified through the many critical works published primarily in the last 25 years. In the second instance, we may note the movement away from traditional literary histories or surveys *en route* to a broad range of textual analyses, including comparative studies, informed as they often are by theoretical models drawn most notably from works in African-American theory from the United States. Third, it could be argued that authors and critics in Afro-Hispanism have refused to seek full integration into the absorbing category of 'Latin American literature', and have instead insisted on the unique specificity of a field that can be accommodated by the larger literary label but must not be subsumed or assimilated. How, then, can we speak directly at all? How can we resist ventriloquism or mimicry – a signal concept in post-colonial studies – unless we first acknowledge the multiplicity of voices through which we speak and the complexity of interlocked terms of which we speak? And how can we raise the voice of feminism without suppressing other critical discourses that to some may seem more natural, more essential, and more authentic?

The authenticity question is one that Afro-Hispanists have frequently brought to bear on their critical practices, something Richard Jackson has so vigorously advocated (Jackson, 1988). It is the concept of authenticity that critics have used in order to distinguish literature written from within the 'true' black experience and literature written from the outside. Feminists of a certain persuasion have employed an analogous concept in their critiques of literature when they seek to uncover women's experience in its authentic manifestations. Feminist theory shows how the tropes and constructions of male normative experience have produced distorted renditions of female presence and experience much as white European hegemonic discourse has colluded to mask or misrepresent Africans' presence and experience in Latin America. Michele Wallace calls this suppression 'the invisibility blues' with respect to African-American women, who have often been silenced, erased, or commodified – and not only by hegemonic white patriarchy (Wallace, 1990). These women gain consciousness of the embattled terrain they must cross in order to emerge into visibility. Their willingness to name the complex forces that conspire to keep some women unseen and unheard constitutes a fundamental risk that not all are required to take. We might find recordings of the 'invisibility blues' in Afro-Hispanic literature in the sense that Afro-Hispanic female characters often are treated only as emblems, examples, or exceptions, which ignores their subjectivities. Afro-Hispanism, if practised in ways that contain rather than challenge, may become part of what Chandra Talpade Mohanty calls the 'Race Industry': 'an industry that is responsible for the management, commodification, and domestication of race on American campuses' (Mohanty, 1989/90, p. 186). Need I add that feminism in Afro-Hispanism risks being assimilated into the 'Gender Industry'? I believe, however, that at this stage Afro-Hispanism can admit a legitimately executed feminist critique, one that seeks to authenticate rather than simply exemplify, and one that resists commodification and domestication. But who can do this work, from what position, and with what motivations?

II

The problem of positionality in relation to feminism has been treated extensively in the growing body of cultural criticism (see Roof and

Wiegman, 1995). According to Anne Balsamo, the sheer diversity of methodologies that have informed feminist scholarship – psychoanalysis, anthropology, post-colonial theory, film studies, literary studies, philosophy, sociology, medical science, and so forth – indicate that feminist cultural studies might best be regarded as 'post-disciplinary', in that they are no longer able or even interested in fully recovering their source disciplines (Balsamo, 1991, p. 50). Feminist cultural studies has taken seriously its responsibility to 'elucidate its own conditions of possibility in an academic institution, as well as its own political accountability to a broader movement' (Balsamo, 1991, p. 52). The notion of 'accountability' is one I wish to recover for feminism within Afro-Hispanism. It seems to me that 'authenticity' alone may lead to a stultified binary: authentic literature or criticism written from within versus inauthentic literature or criticism written from without. I realize that in saying this I am reducing the potential of 'authenticity' as a critical concept. In fact, scholars like James Clifford imbue the term with expanded powers:

> A significant provocation for these changes of orientation [in culture] has clearly been the emergence of non-western and feminist subjects whose works and discourses are different, strong and complex but clearly not 'authentic' in conventional ways. ... [A]uthenticity is reconceived as hybrid, creative activity in a local present-becoming-future. (Clifford, 1987, p. 126)

Accountability, however, does not foreclose on the concept of authenticity: it demands that critics examine the shifting contexts in which they position themselves, in which they are positioned. And it asks them to give a reliable account of their particular forms of knowledge, which Donna Haraway has deemed the privilege of partial perspective. Feminist objectivity, according to Haraway, 'is about limited location and situated knowledge, not about transcendence and splitting of subject and object. It allows us to become answerable for what we learn how to see' (Haraway, 1988, p. 583). If, on the other hand, critics search for a full and total position, that is, the standpoint of the master, the Man, the One God, then they are likely to produce 'the fetishized perfect subject of oppositional history, sometimes appearing in feminist theory as the essentialized Third World Woman' (Haraway, 1988, pp. 587–88). It is clear that whatever the feminist methodologies we employ to study Afro-Hispanic literature, these are best mobilized when they serve to crack apart the generality of the 'Third World Woman'. This task may be accomplished through a deep investment in the specificity of the subject, an integral aspect of most post-colonial feminist theory.

I now want to plot several theoretical crossroads on the terrain of feminism within Afro-Hispanism with an eye toward possible future praxis. The first position entails a coming into consciousness on the part of practitioners of Afro-Hispanic writing, one possible link to accountable critical activity by scholars of this literature. Since there is no unified feminist movement among Afro-Hispanic women, we need to identify specific historical conditions that can produce a feminist *ambiente*, that is, a climate, an environment, or a sense of solidarity that responds to urgencies of all kinds: political, ideological, racial, nationalist. When conditions propitious to a feminist *ambiente* have been established, we then might look at writing as both the product and the process, that is, the result of consciousness and the vehicle through which this consciousness is created, sustained and transmitted. This in turn ushers in a second-stage level of critique, one that goes beyond the 'images of women' model so prevalent in early feminist critical approaches to Afro-Hispanic literature; it does so because the literature itself becomes a site of potent ideological reformation, and refuses to engage in essentialist stereotypical imaging – or imagining – of women's diverse experiences. Feminist critics have performed incisive readings of those images as they appear in the works of authors such as Adalberto Ortiz (Ecuador) or Nicolás Guillén (Cuba), but when confronted with the complex portraits of female characters of African heritage from the Spanish-speaking Caribbean in the works of an author such as Aída Cartagena Portalatín (Dominican Republic), a different strategy is called for, one that can fully interrogate the post-colonial subject. Subjectivity and language might thus serve as a basis from which to question the complex forces of race, nation, gender and social position, such that the relationship between inner self and outer world becomes less of a dichotomy and more of a dynamic interaction worthy of a multipronged analysis. It is this type of analysis that the future of Afro-Hispanic studies can readily anticipate, based on a synthetic glance back to the theoretical and practical issues that have served to build a foundational ground over which to cross.

Or to cross over. I'd like to borrow the notion of 'cross over' in this discussion, since many of the writers who have experienced a feminist *ambiente* speak of that uneasy position they assume when they cease to conform to cultural norms and expectations specifically pertaining to their gender. They may become self-named outcasts or misfits who inhabit a 'no woman's land' as they travel to different countries – often the US – and come in contact with other currents of feminism and activism. While this condition is not unique to women writers of African descent in Spanish America, there is one defining aspect that touches directly on the question of race, as expressed eloquently by the

Dominican writer Sherezada (Chiqui) Vicioso: 'In the United States, there is no space for fine distinctions of race, and one goes from being "trigüeño" [sic] or "indio" to being "mulatto" or "Black" or "Hispanic." This was an excellent experience for me. From that point on I discovered myself as a Caribbean *mulata* and adopted the Black identity as a gesture of solidarity' (Vicioso, 1989, p. 231). Vicioso states that her travels to Africa restored her essence as a *caribeña*, but she recounts her painful return to the Dominican Republic, where her new-found consciousness of her ethnicity and her feminism incurs hostility, harassment and, not surprisingly, rejection on the part of other women, whom she names 'the principal *machistas*' (Vicioso, 1989, p. 233). Vicioso depicts herself as one who is caught at the crossroads, accused of double-crossing her cultural heritage precisely as she strives to uncover and rename her own ontological multiplicities. A similar struggle is encoded in works by other Afro-Caribbean women writers, such as Jamaica Kincaid, in her 'Antigua Crossings': Kincaid remarks 'When I left Antigua I thought: I'm free of this! But I couldn't be free of it in my head. I would carry it around with me' (Kincaid, 1990, p. 227).

The crossings of these two writers bring me to my next intersection: the links between feminist Afro-Hispanic consciousness and that of the many sisters in diaspora culture. Feminism in Afro-Hispanism will seek to make these links more explicit from a historical and literary perspective, and in so doing will arrive at the common threads that bind these women writers. One obvious analytical vehicle would be a post-colonial interrogation of diaspora cultures as they pertain to women's experiences. An analysis along these lines might focus on the relation between literacy, culture and writing by women who have been educated (or sentenced to ignorance) under the inherited systems of colonial forces to show the ways in which women have adopted double, even triple-voiced discourses through which to create themselves as authors. In cultures where male writers have traditionally held positions of political power and intellectual prestige, what of the women who take up the word in resistance to their dominated condition? Some, like Cuba's Nancy Morejón, find a place in official revolutionary culture; others, like Vicioso, dream of the time when women in the Dominican Republic will discover their power as consumers and producers of books, and as mutual supporters in solidarity with one another. In examining Afro-Hispanic literature from a feminist perspective, an accountable response would probe the broad spectrum of identity politics as they are configured in order to elucidate the feminist *ambiente* in all its potency, with all its obstacles, and for all its differences.

In its incipient stages, Afro-Hispanic literary criticism deliberately sought, for the most part, to remain close to the text and faithful to the context from which it emerged, perhaps digressing to make links with fraternal works from other diaspora literatures. This largely humanistic effort proved to be a liberating break from the hegemonic European literary traditions, but it placed restrictions of its own on Afro-Hispanic critical activity. Having demonstrated a carefully constructed faith, critics now may dare to deconstruct, in all senses. What this might mean to the future of the field is an opening up to currents in intellectual discourse that have the potential to illuminate Afro-Hispanic texts in decidedly new ways. I am thinking here of an appropriation of theories derived concretely from psychoanalysis and philosophy, not as reinscriptions of oppressive discourses, but as revisionary practice that says something about post-colonialism, history and white racism, while also highlighting gender considerations. Works in the psychoanalytic and philosophical traditions that foreground specificity and subjectivity may be sensitively applied to Afro-Hispanic studies in such a way that the notions of 'universality' or 'authenticity' take on new meaning. As lesbian theorist Monique Wittig points out in a stunning reversal of well-worn tropes, 'a text by a minority writer is effective only if it succeeds in making the minority point of view universal. ... one must assume both a particular *and* a universal point of view, at least to be part of literature' (Wittig, 1992, pp. 64, 67). And to be part of the future of literary criticism, I would add. Feminist interventions in Afro-Hispanism can successfully negotiate the crossroads I have outlined when they border the specific with a clear sense of a far-reaching purpose: not to imitate or link on to so-called universalist or masculinist discourse, but to contest it from the ground up, to point out where the meanings are, and to make visible – and primary – figures of Afro-Hispanic women who in the past have been relegated to the status of the other 'other' (Durham, 1990).

III

I would like to shift direction at this point to address matters of canonicity in greater detail, since most of us who study Afro-Hispanic literature in North America work to 'change the world', to use Sherley Anne Williams's words, through our writing and teaching. My particular focus centres on applying theories of race and gender through Afro-Hispanic literature, an endeavour I have carried out with respect to the fields of comparative literature, women's studies and Spanish. In bringing together such diverse areas, methodologies and materials in a research and classroom setting, I have kept in mind Paula Treichler's notions about the production and presentation of theory in the context of women's studies, where it becomes a question of 'a space for self-conscious attention to the nature, scope, traditions, and consequences of theorizing itself' (Treichler, 1986, p. 93). Treichler notes that feminist theory entails not only a vigorous 'looking-at', but also construction of a site where sexual differences can be enacted and debated. Since feminist theory 'is a falsely generic rubric incorporating diverse and sometimes contradictory discursive practices', Treichler argues, 'we need not seek to resolve or disguise contradictions and competing claims: these contests are inherent in the notion of feminist theoretical production' (Treichler, 1986, p. 98). To stage this site of resistance and difference, I have experimented with a non-essentialist, non-canonical approach to Afro-Hispanic literature, which I discuss in what follows.

Diana Fuss lucidly distils the concepts of essentialism and constructionism in her *Essentially Speaking: Feminism, Nature and Difference* (1989). Essentialism is commonly understood 'as a belief in the real, true essence of things, the invariable and fixed properties which define the "whatness" of a given entity' (Fuss, 1989, p. xi). In feminist theory, essentialism is articulated through a number of assumptions: it can be located in a belief in a pure or original femininity that dwells outside the boundaries of the social order; it can be legible in accounts of universal oppression of women throughout cultures and throughout histories; and it can lay claims to a unique feminine language, or voice: to Fuss's list we may add a unique psychology, a unique morality, and so forth (Fuss, 1989, p. 2). Constructionism, on the other hand, argues that essence itself is a historical construction, and seeks to examine how previously assumed kinds have been produced by a complex web of discursive practices. Constructionists interrogate the ways in which these processes deliver the seemingly 'natural': they examine representational systems and codes, ideological practices and effects in an attempt to understand the production and organization of differences (Fuss, 1989, p. 2). Fuss does not fall into the 'essentialist' trap of viewing constructionism as inherently more able to articulate differences: rather, she carefully delineates the underlying assumptions in these systems of knowledge that simultaneously conflict and coincide at crucial points (see also Grosz, 1989, and Butler-Evans, 1989).

The non-essentialist challenge for the Afro-Hispanic canon consists of the following. If we agree that there is no invariable, fixed, essence to '*the* Afro-Hispanic', then how do we plot the intersections of race, gender, historical and material realities, social position and linguistic discourse on to the body of works we study? What are the representational systems and codes through which the images of Afro-Hispanic women are filtered? Through what eyes do we see, and how is our vision constructed? To aid us in our thinking, we should examine essays on theory in a similar fashion. What are the biases that inform scholarship on gender and race, including feminist work? What epistemologies undergird an author's formulation and exposition of ideas? How are the notions of essentialism and constructionism deployed in the theoretical model under consideration? This process of interrogating the author's theoretical positionality may be applied to the literary texts we read, and to ourselves as we read them. That is, in this triangular formation of consciousness and self-consciousness, we continually shift from applying theory to examining its constructions of the subject; we weave between interpreting the text and identifying our interpretative frames; we go from gathering experience to questioning how we come to know and transmit that history.

My experiments in developing 'non-essentialist' approaches to Afro-Hispanic literature go hand in hand with a non-canonical assemblage of texts. It seems to me that to adhere to a canon – that is, an authorized body of works that are deemed stable by virtue of their status, their conformity to category, and their shared history – would be to foreclose on some of the major goals of a post-colonial feminist analysis. Although a 'literary history' of Afro-Hispanic literature can produce excellent results, I seek to conduct readings that bring tensions of race, gender and theory to the forefront, sometimes even at the stated expense of chronology, history and tradition. First, however, we should acknowledge that an 'Afro-Hispanic canon' is a recent development, as I outlined in the first part of this chapter (see Kutzinski, 1996). When we write about or teach Afro-Hispanic literature in a canonical fashion, we have a structure that allows us to pay special tribute to the historical and cultural traditions of Africans in the Spanish-speaking Americas. We analyse the ties between the literary texts; we cover a broad, representative spectrum of what we call the 'major works' in the field; and we introduce some of the 'new voices' that are fast gaining admittance to the established canon. A canonical approach contests the body of mainstream Latin American literature as it is typically presented in North American universities, where, until recently, the only Afro-Hispanic who regularly surfaced was Nicolás Guillén. And precisely because the formation of a recognizable canon of Afro-Hispanic literature is a necessary and worthwhile project, one that has been solidified in the past few decades, I can take it into account (and account for it) when I decide to work outside its conventions. To perform accountable feminist criticism, I have staged textual and theoretical encounters in non-canonical fashion from which a process of intellectual inquiry might emerge.

I will give a few examples of encounters of this sort and point to some of their consequences for research and teaching. In looking at nineteenth-century Cuban Juan Francisco Manzano's *Autobiography*, we might simultaneously consider Manuel Moreno Fraginals's essay on 'Cultural Contributions and Deculturation' (1984) and bell hooks's 'Sexism and the Black Female Slave Experience' from *Ain't I A Woman* (1981). While Moreno Fraginals presents a sociological and historical context for understanding the experience of Africans displaced into 'the culture sugar created' in Cuba, bell hooks examines the experience of black women slaves in North America as compared with their male counterparts. Moreno Fraginals employs rather standard scholarly prose and methodologies; bell hooks writes in an angry, passionate tone that caused her editors, when she finally found a press willing to publish her first book, to fret over her 'negativity'. The content of both these essays offers direct relevance to the autobiography of the Cuban slave, but requires a re-contextualization in both cases, and, in the 'Sexism' essay, demands that we consider whether issues indigenous to the North American slave experience may be applied transculturally to Manzano's account. By bringing in feminist criticism, we may make Manzano's text yield unexpected avenues of inquiry, such as the following. How did gender issues shape his vision of the world and the construction of his narrative? Can we consider Manzano 'typical' of Cuban slaves, and in what sense? What is Manzano's relation to writing, which, according to Henry Louis Gates, Jr., was 'the commodity which slaves were forced to trade for their humanity '(Gates, 1986, p. 9), and how did he gain access to literacy? Did female slaves do likewise? What was Manzano's relationship to his *amas* (female owners), and what does their treatment of him have to say about the ways in which gender and race interact in that social setting? As we explore these issues, we might arrive at a sense of ambivalence, even anger, with respect to the figure of Manzano as he depicts himself in his autobiography. His conduct may seem inexplicable or unjustifiable, and, inspired by *Ain't I A Woman*, we would want to fill in the gaps of his narrative with the invisible black women. An accountable feminist critique permits us to pose these disparate questions, but requires that we formulate situated responses. Thus when we pay attention to culturally based psychological considerations that would elucidate some aspects of Manzano's conduct as a co-opted participant in a hierarchical web of racial and social oppressions, the interrelated roles of the *amas* and the invisible sisters in bondage emerge with more clarity.

To offer another illustration: the prose fiction of Afro-Dominican Aída Cartagena Portalatín has been the subject of some highly suggestive criticism carried out by Miriam DeCosta-Willis, who works at the intersections of feminist theory, discourse analysis and close textual readings. DeCosta-Willis shows how sensitivity to theoretical questions of feminism, ethnicity and class need not install a paralysing hierarchy, but instead may motivate an accountable interpretation of these complex, intertwined forces as they are represented through Cartagena Portalatín's writing. In studying texts such as the stories in *Tablero*, and in reading works of critics such as DeCosta-Willis, one might set up a dialogue with the theoretical debates that have been played out in the pages of *New Literary History* (Winter, 1987), which offer a fertile parallel. To read the impassioned words of Joyce Joyce, Henry Louis Gates, Jr., and Houston Baker, along with Barbara Christian's views on 'The Race for Theory', is to come face-to-face with the essential differences that have marked the field of African diasporic literatures. These debates on 'imported European theory', 'the construct of race' and 'the black feminist critic' could be applied to Afro-Hispanic literature and the scholars who study it or theorize it, an enterprise that in turn would oblige us to note newly formed boundaries of difference. We could then turn to more recent attempts at reconciling (or problematizing) the relation of African American theory and criticism to feminism, which would assist us in formulating new questions about how black subjectivity and white subjectivity are constituted, and how they are related to sexual identity and sexual difference. The stories by Cartagena Portalatín yield up their potential for wide-ranging interpretative strategies when we read them conjointly with these essays on matters of theory. I think of Colita, the young woman protagonist in 'La llamaban Aurora (Pasión por Donna Summer)' 'They Called her Aurora: Passion for Donna Summer', who as a domestic in New York suffers discrimination and alienation, as a part of a narrative that embodies the problems in subjectivity as outlined by thinkers such as Carby, Spillers, McDowell, Christian, and bell hooks, all of whose work suggests ways to 'talk sense' and to 'talk back' through a feminist critique. Colita, the girl who resists the discourse of domination voiced by señora Sarah with screams of 'No, noo, and noo', hears in return the accusation of her employer when she shouts 'you talk nonsense' (Cartagena Portalatín, 1978, p. 17). As we simultaneously read the debates in *New Literary History* and those about black feminist criticism, we should become attuned to protests and accusations of a particular sort, one that demands accountable tools with which to do our analyses so we can tell what talking nonsense means in context.

In an essay that follows her 'The Race for Theory', Barbara Christian delineates 'The Highs and Lows of Black Feminist Criticism' in terms of three worlds: the 'high world of lit crit books, journals and conferences, the middle world of classrooms and graduate students, and the low world of bookstores, communities, and creative writers' (Christian, 1990, p. 50). The high world, for Christian, confers status on those who pay homage to its icons (theory, discourse, the canon, the boys); the middle world accommodates research, reading of texts, and sometimes creative writing, but can lead 'up' to the race for theory; the low world is filled with stories, poems, plays, the language of the folk, and invites responses such as 'I sure know what she's talking about' or 'I don't want to hear that' (Christian, 1990, p. 51). When put into practice, these categories might prove more fluid than Christian may have envisioned. An accountable feminist critique will assist in discovering how these 'highs' and 'lows' are constructed in the first place, and who or what gains admittance to each world. Christian's schema is particularly interesting to examine with respect to Afro-Hispanic literature, where creative writers rarely 'ascend' to the world of 'lit crit' books or the canon, but rather remain, at times wilfully, like Manuel Zapata Olivella, 'en la bodega del barco negrero' – 'in the hold of the slave ship'. At the writers' roundtable at the 1991 International Symposium on Afro-Hispanic Literature, Zapata Olivella eloquently declares his perpetual existence in a place that marks refuge-in-bondage from a society that has denied blacks the possibility of being free: 'Despierta en mí el deseo de afirmar mi condición de negro, de expatriado de Africa. Me mantengo en la bodega para que mi pueblo esté libre' – 'In me there awakens the desire to affirm my condition as a black, as an expatriate from Africa. I remain in the ship's hold so that my people can be free' (Olivella, 1991). In closing my article on 'Feminism and Afro-Hispanism', I used a similar metaphor to claim that 'we should take the trip to the margin, not as first-class passengers but as indentured servants: we can strive to "become minor"' (Feal, 1991b, p. 28). While I sound a similar ending note in this chapter, I hope it is apparent here in what ways I am revising, expanding and 'unlearning' my earlier thinking. Finally, I deliberately leave open the question of how 'becoming minor' – even if it were possible or desirable – relates to claiming 'marginality as site of resistance', as bell hooks terms it. As this final doubt shows, a feminist post-colonial approach to Afro-Hispanic literary and cultural studies constitutes a rehearsal of questions with current theoretical import that resonate well beyond the arena that gave them their first articulation.

Works Cited

Balsamo, Anne, 1991. 'Feminism and Cultural Studies', *The Journal of the Midwest Modern Language Association*, vol. 24, no. 1, pp. 50–73.
Butler-Evans, Elliott, 1989. 'Beyond Essentialism: Rethinking Afro-American Cultural Theory', *Inscriptions*, vol. 5, pp. 121–34.
Cartagena Portalatín, Aída, 1978. *Tablero*, Santo Domingo: Taller.

Christian, Barbara, 1990. 'The Highs and Lows of Black Feminist Criticism', in Henry Louis Gates, Jr. (ed.), *Reading Black, Reading Feminist: A Critical Anthology*, New York: Meridian, pp. 44–51.

Clifford, James, 1987. 'Of Other Peoples: Beyond the "Salvage" Paradigm', in Hal Foster (ed.), *Dia Art Foundation Discussions in Contemporary Culture*, vol. 1, Seattle: Bay Press, pp. 121–30.

Degler, Carl N., 1971. *Neither Black Nor White: Slavery and Race Relations in Brazil and the United States*, Madison: University of Wisconsin Press, 1986.

Durham, Carolyn Richardson, 1990. 'Teaching the Other "Other": The Black Woman in Latin America', Modern Language Association Convention, Chicago, 27 December.

Feal, Rosemary Geisdorfer, 1991a. 'Feminism and Afro-Hispanism: The Double Bind', *Afro-Hispanic Review*, vol. 10, no. 1, pp. 25–29.

Feal, Rosemary Geisdorfer, 1991b. 'Feminist Interventions in the Race for Theory: Neither Black Nor White', *Afro-Hispanic Review*, vol. 10, no. 3, pp. 11–20.

Feal, Rosemary Geisdorfer, 1995. 'Reading Against the Cane: Afro-Hispanic Studies and *Mestizaje*', *Diacritics*, vol. 25, no.1, pp. 82–98.

Fuss, Diana, 1989. *Essentially Speaking: Feminism, Nature and Difference*, New York: Routledge.

Gates, Henry Louis, Jr., 1986. 'Introduction: Writing "Race" and the Difference it Makes', in Henry Louis Gates, Jr. (ed.), *'Race', Writing, and Difference*, Chicago: University of Chicago Press, pp. 1–20.

Grosz, Elizabeth, 1989. 'Sexual Difference and the Problem of Essentialism', *Inscriptions*, vol. 5, pp. 86–101.

Haraway, Donna, 1988. 'Situated Knowledges: The Science Question in Feminism and the Privilege of Partial Perspective', *Feminist Studies*, vol. 14, pp. 575–99.

hooks, bell, 1981. *Ain't I A Woman: Black Women and Feminism*, Boston: South End Press.

hooks, bell, 1989. *Talking Back: Thinking Feminist, Thinking Black*, Boston: South End Press.

Jackson, Richard L., 1988. *Black Literature and Humanism in Latin America*, Athens: University of Georgia Press.

Jackson, Richard L., 1989. *The Afro-Spanish American Author II: The 1980s. An Annotated Bibliography of Recent Criticism*, West Cornwall, CT: Locust Hill Press.

Kincaid, Jamaica, 1990. 'Jamaica Kincaid and the Modernist Project: An Interview', with Selwyn R. Cudjoe, in Selwyn R. Cudjoe (ed.), *Caribbean Women Writers: Essays from the First International Conference*, Wellesley, MA: Calaloux, pp. 215–32.

Kutzinski, Vera, 1996. 'Afro-Hispanic American Literature', in Roberto González Echevarría and Enrique Pupo-Walker (eds), *The Cambridge History of Latin American Literature*, vol. 2, Cambridge: Cambridge University Press, pp. 164–94.

Liberal Learning and the Women's Studies Major, 1991. College Park, MD: National Women's Studies Association.

Lorde, Audre, 1983. 'The Master's Tools Will Never Dismantle the Master's House', in Cherríe Moraga and Gloria Anzaldúa (eds), *This Bridge Called My Back: Writings by Radical Women of Color*, 2nd edn. New York: Kitchen Table, pp. 98–101.

Mohanty, Chandra Talpade, 1989/90. 'On Race and Voice: Challenges for Liberal Education in the 1990s', *Cultural Critique*, vol. 14, pp. 179–208.

Moreno Fraginals, Manuel, 1984. 'Cultural Contributions and Deculturation', in Moreno Fraginals (ed.), trans. Leonor Blum, *Africa in Latin America: Essays on History, Culture, and Socialization*, New York: Holmes and Meier, pp. 5–22.

Olivella, Manuel Zapata, 1991. Remarks at writers' roundtable, International Symposium on Afro-Hispanic Literature, 28 February – 2 March, University of Missouri, Columbia, unpub. ms.

Roof, Judith and Robin Wiegman (eds), 1995. *Who Can Speak: Authority and Critical Identity*, Urbana: University of Illinois Press.

Smart, Ian I., 1989. 'The *Afro-Hispanic Review*', in Jorge J. E. Gracia and Mireya Camurati (eds), *Philosophy and Literature in Latin America: A Critical Assessment of the Current Situation*, Albany: State University of New York Press, pp. 194–200.

Treichler, Paula A., 1986. 'Teaching Feminist Theory', in Cary Nelson (ed.), *Theory in the Classroom*, Urbana: University of Illinois Press, pp. 57–128.

Vicioso, Sherezada (Chiqui), 1989. 'An Oral History (Testimonio)', in Asunción Horno-Delgado et al. (eds), *Breaking Boundaries: Latina Writings and Critical Readings*, Amherst: University of Massachusetts Press, pp. 229–34.

Wallace, Michele, 1990. *Invisibility Blues: From Pop to Theory*, London: Verso.

Williams, Sherley Anne, 1990. 'Some Implications of Womanist Theory', in Henry Louis Gates, Jr. (ed.), *Reading Black Reading Feminist: A Critical Anthology*, New York: Meridian, pp. 68–75.

Wittig, Monique, 1992. *The Straight Mind and Other Essays*, Boston: Beacon.

12
Chicano/a Literature: 'An Active Interanimating of Competing Discourses'

Candida N. Hepworth

Chicano/a literature affords the reader valuable insight in the debate as to whether the discourse of post-colonialism contributes to the reception of multiethnic writing in the United States. Commonly conceived of as one of the nation's many ethnic-resistance literatures – resisting, that is, the hegemonic ideology concerning what it is to be an 'American' – the complex colonial inheritance of the Chicano/a means that their literary production actually exists as the product of a far more fascinating dialectic. Where it is possible to contend, as Edward W. Said does in *Culture and Imperialism*, that all too often '[t]he space between the bashing of other religions and cultures and deeply conservative self-praise has not been filled with edifying analysis or discussion' (Said, 1994, p. 397), the circumstances which create Chicano/a literature challenge this tendency towards the binary consciousness of 'us' and 'them'. Reminding us that 'text' is a word which derives from the Latin *textus*, meaning to weave, as Nelly Furman explains, the relationship between writer and reader always establishes literature as 'a place of transition, an area which either leads to something different or a space where change is occurring' (Furman, 1980, p. 49). Within what Bruce-Novoa has called 'The Space of Chicano Literature' (Bruce-Novoa, 1990, p. 93), the opportunities for the weaving of a relationship which can promote change are even more pronounced. As the product of what D. Emily Hicks refers to as 'border writing', according to which the writer offers the reader 'the opportunity to practice multidimensional perception ... quite literally the ability to see not just from one side of a border, but from the other side as well' (Hicks, 1991, p. xxiii), in the context of the United States' reception of multiethnic literature, Chicano/a literature resists the binary order of self and other and promotes instead a 'region of encounter in between, an area of contest but also of consort between cultures' (Faragher, 1993, p. 75). In claiming such powers for Chicano/a literature, then, it becomes necessary to explain who the Chicano/a is. By virtue of doing this, moreover, the extent to which it is crucial to acknowledge the significance of their colonial inheritance soon becomes apparent.

The etymological origin of the term Chicano/a is open to debate. In their introduction to *Chicano Literature: A Reference Guide*, Julio A. Martínez and Francisco A. Lomelí articulate the more popular theory that it derives from a corruption of the word *mexicano* which, in the process of linguistic evolution, came in the sixteenth century to be pronounced *meschicano* or *mechicano*. Yet without an appreciation of subsequent historical-political circumstances, such speculation does not shed light on the association of Mexico with the United States and neither, in turn, does it explain how the word has come frequently to be regarded as synonymous with the description Mexican American. Bruce-Novoa may therefore provide a more enlightening definition. The Chicano/a, he explains, exists in the 'intercultural space' (Bruce-Novoa, 1990, p. 71) between Mexico and the United States: 'no one would deny the predominance of the Mexican and the US influences', he writes, 'yet we are neither ... we are the space (not the hyphen) between the two' (Bruce-Novoa, 1990, p. 98).

That the Chicano/a *is* distinct from the Mexican American is a circumstance that Bruce-Novoa, amongst others, is keen to stress. 'A person of Mexican parentage becomes a "Mexican American" by being born in [the United States] ... or by attaining a certificate of citizenship', remarks Albert S. Herrera in his essay 'The Mexican American in Two Cultures' (Herrera, 1973, p. 249), but this description encompasses a diversity of experiences as well as a wide array of psychological outlooks. According to Carlos Muñoz, it is from this latter dynamic that one may distinguish between the Mexican American, the (hyphenated) Mexican-American and the Chicano/a. In the system of nomenclature advanced by Muñoz, reference to the unhyphenated Mexican American constitutes a generic allusion to anyone of Mexican descent born or resident in the United States. The hyphenated Mexican-American, by contrast, denotes the generation shaped by the political ideology that prevailed in the United States in the 1930s and 1940s. With benefits accruing from Franklin Delano Roosevelt's New Deal programmes and with the Second World War having created openings in employment and education, Muñoz claims that an entire generation was fostered whose behaviour was shaped by a perception that 'Mexican Americans were finally about to profit from democracy and the "American way of life"' (Muñoz, 1989, p. 44). The atmosphere and events of the 1950s then compounded this outlook further, since the politics of the decade could hardly be regarded as conducive to the expression of attitudes that might be looked upon as 'Un-American'.

If Muñoz applies the hyphen only to a specific group of Mexican Americans, his use of the designation Chicano/a is equally selective. Having begun by mentioning that the terms are often used synonymously, we are now close to appreciating the logic at work behind Edward Simmen's statement that 'while it will be readily agreed that all Chicanos are Mexican Americans, it will not be agreed that *all* Mexican Americans are Chicanos' (Simmen, 1971, pp. xii–xiii). To use the terminology of Luis Leal, Chicano/a was a term which became 'naturalized' (Leal, 1979, p. 21) in the 1960s. In keeping with the spirit of the times, and unlike Mexican-Americans, Chicano/as preferred 'to live out their intercultural essence openly', laying claim to their 'legitimate residence in the space between the poles' (Bruce-Novoa, 1990, p. 38). Concomitant with the sentiments articulated by their newly created Movement, Chicano/a became 'a word self-consciously selected by many persons as symbolic of positive identification with a unique cultural heritage' (Mirandé, 1985, p. 2).

Fundamental to the Chicano/as' 'positive identification with a unique cultural heritage' is their awareness of the historical-political situation of colonialism. Edward Said has observed that 'if there is anything that radically distinguishes the imagination of anti-imperialism it is the primacy of the geographical in it' (Said, 1990, p. 77) and as Alfred Arteaga remarks in *Chicano Poetics*, the ideology of the Chicano/a is informed by two concepts of territorial space. Not only have they experienced colonization once, moreover; rather, they are the 'products of two colonial contexts' (Arteaga, 1997, p. 81). Aztlán represents the site of the first of these and although now it exists only in the realm of legend, its existence can be said to have had 'a formative and continuing influence on the collective Chicano mind' (Chávez, 1989, p. 1). Traditionally supposed to lie in the area now known as the Southwestern United States, it is reputed to have been the ancient homeland of the Aztecs. Gloria Anzaldúa relates that in 1168 the Aztecs left their 'Edenic place of origin' (Anzaldúa, 1987, p. 4) and began to move progressively southwards. Guided by the prophecy of Huitzilopochtli, the Aztec God of War, eventually, in 1325, they arrived at a group of islands in Lake Texcoco where they found the scene for which they had been searching: an eagle, perched atop a cactus, holding a serpent in its beak. Thereupon the Aztecs set about the process of establishing their empire which, according to Miguel Leon-Portilla, came to extend all the way from the Gulf Coast to the Pacific Ocean and as far south as Guatemala. Centred upon the city of Tenochtitlán, site of present-day

Mexico City, it was to this prestigious city of wealth that the Spanish-sponsored Hernán Cortés beat his path, having arrived with a small Spanish army at Vera Cruz in April 1519. Through a series of events related in the codices that have given rise to Leon-Portilla's publication, *The Broken Spears: The Aztec Account of the Conquest of Mexico*, in August 1521, Cortés claimed both the city and the empire for Spain and so began the first colonial encounter.

As a consequence of the legend of Aztlán, the Aztecs and their original homeland are held to lie at the root of the Chicano/a culture. It is for this reason that 'the Indian presence affects the act of being Chicano' (Arteaga, 1997, p. 8). Given that Spain ruled over the empire for a period of 300 years, moreover, the process of miscegenation, or *mestizaje*, meant that the racial characteristics of the Spaniard and the Indian were, in Arteaga's words, to 'compete for presence' (Arteaga, 1997, p. 10) in the physiognomy of the *mestizo*. Writing in the early 1980s, in a section of *Hunger of Memory* entitled 'Complexion', Richard Rodriguez is therefore able to remark:

> Regarding my family, I see faces that do not closely resemble my own. Like some other Mexican families, my family suggests Mexico's confused colonial past. Gathered around a table, we appear to be from separate continents ... I am the only one in the family whose face is severely cut to the line of ancient Indian ancestors. My face is mournfully long, in the classical Indian manner; my profile suggests one of those beak-nosed Mayan sculptures – the eaglelike face upturned, open-mouthed, against the deserted, primitive sky. (Rodriguez, 1988, pp. 114–15)

In 1810, with the population having become restless under Spanish rule, when priest Miguel Hidalgo y Costilla uttered the now famous Grito de Dolores – 'Viva Nuestra Señora de Guadalupe y muera al mal gobierno' – he kindled the impetus for the Revolution against the Spanish oppressors which finally, in 1821, saw the declaration of Mexico's independence. Yet as Rodriguez records in his article 'Night and Day', the country was still subject to foreign intervention, even if it could not be characterized as colonization. The 'pageant of nineteenth-century Mexican history was a confusing succession of ideological banns', he writes (Rodriguez, 1990, p. 206). Characterizing Mexico as 'the richest daughter of the King of Spain', she was courted, we are told, by 'many suitors'; the French invaded, British bankers inveigled her, an Austrian archduke even 'came to marry Mexico with full panoply of candles and bishops'. And all the while, 'America reached under Mexico's skirt every chance we got' (Rodriguez, 1990, p. 206).

The second colonial context against which the Chicano/as determine their identity concerns, indeed, the actions of the United States. As

Arteaga expresses it, 'the Chicano derives *being* not only from the Spanish colonial intervention but also from Anglo-American colonialism' (Arteaga, 1997, p. 27). Anglo-Americans, particularly after the purchase of Louisiana from the French in 1803, were encroaching in ever-increasing numbers into the northern reaches of what, as has been said, in 1821 became Mexico. Driven by the spirit which would later be encapsulated within the doctrine of Manifest Destiny and attracted by the *empresario* land grants which the Mexican government had issued in order to encourage Mexican settlement of its sparsely populated northern reaches, the Anglo-Americans soon came in such numbers that the Mexicans were outnumbered. In 1830, Mexico passed a law that sought to forbid immigration from the United States into the area now known as Texas. Immigration continued, however, and according to Andreas Reichstein, when a population survey was conducted in 1834, of the 24,700 people registered only 4,000 were listed as being Mexican. On 2 March 1836, in fact, the territory severed its links with Mexico and declared itself a republic.

The president of Mexico himself, General Antonio López de Santa Anna, led an army of approximately 6,000 professional soldiers against what he considered the seditious revolt of Texas. On 6 March 1836, the San Antonio mission, the Alamo, fell to Santa Anna and his troops, but the following month Samuel Houston and his men caught the Mexicans by surprise on the banks of the San Jacinto river and effectively brought that stage of the confrontation to a close. Santa Anna signed the Treaty of Velasco in return for his release and Texas was recognized as independent until it went on to be annexed to the United States in 1845. Doña Mauricia Puig, a character in Rolando Hinojosa's novel *Becky and Her Friends*, testifies to the confusing history of the area: 'born a Spanish subject in 1814; at age ten she was a Mexican citizen; by the summer of 1836, she was a Texan. Later, in 1845, an American when Texas was annexed that December 21st' (Hinojosa, 1990, p. 107).

Still smarting from the ignominious defeat of Santa Anna and the acceptance of Texas into the Union, Mexico was in no mood to tolerate the activities of President James K. Polk, a man whom Chicano histories have branded an 'aggressive expansionist' (Shirley, 1989, p. 298). Having attempted, in vain, financially to appropriate the area now represented by the states of California and New Mexico, Polk sought to acquire them by force instead. When hostilities began in May 1846, so did what Bruce-Novoa has described as 'the definitive historical event in Chicano history' (Bruce-Novoa, 1982, p. 61). For almost two years the countries were at war with one another and with the signing of the Treaty of Guadalupe Hidalgo on 2 February 1848, the United States emerged the victor. Under the terms of this treaty, Mexico effectively surrendered her claims to approximately one million square miles of land, territory that today broadly forms the states of California, Nevada, New Mexico and parts of Utah, Arizona and Colorado. Article VIII of the treaty, moreover, gave the people who were resident in that territory a twelve-month period in which to decide whether or not they wished to become 'American', and as historians Matt Meier and Feliciano Ribera record, 'nearly all 80,000 Mexicans living in the ceded territory ultimately became U.S. nationals' (Meier and Ribera, 1993, p. 66). The Mexican inhabitants of this annexed land, the first Mexican Americans, thus found themselves, in Bruce-Novoa's words, 'living in the Other's space' (Bruce-Novoa, 1982, p. 49).

In spite of the fact that, officially at least, Article IX of the Treaty of Guadalupe Hidalgo promised that these new citizens of the United States would 'be maintained and protected in the enjoyment of their liberty, their property, and the civil rights now vested in them according to the Mexican laws' (Duran and Bernard, 1973, p. 206), the actual repercussions after the war provided the context for what the Chicano/as perceive to be their second colonial encounter. 'Beginning with the premise that Chicanos are not a recent immigrant group but native to the Southwest and the American continent', writes Mirandé, 'the relationship between Chicanos and the dominant society becomes one, not of a voluntary, mobile immigrant group and a host society, but of an indigenous people and an invading nation' (Mirandé, 1985, p. 4). The poem 'We Call Them Greasers' in Anzaldúa's *Borderlands/La Frontera*, for example, reiterates this sensation of there having been an 'invasion'. Written in the voice of an Anglo-American, the narrator's lack of respect is quickly apparent: 'why they didn't even own the land but shared it. / Wasn't hard to drive them off, / cowards, they were, no backbone' (Anzaldúa, 1987, p. 134). As the titles of such histories as John Chávez's *The Lost Land* and Rudolfo Acuña's *Occupied America* attest, then, by virtue both of Aztlán and the war of 1846–48, Chicano/as regard themselves as 'indigenous to and dispossessed of their homeland' (Chávez, 1989, p. 3).

It is this second experience of colonization that carries the greatest impression of violent colonial encounter, however. With the imposition of a new geopolitical borderline at the end of the war, 'the facts of violence and cultural conflict within the interface between nations' (Arteaga, 1997, p. 14) were emphasized. To underestimate the significance of the border to the Chicano/a is almost impossible, in fact. It permeates their conception of self. In the same manner that Sandra Cisneros internalizes the historical-political legacy within the 'forty-pound body' of her *Woman Hollering Creek* character Salvador, marked by 'its geography of scars, its history of hurt' (Cisneros, 1991b, p. 10), so Anzaldúa characterizes the border as a '1,950 mile-long open wound / dividing a *pueblo*, a culture, / running down the length of my body, / staking fence rods in my flesh' (Anzaldúa, 1987, p. 2). Indeed, a popular motif is to characterize the border as, again the words of Anzaldúa, '*una herida abierta*, where the Third World grates against the first and bleeds' (Anzaldúa, 1987, p. 3). And it is within the image of the Chicano/a as 'the lifeblood of two worlds merging to form a third country – a border culture' (Anzaldúa, 1987, p. 3) that the notion of their post-colonial hybridity is rendered once again particularly apparent. In addition to the hybridity of *miscegenation* from the Spanish colonial intervention, this new mingling of blood, drawn from the body politic of Mexico and the United States alike, further 'reflects the intercultural dynamics at play in constructing Chicano identity' (Arteaga, 1997, p. 68).

In the context of making a positive contribution to the reception of multiethnic literature in the United States, the fact of this hybridity is crucial to the promotion of 'multidimensional perception'. Chicano/a literature can be characterized as having the potential of what Hicks describes as 'border writing' because, as their post-colonial situation makes clear, Chicano/as are a cultural group for whom the notion of existing at an 'intersection' is particularly significant. Yet simultaneously, the same factors are responsible for making the reception of Chicano/as problematic. Products of both a hybrid and a border culture, they exist in a complex relationship to any clear sense of national identity. As Arteaga puts it, 'inhabitants of the border zone who partake in messy cultural interplay cannot be contained on a narrow conceptual axis of monologic nationalism' (Arteaga, 1997, p. 94).

'To live in the Borderlands means you / are neither *hispana india negra española* / *ni gabacha, eres mestiza, mulata*, half-breed / caught in the crossfire between camps / while carrying all five races on your back', writes Anzaldúa (1987, p. 194). Where a 'thin and severe borderline is an essential component in the narrative of the nation' (Arteaga, 1997, p. 92), the ability to comprehend this blurring of national cultures lies beyond what might be described as our 'neurological threshold' (Rieff, 1988, p. 82); 'the notion of a broader zone, a borderlands, is incomprehensible' (Arteaga, 1997, p. 92). To live in a situation in which the 'provision of periphery' (Ardrey, 1966, p. 170) is so ambiguous proves too unsettling. Man, as a territorial animal, looks for the existence of a border which 'surrounds and sets bounds', bringing 'security and stability' (Paz, 1990, p. 32). The absence of a clearly defined border therefore has a profound impact upon the configuration of self. In the words of Rolando J. Romero, the 'space of the self is also the space of sanity' (Romero, 1993, p. 63).

Robert Ardrey's research in the writing of *The Territorial Imperative* has suggested that the following territorial behaviour is so endemic as to be credited with the status of a law:

> A proprietor's confidence is at its peak in the heartland, as is an intruder's at its lowest ... That confidence, however, will wane as the proprietor approaches his border, vanish as he crosses it. Having entered his neighbor's yard, an urge to flee will replace his urge to fight, just as his neighbor's confidence and fighting urge will be restored by the touch of his vested soil. (Ardrey, 1966, p. 90)

Hence there are areas within the dimensions of one's territory which are endowed with different psychological attributes. The centre – what Ardrey calls the heartland – affords the site of greatest security, while the border regions enhance anxiety. So when Anzaldúa remarks that '[b]orders are set up to define the places that are safe and unsafe, to distinguish *us* from *them*' (Anzaldúa, 1987, p. 3), she not only reiterates Ardrey's findings but also provides an insight into how the very concept of hybridity can cause consternation amongst those who perceive their nationality as a clear-cut case. Octavio Paz, speaking as a Mexican national, feels able to declare that '[w]e can all reach the point of knowing ourselves to be Mexicans. It is enough, for example, simply to cross the border' (Paz, 1990, p. 12). The politics of identity in this scenario take the borderline 'simply' to represent the point at which exclusions of membership are made; for Paz, Mexican identity exists in a relationship of difference to the United States. For the Chicano/a, meanwhile, this is not a feasible attitude. It cannot accommodate a culture in which the people are literate in two or more 'referential codes' (Hicks, 1991, p. 10), for 'denying the Anglo inside you / is as bad as having denied the Indian' (Anzaldúa, 1987, p. 194).

The United States may well be multiethnic, then, but its sense of nationhood survives through the protection of what may be characterized as the 'sanctioned narratives' (Said, 1994, p. 380) of its heartland. Fundamental to the success of this project is the maintenance of an 'interpretive master code' (Jameson, 1993, p. 10) on the basis of which the nation decides what is, and what is not, 'American'. Multiculturalism, therefore, at least as it is understood by Robert Hughes, is a condition which makes the United States uncomfortable, since it asserts

> that people with different roots can co-exist, that they can learn to read the image-banks of others, that they can and should look across the frontiers of race, language, gender and age without prejudice or illusion, and learn to think against the background of a hybridized society. (Hughes, 1993, p. 83)

From their place not so much on the border as in the borderlands, then, Chicano/as bring this challenge to the nation; they contest the monologism of the closed text. Given their historical condition, moreover, since the hegemony's 'discursive practice does not simply represent colonialism after the fact but functions as the means to order colonial relations' (Arteaga, 1997, p. 76), post-colonialism becomes a powerful notion by which to describe the multiple layers of oppression represented in their literature.

'The power to narrate, or to block other narratives from forming and emerging' is, states Said, 'very important to culture and imperialism' (Said, 1994, p. xiii). Although, through the process of internal colonialism, the Chicano/as may have been made to feel 'at home, a stranger' (Anzaldúa, 1987, p. 194), and although they may view Rodriguez as something of a controversial figure, like him they are determined to acquire for themselves a public voice. When, in *Hunger of Memory*, Rodriguez recalls his encounter with a group of Mexican nationals who have been employed in the United States as manual labourers, the overwhelming impression he carries away with him is that of their silence: 'Only, the quiet. Something uncanny about it. Its compliance. Vulnerability' (Rodriguez, 1988, p. 139). Whereas it is not the intention of the Chicano/as to be passive, they are not prepared to have it said that '[s]ilence remains to oppress them' (Rodriguez, 1988, p. 185). Their stories, as Said suggests, are 'the method the colonized people use to assert their own identity and the existence of their own history' (1994, p. xiii).

Crucial to the post-colonial circumstance of the Chicano/a is the knowledge that they must contend with 'the discursive confrontation of versions of history' (Bruce-Novoa, 1987, p. 29). In the Western world, which has become adept at perceiving the passage of time as a linear phenomenon, one needs to be cautioned against accepting the idea that there is only one past. It is 'misleading', writes Paz, to speak of previous times in the singular; 'rather, they are many, they are all alive, and they continually fight within us' (Paz, 1972, p. 70). Whilst R. W. B. Lewis proposes an analogy between 'the history of a culture – or of its thought and literature – and the unfolding course of a dialogue' (Lewis, 1955, p. 1), therefore, from the perspective of a colonial subject such as the Chicano/a, the historical discourse advocated by the United States more closely resembles a monologue. In Rodolfo Gonzales's epic poem of 1967, 'I Am Joaquín', the narrative voice, for example, records how he lives in 'a country that has wiped out / all my history' (1991, p. 6). In fact, however, according to Peter Worsley, the situation which develops in a colonial relationship will always be the product of a 'dialectic, a synthesis, not just a simple imposition' (quoted by Harlow,

1987, p. 5), but since the 'spotlight we flash into the darkness of the past is guided by our own concerns in the present' (Schlesinger, 1992, p. 46) it is hardly surprising that what the United States promotes as its history tends to be 'the story of what the White man did' (Harlow, 1987, p. 5).

It is on account of this circumstance that Chicano/as seek to rearticulate their place in history. When Esperanza, the young Chicana narrator of Cisneros's *The House on Mango Street*, tells her Mexican friend Alicia, 'You have a home ... and one day you'll go there, to a town you remember, but me I have never had a house' (Cisneros, 1991a, p. 106), what she reveals is the extent to which she has not been made to feel she belongs. Throughout the book, Esperanza's repeated desire is to have a house 'all my own ... a space for myself to go' (Cisneros, 1991a, p. 108) and her ambition echoes that of her creator in that they may both be said to be 'trying to create within colonial space the space for [their] own community' (Crawford, 1990, p. 91). *The House on Mango Street* stands, then, as but one of many Chicano/a texts which enable us to understand why Bruce-Novoa should envisage Chicano/a literature as 'a geographic rescue operation' (Bruce-Novoa, 1990, p. 102) and why, allied to this, it has been alleged that the need to recuperate historical knowledge became, at an early stage, 'the most significant context of the Chicano literary project' (Bruce-Novoa, 1987, p. 33). As Said contends in his essay 'Yeats and Decolonization', for the person whose 'colonial servitude is inaugurated by the loss to an outsider of the local place ... there is a pressing need for the recovery of the land'. Moreover, 'because of the presence of the colonizing outsider', this 'is recoverable at first only through the imagination' (Said, 1990, p. 77). Given the particulars of their post-colonial circumstance, for the Chicano/a the literary space of that imaginative retrieval becomes 'the frame of reference within which one begins to know oneself and the world in which one lives' (Winchell, 1980, p. 75). It is of especial significance, moreover, because for the Chicano/a an *imaginative* retrieval of what has historically been lost is all that is accessible.

When Frantz Fanon, in *The Wretched of the Earth*, discusses the control of historical discourse in situations of colonialism, the course of action for both parties appears relatively straightforward. The project of the colonial power, with regard to those people whom it has colonized, lies in 'either expelling them from history or preventing them from taking root in it' (Fanon, 1968, p. 169). The person oppressed, on the other hand, is portrayed as the 'fighter [who] carried his warring country between his bare toes' (Fanon, 1968, p. 135). To some extent, an analogy seems plausible between this depiction and the colonial situation of the Chicano/a. In Cisneros's story 'Four Skinny Trees', part of *The House on*

Mango Street, the trees that are struggling to survive in the city cling to life, like the Chicano/as, 'despite concrete' laid over them; both 'send ferocious roots beneath the ground ... and grab the earth between their ... toes ... and never quit their anger'. This, the reader is told, 'is how they keep' (Cisneros, 1991a, p. 74). Also, in Raymond Barrio's *The Plum Plum Pickers*, a novel that was popular at the height of the Chicano Movement, there is a character by the name of Ramiro Sánchez who appears to be the epitome of Fanon's 'fighter'. He watches, he waits, he bides his time, waiting until the moment is right to strike out against his oppressor. 'The grito of Padre Hidalgo still echoing in his soul, lay still, and unanswered' (Barrio, 1984, p. 49), we are told. With 'muscle-hardened flesh ... fingers made deft and flinty and wrists locked hard', Ramiro proclaims that he 'would rather be outlawed than be embraced and smothered' (Barrio, 1984, p. 217). Yet for the Chicano/a, fighting back against the culture of exclusion is not this simple. The 'anger' of the Chicano/as can only function through literature to maintain an ethnic and historical 'space' that would otherwise be subsumed by the so-called mainstream culture. It cannot be 'anger' which is directed at the outsider with the intention that he or she be 'put ... out of the picture' (Fanon, 1968, p. 44) because in their post-colonial circumstance, such wholesale rejection of the outsider is impossible. 'To attempt to eliminate completely one or the other [of the influences of the United States or Mexico] is to cease to be Chicano' (Bruce-Novoa, 1990, p. 31). For the Chicano/as, in other words, their oppressors have come to constitute an integral part of their cultural heritage.

Since the Chicano/a subject 'comes about through the interplay of different social "texts," analogously, through *heterotextual* reproduction' (Arteaga, 1997, p. 25), Arteaga suggests that we may envisage their literature as one which is articulated through 'the trope of chiasmus' (Arteaga, 1997, p. 48). Chiasmus, a word derived from the Greek *chiasma*, signifies a cross-shaped mark, like the Greek letter X, *chi*. This proves to be a powerful tool by which to interpret Chicano/a literature because, if each line of the cross is taken to represent one of the Chicano/as' two 'referential codes' (Hicks, 1991, p. 10) – that is to say, the influences of the United States and also those of Mexico – then chiasmus becomes a trick by which one can overcome 'the silencing of the other by articulating marginalized discourses that cross, but do not supplant, the dominant discourse' (Arteaga, 1997, p. 49). The dominant voice of the 'American' is present, but the marginalized voice of the Mexican experience also persists. One medium through which the tolerance of this 'heterotextuality' is made immediately apparent is the medium of language, notably, the co-existence in much Chicano/a literature of Nahuatl (the ancient language of the Aztecs), Spanish and English.

When the new geopolitical border cut across Mexico in 1848, in the land to the north 'Spanish, the great metropolitan language of the region, was reduced to a foreign tongue, the language of the outskirts, the language of the gibbering poor, thus gibberish' (Rodriguez, 1990, pp. 206–207). As is made manifest in 'Sometimes It Just Happens That Way', a section of Rolando Hinojosa's novel *The Valley*, the world of authority became an Anglo-American affair – the Assistant District Attorney is Mr Robert A. Chapman, the judge a man by the name of Harrison Phelps, the employer a Mr Royce – and business in this world is conducted in English, with the voice of the Spanish speaker marginalized. In the words of Rodriguez, therefore, the imposition of the English language came to signify 'the triumphal crushing metaphor' (1990, pp. 206–207). The English language attained the reputation of being 'the primary linguistic medium through which the Chicano is oppressed' (Peñalosa, 1980, p. 115) and the insensitivity of the colonial power to this circumstance is concisely illustrated in another of Hinojosa's texts, *Rites and Witnesses*. Speaking from his fictional creation of Belken County, Texas, a relatively minor Anglo-American character, Rebecca Ruth Verser, declares: '[I]f they like Spanish so much, why don't they go to Mexico? It's right there. It's right *there*, right on top of us, for crying out loud' (Hinojosa, 1989, p. 97). In contrast to this character's insistence upon maintaining the purity of linguistic borders, however, by dint of employing 'the hybrid cross of xicanimso' (Arteaga, 1997, p. 154), much Chicano/a literature sustains a linguistic phenomenon that both 'engages' and 'crosses the [English] line of authority' (Arteaga, 1997, p. 65). This device may be characterized as 'interlingualism' or 'code-switching' – that is to say, 'the use in one speech act [such as a sentence] of two or more languages' (Smith, 1992, p. 245).

Sociolinguists have identified two motivations for the code-switch. The first of these, the mechanical switch, is used when the requisite vocabulary is unknown to the speaker, as when Nurse Luciano, in Denise Chávez's *The Last of the Menu Girls*, enquires: 'Cómo se dice when was the last time you had a bowel movement?' (Chávez, 1986, p. 31). The second, which is more pertinent to the argument here, is the connotative or deliberate switch, employed when the speaker does have command of the language but chooses, for reasons of situation, style or effect, to vary his or her use of the language codes. In the same novel, then, we see a character called Braulia who, forsaken for another woman, switches from English into Spanish in order to express the measure of her contempt: as she tells her friend Nieves, Regino has 'gone. And now he's living with some *desgraciada pintada chorreada* and she isn't even young, *comadre*' (Chávez, 1986, p. 162). That the monolingual English speaker cannot understand exactly what she is saying is largely irrelevant; the gist of her scorn for the other woman is readily apparent. What *is* significant from the point of view of the reader is that code-switching can have a 'boundary levelling function' since it caters to both Spanish and English and thus allows for the 'widest possible audience participation' (Smith, 1992, p. 255). The humorous aspect of these examples aside, what code-switching conceals is a far more serious achievement: the dominant code may well be English, but the Spanish voice of the Chicano/a refuses to be silenced.

In conclusion, to 'be Chicano in the borderlands is to make oneself from among the competing definitions of nation, culture, language, race, ethnicity, and so on' (Arteaga, 1997, p. 10). From the complexity of their colonial legacy, the Chicano/a 'takes the notion of chaos and transforms it from a spectre to a creative source of being' (Rodríguez, 1981, p. 67). It is through this act that their post-colonial discourse makes such a valuable contribution to the manner in which multiethnic literature is received in the United States. Precisely because to '*be* Chicano is to negotiate difference', is 'an active interanimating of competing discourses' (Arteaga, 1997, p. 95), the recording and transmission of their colonial legacy encapsulate great possibilities for the interpretation of their writing actively to promote 'consort between cultures'. It is this spirit which informs the Preface to Anzaldúa's *Borderlands/La Frontera*, in which she offers her work as 'our invitation to you' (Anzaldúa, 1987). Readers are invited to become 'border crossers' (Hicks, 1991, p. xxvi), are invited, in the spirit of multiculturalism, to 'learn to read the image-banks of others' (Hughes, 1993, p. 116) and engage in the 'dynamics of intercultural knowledge' (Fischer, 1986, p. 201). The lesson which the mainstream readership can therefore learn from post-colonial Chicano/a literature is that in which Ultima instructs Antonio in Rudolfo Anaya's *Bless Me, Ultima*: '*The waters are one, Antonio ... You have been seeing only parts ... and not looking into the great cycle that binds us all*' (Anaya's italics) (Anaya, 1989, p. 113).

Works Cited

Anaya, Rudolfo A., 1989. *Bless Me, Ultima*, Berkeley, CA: Tonatiuh-Quinto Sol International, rpt.
Anzaldúa, Gloria, 1987. *Borderlands/La Frontera: The New Mestiza*, San Francisco: Spinsters/Aunt Lute.
Ardrey, Robert, 1966. *The Territorial Imperative: A Personal Inquiry into the Animal Origins of Property and Nations*, New York: Delta, Dell Publishing Co., Inc.
Arteaga, Alfred, 1997. *Chicano Poetics: Heterotexts and Hybridities*, Cambridge: Cambridge University Press.

Barrio, Raymond, 1984. *The Plum Plum Pickers*, Binghamton, NY: Bilingual Press/Editorial Bilingüe.
Bruce-Novoa, 1982. 'The Heroics of Sacrifice: *I Am Joaquín*', in *Chicano Poetry: A Response to Chaos*, Austin: University of Texas Press, pp. 48–68.
Bruce-Novoa, 1987. 'History as Content, History as Act: The Chicano Novel', *Aztlán: A Journal of Chicano Studies*, vol. 18, no. 1 (Spring), pp. 29–44.
Bruce-Novoa, 1990. *RetroSpace: Collected Essays on Chicano Literature, Theory and History*, Houston: Arte Público Press.
Chávez, Denise, 1986. *The Last of the Menu Girls*, Houston: Arte Público Press.
Chávez, John R., 1989. *The Lost Land: The Chicano Image of the Southwest*, Albuquerque: University of New Mexico Press, rpt.
Cisneros, Sandra, 1991a. *The House on Mango Street*, New York: Vintage Books.
Cisneros, Sandra, 1991b. *Woman Hollering Creek and Other Stories*, New York: Random House.
Crawford, John, 1990. 'Rudolfo Anaya', in *This Is About Vision: Interviews with Southwestern Writers*, William Balassi, John F. Crawford and Annie O. Eysturoy (eds), Albuquerque: University of New Mexico Press, pp. 82–93.
Duran, Livie Isauro and H. Russell Bernard (eds), 1973. *Introduction to Chicano Studies: A Reader*, New York: Macmillan Publishing Co., Inc.
Fanon, Frantz, 1968. *The Wretched of the Earth*, New York: Grove Press.
Faragher, John Mack, 1993. 'A Nation Thrown Back Upon Itself: Turner and the Frontier', *Culturefront*, vol. 2, no. 2 (Summer), pp. 5–9 and continued on p. 75.
Fischer, Michael M. J., 1986. 'Ethnicity and the Post-Modern Arts of Memory', in James Clifford and George E. Marcus (eds), *Writing Culture: The Poetics and Politics of Ethnography*, Berkeley, Los Angeles and London: University of California Press, pp. 194–233.
Furman, Nelly, 1980. 'Textual Feminism', in Sally McConnell-Ginet, Ruth Borker and Nelly Furman (eds), *Women and Language in Literature and Society*, New York: Praeger, pp. 46–53.
Gonzales, Rodolfo, 1991. *I Am Joaquín*, El Gallo Newspaper.
Harlow, Barbara, 1987. *Resistance Literature*, New York and London: Methuen.
Herrera, Albert S., 1973. 'The Mexican American in Two Cultures', in Ed Ludwig and James Santibañez (eds), *The Chicanos: Mexican American Voices*, Baltimore: Penguin Books, Inc., pp. 249–54.
Hicks, D. Emily, 1991. *Border Writing: The Multidimensional Text*, Minneapolis and Oxford: University of Minnesota Press.

Hinojosa, Rolando, 1983. *The Valley*, Ypsilanti, MI: Bilingual Press/Editorial Bilingüe Press.
Hinojosa, Rolando, 1989. *Rites and Witnesses: A Comedy*, Houston: Arte Público Press, rpt.
Hinojosa, Rolando, 1990. *Becky and Her Friends*, Houston: Arte Público Press.
Hughes, Robert, 1993. *Culture of Complaint: The Fraying of America*, New York and Oxford: Oxford University Press.
Jameson, Fredric, 1993. *The Political Unconscious: Narrative as a Socially Symbolic Act*, London: Routledge, rpt.
Leal, Luis, 1979. 'Mexican American Literature: A Historical Perspective', in Joseph Sommers and Tomás Ybarra-Frausto (eds), *Modern Chicano Writers: A Collection of Critical Essays*, Englewood Cliffs, NJ: Prentice-Hall, Inc., pp. 18–30.
Leon-Portilla, Miguel, 1990. *The Broken Spears: The Aztec Account of the Conquest of Mexico*, Boston: Beacon Press.
Lewis, R. W. B., 1955. *The American Adam: Innocence, Tragedy and Tradition in the Nineteenth Century*, Chicago: Chicago University Press.
Martínez, Julio A. and Francisco A. Lomelí, 1985. *Chicano Literature: A Reference Guide*, Westport, CT: Greenwood Press.
Meier, Matt S. and Feliciano Ribera, 1993. *Mexican Americans/American Mexicans: From Conquistadors to Chicanos*, New York: Hill and Wang.
Mirandé, Alfredo, 1985. *The Chicano Experience: An Alternative Perspective*, Notre Dame, IN: University of Notre Dame Press.
Muñoz, Carlos, 1989. *Youth, Identity, Power: The Chicano Movement*, London and New York: Verso.
Paz, Octavio, 1972. 'Eroticism and Gastrosophy', *Daedalus: Journal of the American Academy of Arts and Sciences*, vol. 101, no. 4 (Fall), pp. 67–85.
Paz, Octavio, 1990. *The Labyrinth of Solitude*, London: Penguin Books.
Peñalosa, Fernando, 1980. *Chicano Sociolinguistics, A Brief Introduction*, Rowley, MA: Newbury House Publishers, Inc.
Reichstein, Andreas, 1989. 'Was there a Revolution in Texas in 1835–1836?', *American Studies International*, vol. XXVII, no. 2 (October), pp. 66–86.
Rieff, David, 1988. *Going to Miami: Exiles, Tourists and Refugees in the New America*, London: Bloomsbury Publishing Ltd.
Rodríguez, Joe, 1981. 'The Chicano Novel and the North American Narrative of Survival', *Denver Quarterly*, vol. 6, no. 3 (Fall), pp. 64–70.
Rodriguez, Richard, 1988. *Hunger of Memory: The Autobiography of Richard Rodriguez*, New York: Bantam Books, rpt.

Rodriguez, Richard, 1990. 'Night and Day', in Ronald Eyre et al. (eds), *Frontiers*, London: BBC Books, pp. 204–39.
Romero, Rolando J., 1993. 'Border of Fear, Border of Desire', *Borderlines: Studies in American Culture*, vol. 1, no. 1 (September), pp. 36–70.
Said, Edward W., 1990. 'Yeats and Decolonization', in Terry Eagleton, Fredric Jameson and Edward W. Said (eds), *Nationalism, Colonialism, and Literature*, Minneapolis: University of Minnesota Press, pp. 69–95.
Said, Edward W., 1994. *Culture and Imperialism*, London: Vintage.
Schlesinger, Arthur M., 1992. *The Disuniting of America: Reflections on a Multicultural Society*, New York and London: W. W. Norton and Co.
Shirley, Carl R., 1989. 'Chicano History', in Francisco A. Lomelí and Carl R. Shirley (eds), *Chicano Writers, First Series*, Detroit: Gale Research Inc., pp. 296–303.
Simmen, Edward (ed.), 1971. *The Chicano: From Caricature to Self-Portrait*, New York: The New American Library, Inc.
Smith, Andrea Lynn, 1992. 'Multi-Functional Code-Switching in North American Rap Songs: A Preliminary Analysis', in *Rediscovering America, 1492–1992: National, Cultural and Disciplinary Boundaries Re-examined*, Selected Proceedings, Louisiana Conference on Hispanic Languages and Literatures. 27–30 February, Louisiana State University, Baton Rouge, pp. 245–60.
Winchell, Mark Royden, 1980. *Joan Didion*, Boston: Twayne Publishers.

13

Border Theory and the Canon
Debra A. Castillo

There is a curious undertone to many recent discussions of border theory in general, and Mexican–US border theory in particular, that profoundly shades how we read border texts, as well as to some degree predetermines what texts enter into this dialogue and thereby constitute the newly forming canon from which we choose our examples. From the Mexican side, one aspect of this phenomenon is the displacement of writers *from* the border – who, subject to small press runs and inadequate distribution, are less well known and tend to be associated with 'regional' themes – by centrist writers *about* the border (Carlos Fuentes's *Frontera de cristal* and Laura Esquivel's *Como agua para chocolate* are salient recent examples) and by border writers displaced to the centre of the country (Silvia Molina's *La familia vino del norte*) whose work is widely read and distributed, while also fitting more neatly into dominant culture constructions/inventions of 'borderness'. From the US side, there is a notable privileging of English-dominant oppositional Chicana thinker-poets like Gloria Anzaldúa in course syllabi, elite journals, and in texts by high-powered theoreticians like Homi Bhabha, in many of which manifestations concrete border consciousness is otherwise unfortunately slight, and reference to Spanish-language border texts and theory even slighter.

Even in well-informed current discussions, Mexico's northern border's remoteness and relative isolation from the two contemporary dominant national discourses (Mexico, US) offer intriguing opportunities for speculative projection from both the Distrito Federal and the District of Columbia. And while these two sets of discussions often occur in a parallel manner, in the best of such work border theorization necessarily requires a transcultural dialogue between these two dominant cultural discourses *and* between the resistant voices within these two dominant cultures by which border culture is invented, projected as an imaginary space, and reread in the engagement between texts. Much of the discourse of/from the border has what I have elsewhere called a 'shadowtext' quality, that is, from a space ambiguously in/outside dominant discourse(s), it echoes those issues that both societies uneasily abject or repress or, curiously, celebrate, often through an exoticizing lens. Thus, from both sides of the US–Mexico border, the region has been submitted to intense scrutiny both as an apocalyptic space of a rejected past/present, which is often nevertheless a perversely attractive one (this is particularly true in popular culture and media representations), and as the best hope for a utopic project for the future (in high theory recuperations of the metaphor of the border as well as in some government projections). At the same time, as Mexican border scholar María-Socorro Tabuenca Córdoba writes, for scholars working in Mexico,

> it is difficult to conceive of the border simply as a metaphor at the very moment in which we are seeking conceptual frameworks for the analysis of border literature. And if border literary expression in Mexico is someday reduced to simply being a metaphor, it will be necessary for us to find out the direction of such metaphor. (Tabuenca Córdoba, 1995/96, p. 151)

While I cannot hope to sort out the complexities of these practices in such a short study, I would like to respond to Tabuenca Córdoba's call for a more rigorous analysis of the vectors of border metaphorizing through a quick review of a few seminal texts in border theory, and to signal the processes by which border theorization seems to necessarily require a transcultural dialogue between dominant cultural discourses in which the border culture is invented or imagined. I will then read a pair of short stories from Alicia Gaspar de Alba's bilingual collection, *The Mystery of Survival* (1993) and conclude with a few speculations on the implications of such works in US and, marginally, Mexican canon construction.

Let us look first at the utopic image familiar to us from so much border theorization. In their introduction to a recent *Border Theory* volume, David Johnson and Scott Michaelson summarize recent contributions to the astonishingly popular theoretical formulation of border studies. They note the hundreds of conferences, articles and books organized around this topic, making it what they call 'one of the grand themes of recent political liberal-to-left work across the humanities and social sciences' in the US. They continue, in a perceptive and pointed conclusion:

> In the majority of this work, interestingly, the entry point of 'the border' or 'the borderlands' goes unquestioned, and, in addition, often is assumed to be a place of politically exciting hybridity, intellectual creativity, and moral possibility. The borderlands, in other words, are *the* privileged locus of hope for a better world. (Johnson and Michaelson, 1997, pp. 2–3)

I think Johnson and Michaelson are absolutely accurate in this summary, and only add to it that, interestingly enough, the general direction of this liberal-to-left work exactly inverts the traditional dominant culture (both US and Mexican) stereotypes about the border as a place of deplorable cultural mixing, intellectual and creative vacuum, and immoral depravity: the equal and alternative apocalyptic vision. In these more recent theoretical recuperations of the border, the characterization as a 'locus for hope' can occur precisely only to the degree that the US–Mexico border's concrete location is undermined and the border region becomes 'u-topic', a floating signifier for a displaced self.

This ambiguously located but vaguely utopic and moralizing quality undergirds Michel de Certeau's 'Californie, un théâtre de passants'. Written for a French audience, upon de Certeau's return to France and French after two-and-a-half years in San Diego, the article describes the author's Californian writing block and the release from that inability to write once back in the homeland, and does so by positioning itself with reference to yet another text, a poem in which California becomes an imaginary space:

> Voici deux ans et demi que je suis en Californie. Jusqu'ici je me suis abstenu d'en écrire. Là-bas, les phrases se perdent dans les rouleaux du Pacifique ... De retour à France, j'ai l'impression que pays lunaire d'où je viens ne peut pas s'introduire ni se dire dans le texte serré de mes villages parisiens .... Peut-être faudrait-il décrire la Californie comme un songe, à la maniére d'Edgar Morin dans son *Journal de Californie*, poème d'un pays imaginaire. (de Certeau, 1981, p. 10)

Strikingly, de Certeau can only write about California from France, for a French audience that is incapable of understanding a place so foreign, approaching it metaphorically through a poem in which California becomes an imaginary country. If, as Tabuenca Córdoba asserts, it is important to discover the direction of the guiding metaphor for the construction of border theory, then de Certeau's orientation is clearly eastward, back in Paris, where writing can occur, rather than in the too-real California that swallows up his commentary. Furthermore, he can only write about California as a certain kind of fictional effect, filtered through the metaphorical appropriations of poetic expression. It is interesting too, to note that the dominant image he chooses to organize this discussion, 'théâtre de passants', evokes US California's most famously stereotypical association with a certain Hollywoodesque theatricalized play of identity, alongside Mexican California's stereotypical association with illegal migrants, who in their efforts to avoid the border patrol not only attempt surreptitious border crossings, but also hope to 'pass' as US nationals.

Certainly it is this multiply textually shadowed French appropriation of an imaginary country that Néstor García Canclini finds so postmodernly productive in his own reading of the border area, and the utopic thrust Johnson and Michaelson identify as typical of much border theory is consonant with work inspired by Néstor García Canclini's much cited *Culturas híbridas (Hybrid Cultures)*. In García Canclini's study, the last chapter, focusing on the border city of Tijuana, describes that urban centre, along with New York City, as 'uno de los mayores laboratorios de la posmodernidad' (García Canclini, 1989, p. 293; 'one of the biggest laboratories of postmodernity' [García Canclini, 1995, p. 233]). It is also, in an alternative metaphor, 'la casa de toda la gente' ('everyone's house'). Here Tijuana is both exceptional and paradigmatic, both not-Mexico and globally transcendent. Tijuana is everyone's house precisely because in this formulation it is not a symbolic house at all, but rather a huge laboratory for aesthetic contemplation from outside, where scientists can go to do field work in postmodern reality effects. I suspect that Welchman, in his study of border culture, would categorize García Canclini's version of a border theory alongside the position he aligns with the Baudrillardian spectacle in which '"home" is thus evaporated' and the '"borderama" is vaunted ... as the governing trope of the postmodern' (Welchman, 1996, p. 175). Please note Welchman's appropriately San Diegan scare quotes as ironic commentaries on this archetypal first world po-mo position which, whether it comes from central Mexico (García Canclini) or mainstream US (the studies cited by Johnson and Michaelson), tend toward a similar evacuation of content in favour of privileging the border region as an abstract site for progressive cultural work.

This finding is also consonant with the conclusions in Walter Mignolo's influential article, 'Posoccidentalismo: el argumento desde América Latina', ('Postoccidentalism: The Argument from Latin America') in which this Latin Americanist scholar proposes the generation of a border epistemology from the various Third World spaces in order to help reconfigure understandings of the legacy of colonialism in the Americas writ large. Mignolo rejects the US-European based 'orientalist' post-colonial model in favour of the concept of 'occidentalism', which he borrows from Venezuelan scholar Fernando Coronil, expanding Coronil's project to a revised epistemological underpinning for the analysis of the colonial enterprise. In this effort, the metaphor of the border serves a crucial role. Mignolo recurs to the old Sarmientian opposition of civilization and barbarism and, tying it to a brief excursus on Anzaldúa, calls for the revindication of la fuerza de la frontera que crea la posibilidad de la barbarie en negarse a sí misma como barbarie-en-la-otredad; de revelar la barbarie-en-la-mismidad que la categoría de civilización ocultó; y de generar un nuevo espacio de reflexión que mantiene y trasciende el concepto moderno de razón. (Mignolo, 1998, p. 157; 'the force of the border which creates the possibility for barbarism to deny itself as barbarism-in-otherness; to reveal the barbarism-in-the-self that the category of civilization occulted; and to generate a new space of reflection that maintains and transcends the modern concept of reason.')

Following upon Mignolo's work in this essay and other related studies, critics like Abril Trigo wax even more abstractly poetic: 'la frontera es marca de la Historia, la frontería habilita memorias fragmentarias; la frontera sutura (a) la epistemologia moderna' (Trigo, 1997, p. 81; 'the border is the mark of History, the borderlands habilitate fragmentary memories; the border sutures modern epistemology'). For writers like Mignolo and Trigo, the border most aptly serves as a foil to define the self, which at the same time suggests its containment within the boundaries of a single human body, and allows it to partake of a free-floating unanchoredness. It has a fluctuating quality that makes it a perfect objective correlative for concepts ranging from liminality and psychic repression to a figure for a Foucauldian heterotopic space. To the degree that border theory approaches the inaccessible edges of pure transgression, it dissolves into an indeterminate quality: something like a transcendental grammar or mathematical formula. Says Trigo: 'la frontera es sólo una función' (Trigo, 1997, p. 72; 'the border is only a function'), and later: 'es fácil, sin duda, incurrir en la fetichización de este no-lugar fronterizo en tanto *locus* privilegiado de producción de conocimiento' (Trigo, 1997, p. 79; 'it is doubtlessly easy, to incur in the fetishization of this no-place borderlands as a privileged locus for the production of knowledge'). In this manner, Trigo takes a debatable statement ('la frontera es sólo una función') and assumes it as the grounding for further extension: functionality as a privileged site, but only if the border is understood as a metaphor rather than a specific place. However, one could argue, *pace* Trigo, that if indeed the border can be reduced to a mere floating functionality, then the oxymoronic quality of a no-place (utopic) space as an alternative site for knowledge production offers not an alternative epistemology, but only a slightly disguised version of the West's most traditional reasoning. This unrecognized complicity with older forms of knowledge production is one of the more worrisome qualities of much abstract theorizing, and points not only to an evacuation of concrete meaning, but also to an unconscious complicity with rejected structures such as the civilization and barbarism model evoked by Mignolo, or the fetishization metaphor deployed by Trigo.

If the border is insufficiently actualized in works like those of Mignolo, Trigo, García Canclini, de Certeau, et al., as a conceptual tool, it poses another kind of problem for the work of other well-known border thinkers, where the concept of the borderlands can be too easily recuperated into a certain type of cultural nationalist discourse. Johnson and Michaelson ask: 'Of what use, finally, are concepts like "culture" and "identity" if their invocation, even in so-called multicultural contexts, is also exclusive, colonial, intolerant?' On the US side, the contributors to Johnson and Michaelson's border theory volume quite rightly question, as the editors note, 'the *value* of the border, both as cultural indicator and as a conceptual tool', finding 'the identity politics of border studies' most prominent instantiations naive and wanting in quite similar ways' (Johnson and Michaelson, 1997, pp. 29, 31). Benjamin Alire Saenz trenchantly argues this point in his critique of Anzaldúa's canonical text *Borderlands/La Frontera*, which he sees as a dangerously escapist romanticization of indigenous cultures, offering little of practical value to today's urban Chicanos/as (Saenz, 1997, pp. 85–86). This problem is, of course, not unique to Anzaldúa; Johnson's article in the same volume describes the process by which Octavio Paz's definition of Mexicanness is produced by crossing the border into the United States and fetishizing that act of crossing as a psychic journey in understanding the national and personal self as a cultural product. Says Johnson:

> On either side of the border, on both sides of the border, there is one cultural identity; however it is defined, in whatever terms it is disclosed, it is nevertheless *one* – it is *our* identity. And even if on either side of the border there is more than one cultural identity, each one will be located within the horizon of a certain discretion; each will be found in its own place, bordered by the dream of its proper univocity. Such is the effect of Paz's border. ... 'we' will only find ourselves there, awaiting us on the other side of the border. (Michaelson and Johnson, 1997, pp. 133–34)

Johnson's reading of Paz reminds us of striking similarities between the Mexican thinker's 1950s meditation on Mexicanness and Mignolo's 1990s discussion of border epistemology as a play of self and other. Despite generational and ideological differences, for both Paz and Mignolo the most salient quality of the border is that the act of crossing serves the psychic function of reflection. The border itself becomes a mirror exacting knowledge of the self and the other, but most importantly, as a reinscription of the self in the other, of knowledge of the self.

This highly abstract and metaphorical theoretical approximation to border theory is not widely accepted by border writers and artists. One concrete example of the operations of this presumed univocity, this unrecognized intolerance, as projected from the Mexican side is provided by the history of the Border Art Workshop/Taller de Arte Fronterizo (BAW/TAF). Founded in 1984 by performance artist Guillermo Gómez Peña to bring together Mexican and US border artists, Chicanos and non-Chicanos, many of the Mexican nationals dropped out. Explains Chicano artist David Avalos:

> some resistance to the BAW/TAF came from Tijuana artists. They said, hey, we don't think that the border is this wonderful place of exchange. We can't dispense with our nationality, so we can't join the parade. ... The BAW/TAF has the perspective of the USA, as do so many of the notions of border that we consume. (Avalos, 1996, p. 198)

Other critics have succinctly pointed out how Gómez Peña's phenomenal success in the US academic scene as the representative border artist/thinker – when, ironically, he is considered in the border area an outsider to their cultural circles – has created the conditions for conjoining dominant cultural discursive practices that define 'hybridity' and determine the value ascribed to this project in the metaphorized community. For example, Eduardo Barrera states, 'Gómez Peña fabricates his border by drinking from the same theoretical watering holes as the academics who test their arguments with his texts. ... Gómez Peña's border turns into the Border of García Canclini and Homi Bhabha. (Barrera, 1995, p. 16), and Tabuenca Córdoba adds: 'it is ironic to note how hegemonic critics such as García Canclini validate Gómez Peña by accepting the latter as "the fronterizo" while presenting Tijuana as the representation of "the" hybrid space' (Tabuenca Córdoba, 1995/96, p. 153). What is needed, these border critics suggest, is that such well-received and respected writers rethink more thoroughly the epistemological status of their own discursive practices. Too often, these theoretical reimaginings, overtly resistant to their respective US and Latin American dominant cultures although writing from within them, define an ideological longing projected on to a specific space that must remain, in this theory at least, both diffusely utopic and concretely sited (but incompletely known). The actual border, so distant from mainstream centres of theory production in both the US and Mexico, offers itself all too neatly as the very metaphor of this desired fluidity for thinkers who have lived with their backs to its concrete reality.

In contrast with the liberal-to-left theory producers, the alternative and more apocalyptic popular culture concern about the border figures an anticipated future that is also and at the same time a refused past. In using the word 'refused' here, I am thinking in terms of refusal as both a noun and a verb (Trinh Minh-ha has already made this connection in another context; 1996, p. 6), as well as an inadequate suturing: re-fuse, fusing together two disparate materials that continually come unstuck. The border in this sense reflects those stereotypes about itself that each society has refused, while readmitting the stereotypes about the refused other; it also reflects the border as a well known site of refusal – the literal and figural dump for each society's urban, industrial, toxic and sexual wastes. And yet, because the refused (repressed) always returns in some future moment, because the refuse is inextricably linked to the most personal and private details of modern life, dominant cultures' refusal is doomed to shadow itself, past and future. Trinh says:

> If, despite their location, noun and verb inhabit the two very different and well-located worlds of designated and designator, the space between them remains a surreptitious site of movement and passage whose open, communal character makes exclusive belonging and long-term residence undesirable, if not impossible. (Trinh, 1996, p. 6)

To speak about the border in such a context is to empty it out, retaining the projected residue of a refused and powerful violence. Cities like Tijuana and Juárez almost too neatly conflate symbolic geographic and moral exclusions from the healthy body of the state. From both sides of the border, these cities represent that tacky and vile and threatening thing that middle-class morality must resist, and cannot stop talking about. This latent violence is echoed even in the US tourist imaginations, where the border frequently figures as a sort of cinematic Wild West outpost, and in centrist Mexican conceptions, where it persists as a convenient trope for provincial cities full of violent men and lawless women.

In her discussion of the sexual interface of colonial encounters, Ann Laura Stoler offers a helpful point of departure for an analysis of this trope. Her work focuses on what she calls the 'analytic slippage between the sexual symbols of power and the politics of sex', and asks the important questions: 'Was sexuality merely a graphic substantiation of who was, so to speak, on the top? Was the medium the message, or did sexual relations always "mean" something else, stand in for other relations, evoke the sense of *other* ... desires?' (Stoler, 1997, p. 346). Despite, or perhaps because of its shocking physicality, control and manipulation of the sexualized trope serves both central Mexico and US dominant discourses as a salient instrument of textual authority in constructing and controlling discussions about the dangerous attractions of a degraded border reality.

Writing from Mexico City, both Néstor García Canclini and Carlos Monsiváis ask about methodologies for associating popular culture with national identity formation. Both writers also signal the danger and opportunity involved in the material and commercial qualities of deploying certain theatricalized roles as saleable iconic representations: what Olalquiaga in her essay on 'Vulture Culture' calls 'the displacement of referentiality by simulation' and the 'valorization of surface, immediate gratification, and highly iconographic codes over the tradition of depth, contemplation, and symbolic abstraction' (Olalquiaga, 1996, pp. 92, 94). Both García Canclini and Monsiváis register and discuss the dominant Mexican culture's concern that a contaminated, Disneyfied version of popular culture will obstruct access to real national culture, and stifle progress. Among the oppositions these authors set up between Mexico and the First World, they signal the still-current debates around the poles of colonizer versus colonized and cosmopolitanism versus nationalism. In a parallel manner, Monsiváis elaborates on the binary oppositions still undergirding official national understandings of the conflict between central Mexico and the provinces. In this view, the conflict capital versus province carries with it the baggage of civilization versus barbarism, culture versus desolation, national consolidation versus aborted history. New complicating factors make these dichotomies harder and harder to maintain; both authors point to demographic explosion, industrial development extending into formerly isolated zones, the influence of mass media, creeping Americanization 'tan temida desde la ingenuidad y tan sacralizada desde el consumo' (Monsiváis, 1992, p. 201; 'so feared by the ingenuous and so sacralized from the point of view of consumption'), and, in more general terms, the 'deslocalización de los productos simbólicos por la electrónica y la telemática, el uso de satélites y computadoras en la difusión cultural' (García Canclini, 1989, p. 289; 'the delocalization of symbolic products by electronics and telematics, and the use of satellites and computers in cultural diffusion' [1995, p. 229]).

Briefly, then, the border becomes the space where popular culture icons of Mexicanness can be reified, refried and sold, so long as these iconic representations also concatenate with US cultural stereotypes of Mexican identity in their Disneyfied variations. It is also that utopic space where high culture dramas of identity can play themselves out. Mexican centrist culture fears border contamination; the border becomes the realm of fearful possibility and of rejected affinities. Yet, by representing for both cultures the place of opportunity and the site of refusal, the border region also slips outside the norming processes of popular culture absorption. As Michel de Certeau notes, '"Popular culture" presupposes an unavowed operation. Before being studied, it had to be censored. Only after its danger had been eliminated did it become an object of interest' (de Certeau, 1986, p. 119). He concludes:

> This takes us to the root of the problem: popular culture can only be grasped in the process of vanishing. ... These blank spots outline a geography of the *forgotten*. They trace the negative silhouette of the problematics displayed on black and white in scholarly books. (de Certeau, 1986, p. 131)

Furthermore, regardless of the effects of industrialization and modernization that have radically changed the economy of the border region, García Canclini finds it necessary to remind his readers of the recent past, if only to tell us that this past is no longer representative of contemporary reality, tracing in a particularly graphic manner this scholarly geography of that which must – and must not – be forgotten. García Canclini dates the reformation of the old image to a recent shift in public perception: 'Desde principios de siglo hasta hace unos quince años, Tijuana había sido conocida por un casino ..., cabarets, dancing halls, liquor stores a donde los norteamericanos llegaban para eludir las prohibiciones sexuales' (García Canclini, 1989, p. 294; 'From the beginning of the century until fifteen years ago, Tijuana was known for a casino ..., cabarets, dance halls, and liquor stores where North Americans came to elude their country's prohibitions on sex' [1995, p. 234]). In this way, the illicit relations between US men and border women are relegated to the past. In effect, then, the Mexico City-based scholar sets up a contrast between the distanced and romanticized calumny that overlays the area through the images of the past as a depraved female and the contrasting image of macho modern industry. The rattled or vampiric whore becomes the rejected image that must be obsessively called to memory along with the abjuration that it is no longer either accurate or adequate.

Interestingly enough, in this manner, the city offers a prominent example of the operations of centrist historical discourse that have been so ably dissected by Benedict Anderson, although Anderson's work develops without the necessary additional nuance of attention to that history's gender politics: 'Having to "have already forgotten" tragedies of which one needs unceasingly to be "reminded" turns out to be a characteristic device in the later construction of national genealogies' (Anderson, 1991, p. 201). Stoler would add to this analysis a reminder of the significance of gender politics in the construction of these historical models. When we turn back to the border with these insights in mind, it is striking how consistently in these discussions images of sneaky invading hordes are linked to phobias about female sexuality and disguised in dominant culture's fears of/celebrations of social change. Striking too is the consistency in evocations of a historical amnesia tied to figures of a refused and denied historicity. These issues are given particularly sharp attention in those works by Mexican- and US-based border writers whose works grapple seriously and directly with the consequences of a doubled linguistic and historical heritage.

Alicia Gaspar de Alba was born in El Paso, and wrote her collection of short stories *The Mystery of Survival* in the 1980s as she moved from El Paso to Juárez to other cities in both Mexico and the US. Her work, both in this collection of stories and in her poems, is less easily recuperable to the emerging Chicana canon than that of fellow creative writers like Helena Viramontes or Sandra Cisneros, partly because her aggressively bilingual style poses a serious course-adoption dilemma to the primarily Anglophone institutional structure for most such courses in the US. At the same time, both US Spanish Departments and the Latin American literature programmes have been slow to grasp the possibilities for exploring literary expression in which the play between two languages and two cultures is at the core. Gaspar de Alba's work can in some sense be compared to that of fellow Texan Rolando Hinojosa Smith, who is one of the central figures in the Chicano canon. Hinojosa Smith's commitment to recuperating the orality of the Texas–Mexico border is evident in aggressively bilingual works like his classic *Klail City y sus alrededores* (winner of the Casa de las Americas prize) and his comic masterpiece *Mi querido Rafa*. However, it is important to note that his work has entered the US canon in the English renditions that precisely and unfortunately flatten out the possibilities of the play of and tensions between the two languages spoken by the characters in his novels. On another front, both sides of the question of the place of Spanish language texts in the US literary canon have been forcefully and clearly argued by Chicano critics in, for example, the difference of opinion between Bruce-Novoa and Arteaga on the one hand, and Calderón and Saldívar on other with reference to the inclusion or exclusion of colonial conqueror-writers like Cabeza de Vaca and Pérez de Villagrá in the Chicano canon. Ironically, Cabeza de Vaca (along with Columbus) is included in *The Heath Anthology* – the exception to the generally unwritten rule that US literature is only what occurs in English. It is neither surprising nor particularly original for me to note that literary canons prefer sharp delineations, both linguistic and national. Using the example of the *Heath Anthology of American Literature* as a typical instance of the ideological underpinnings of canon consolidation, Johnson observes:

> Mexican literature, on the one hand, will be written in the shadow of the border; US literature, or so-called American literature, on the other hand, will

also take place there, but on the other side, on *our side*. ... The borders separating these two literatures remain necessarily secure. ... *The Heath Anthology* extends the notion of American literature only as far as English allows it: there will be no text, no 'literature' included in the *Heath* that does not appear in English. There will be no text produced on the other side, *el otro lado*. ... [T]here will be no American literature in any other language, in any other place. (Johnson, 1997, p. 147)

The same point can be made with respect to the Mexican literary establishment, which has generally relegated border writing to some space outside the canon of national literature in that country. Certainly it is true that border theoreticians tend to explicitly reject this monolingual and hegemonic vision in favour of a more fluid model that asks for a consideration of the borderlands as a bi-national and bilingual space of physical crossing and cultural translation. Yet, frequently, as Tabuenca Córdoba acutely observes, actual literary and cultural practice remains firmly within national boundaries. Using Héctor Calderón and José David Saldívar's *Criticism in the Borderlands* as an instance of this unexplored national bias even in explicitly contestatory texts, she writes:

en efecto, el libro se dedica a desarticular las fronteras del discurso monolítico de la 'American Literature'. ... Sin embargo, la distribución de planos de ese mapa global se ciñe sólo a lo local: a Estados Unidos, y su 'criticism *on* the borderlands' se restringe a las fronteras del sistema sociopolítico estadunidense. (Tabuenca Córdoba, 1997, p. 88; 'in effect, the book dedicates itself to disarticulating the borders of the monolithic discourse of American Literature. ... Nevertheless, the distribution of planes on this global map is tied only to the local: to the United States, and their criticism on the borderlands restricts itself to the borders of the US sociopolitical system.')

Johnson and Michaelson would agree. In their terms, such analyses define a practice by which 'a border is always crossed and double-crossed, without the possibility of the "trans"cultural' (Johnson and Michaelson, 1997, p. 15).

Two of the eleven stories in *Mystery of Survival* are written entirely in Spanish. One, 'El pavo', focuses on a child's anticipation of the mainstream US holiday of Thanksgiving; the other, 'Los derechos de la Malinche', offers a poetic meditation on that much discussed indigenous woman from the early sixteenth-century conquest of Mexico by Spain. Another sequence of stories, focused on the *curandera* Estrella González, rely for their impact on a de-exoticized acceptance of the powers of this traditional healer. In each case, the weighted choice of Spanish or English or 'Spanglish' in these stories evokes the tensions of living in two languages and two cultures, languages that conflict not only with each other, but also with the presumed cultural underpinnings that, in the border zone, are frequently highly charged. This tension is heightened by the interlinked nature of the stories which gives them, as Cordelia Candelaria has already noted in her introduction to the volume, the quality of a 'loosely woven novel' (Candelaria, 1993, p. 3), creating even more of an awareness of the jostling of different voices and different languages against each other.

In effect, as the counterposition of the Thanksgiving and the Malinche stories suggests, at question in Gaspar de Alba's work is a deeper interrogation of the nature of historical origins for national and cultural identity claims. Gaspar de Alba's narrative is marked in a particular manner by her own social commitment, her own imbrication in a border reality that has left the northern border of Mexico out of official histories of that country, and at the same time has left Chicano history out of official histories of the United States. Doubly set adrift from official historiography, the Chicana writer attempts to piece together an alternative, rooted, genealogical tale, only to come up against the flotsam and jetsam of haunted shadowtexts from both sides of the border (the Pilgrims, the conquistadors) that tend to substitute for other forms of historical reconstruction.

The twinned themes of memory and destiny are repeated over and over in the book, in Spanish and in English, often associated with some variation of the proverb that serves as epigraph to the collection and appears textually in the first story, stencilled on to a whitewashed wall in Querétaro: 'El pueblo que pierde su memoria pierde su destino'. The child narrator in that story asks her mother what it means, and her mother impatiently responds: 'I don't know. ... Mexican proverbs don't mean anything anymore' (Gaspar de Alba, 1993, p. 12). Pointedly, the loss of meaning has a good deal to do with the loss of language, and also with the willed memory loss involving the mother's refusal to acknowledge her daughter's abuse at the hands of her stepfather. This intentional forgetfulness, this encrypting of memory, results in the creation of the Pandora's box or memory piñata that serves as one of the book's leitmotivs. By the end of the volume, with 'Facing the Mariachis', one of the linked series of stories involving Estrella Gónzalez, the author adds to this discussion the nuanced and explicitly female alternative genealogical tale involving a recuperation of memory through the deliberate creation of the child/future story-teller, Xochitl, implicitly counterposing Xochitl to Malinche as alternative textual strategies.

In the classic telling of the Malinche story/myth, the indigenous woman betrays her people to the Spanish conqueror by serving both as interpreter and mistress for Hernán Cortés; 'malinchista' in Mexican usage evokes the sense of an unpatriotic betrayal of the nation to foreign interests. Octavio Paz's seminal analysis of Malinche as the icon of Mexicanness focuses on this psychological trauma of a national identity based on a foundational betrayal that is both political and sexual. As Paz notes, the cry, '¡Viva México, hijos de la Chingada!' recognizes the implicit underlying connection between the nation and Malinche as the figure of the raped indigenous woman, between the Mexican male force and the children born of violence. In this reading, Mexicans, metaphorically born to the rape victim ('la chingada'), wake up to find themselves victims of the evil betrayer, and so have no recourse but to commit violence, including sexual violence, against women and against their fellow man so as to shore up a sagging and threatened identity as the possessor of a powerful and inviolable male body. And yet, as Paz says, in these paranoid constructions of gender and sexual norms, while 'la Chingada' is ineluctably associated with the mother, her very passivity leeches her identity and her name; she is nothing and no one; 'es la Nada' (Paz, 1959, p. 68; 'she is Nothingness' [Paz, 1961, p. 72]). If, in the complexities of national myth, the nation is both mother and whore, then national pride and perceived deficiencies in the national character derive from a common cause. Moreover, if racially inferior and sexually available women are to blame – literally or metaphorically – for society's problems, tacitly national pride is also bound up in the admission that nothing can be done to improve the situation since the powerful, handsome, yearned-for father is always already gone.

Chicano, and especially Chicana, critics and writers, including Norma Alarcón, Gloria Anzaldúa, and Ana Castillo, have turned this negative image of the indigenous woman on its head, rewriting her story as that of an empowered woman. Cortés called Malinche 'mi lengua' (my tongue), and the Chicana recuperations of the power of her native tongue and her indigenous body offer an iconic example for the potentiality of a woman who escapes the confines of the home and allows herself to speak. Thus, the image that in Mexico figures shame and betrayal becomes in Chicana theory a figure of pride and empowerment, as well as a metaphor for the bilingual resistances of the contemporary Chicana woman who is faced with a second colonial threat through the pressures of US-Anglo culture and the English language that threaten to efface her from the national Imaginary. Alfred Arteaga sees this recuperation of a usable image for cultural consolidation as a particularly urgent project in the fraught cultural contact zones of the border region:

For Mexicans and for Chicanos subjectivity is reproduced anew in the self-fashioning act of heterotextual interaction. But this sense is more acute for the Chicano than for the Mexican because the Chicano derives *being* not only from the Spanish colonial intervention but also from Anglo-American colonialism: for not only was Mexico conquered by Spain, but Northern Mexico by the United States. (Arteaga, 1997, p. 27)

At the same time, Arteaga quite rightly points out the stress points in current poetic and theoretical re-elaborations of the myth of the Malinche, especially in its most celebrated forms where, ironically, prominent Chicana lesbians (Gaspar de Alba would also be included in this distinguished body) fall back into a heterosexual metaphor of national and textual production: once again, as in Paz, textual production devolves back on to the absent authority figure, the white father.

Gaspar de Alba's story 'Los derechos de la Malinche' offers her take on this vexed international and interlingual problematic genealogy, exploring the issue of a usable past by way of an aggressively feminocentric tale that nevertheless must cede its authority to the 'barbudos', the Spanish and gringo male-dominant heterotexts. 'Los derechos de la Malinche' opens *in medias res* with the voice of the female narrator, raising at the very beginning of the narrative the question that, while suppressed, will haunt and destabilize the whole of the succeeding text: 'No me voy a disculpar. Después de tantos años, hasta nuestra lengua ha cambiado. Es posible que ni me entiendas. Es posible que mis palabras todavía estén coaguladas' (Gaspar de Alba, 1993, p. 47; 'I am not going to ask for pardon. After so many years, even our language has changed. It is possible that you don't even understand me. It is possible that my words are still coagulated'). Economically, with these few and tightly constructed phrases, Gaspar de Alba outlines the central problematics and metaphorics of this story: the response to an implicit demand for contrition, the problem of communicating across languages, the image of the blood clot that stands in for a choked narration. The narrative voice, abruptly interrupting the English flow of the majority of the stories in this volume, begins aggressively refusing to ask forgiveness. But forgiveness for what? For a traitorous reputation? A linguistic transgression? A sexual one? The uncontrite voice in refusing to ask nevertheless evokes an unstated history in which such forgiveness would more typically be begged – and perhaps grudgingly given. And yet, in the very next sentence, we are invited to wonder if indeed 'disculpas' are exactly what are at issue here – perhaps we misunderstand; after all, the language has changed: 'our' language has changed. But which language? The historical Malinche originally translated Maya to Nahuatl, and later, as her abilities grow, Nahuatl to Spanish. The narrator in this story shifts to Spanish in an Anglophone context and a predominantly English-language collection. And yet, the story is there, on the page, stubbornly written in Spanish, defiantly non-US oriented in its metaphoric base; there, as María Lugones has said in reference to her own use of bilinguality in her theoretical texts, to be understood or to be missed, so that in both sharing an understanding, and in having to skip over the text because of linguistic inability, there is an important meaning.

> If you do not understand my many tongues, you begin to understand why I speak them. ... It [introductory monologue in Spanish] is here to be appreciated or missed, and both the appreciation and the missing are significant. The more fully this playfulness is appreciated, the less broken I am to you, the more dimensional I am to you. (Lugones, 1990, p. 46)

This contestatory stance introduces a narrator who is simultaneously a contemporary woman and that much maligned and celebrated indigenous figure. In its historical evocation of the conquest tale, the story details a change of language and change of name through involuntary baptism and the imposition of a foreign spirituality: Malintzín becomes Malinche and then Marina in the wholly unwanted, terrified gesture of 'el vendido' ('the sell out') who tosses his 'gotas de ácido' ('drops of acid') in her direction in an attempt to control her (Gaspar de Alba, 1993, pp. 50–51). This cultural rape is paired with sexual abuse; indeed, sexual intercourse with the conqueror follows immediately upon baptism. Importantly, moreover, this doubled violence figures the narrator's entry into the space of narration. In the overlapping of colonial and contemporary times, of Malinche and her modern counterpart, these two elements of a spurious Catholicism and sexual abuse remain paired. Thus, the modern woman refers elliptically to sexual abuse by her father in the sordid surroundings of a movie matinee, through a parody of the Lord's Prayer: 'Tú, padre nuestro que estás en el cielo ... me alzabas la falda y me dabas el pan de cada día' (Gaspar de Alba, 1993, p. 52; 'You, our father who art in heaven ... lifted my skirt and gave me our daily bread'). Likewise, the Spanish conqueror's entirely expected use of Malinche's body is paired with the modern woman's distaste for the pressured sexual relations with her gringo boyfriend, and both experiences are dismissed with the same phrase: 'lo que pasó que ese barbudo no fue más que otro tributo a otro conquistador' (Gaspar de Alba, 1993, p. 52; 'what happened with that bearded man was no more than another tribute to another conqueror').

Yet, at the same time as the colonial Malinche and her Chicana counterpart dismiss complicity in their own abuse, they are profoundly aware of the social context in which the colonial woman, like the modern abuse victim, is made responsible for her victimization. The opening sentence of the story, with its implication that typically forgiveness would need to be given for the unstated offence, offers a clear index to this social construction by which the woman is sullied (in social terms) by the abuse visited upon her. Moreover, the bloody clot of words – an unspoken story, in another tongue – reminds us that at least at one level the rape victim is expected to keep silent and suffer in shame for her violation.

For both women, the first sign of this impending conquest is a linguistic catachresis followed by physical disgust and vomiting:

> Malintzín se empezó a marear. Le venía un ataque de palabras raras, palabras que no conocía, palabras secretas de las diosas. No quería que el extranjero escuchara su canto. ... Se le convulsionó el estomago y echó un líquido amargo a los pies del barbudo. Ya le venían las primeras sílabas. (Gaspar de Alba, 1993, p. 51; 'Malintzín began to get nauseous. An attack of strange words came upon her, words she didn't know, the secret words of the goddesses. She did not want the foreigner to hear her song. ... Her stomach convulsed and she threw up a bitter liquid at the bearded man's feet. Then the first syllables came out.')

Derrida is on the right track when he theorizes, in a discussion of Kant, the relation of the aesthetic category of the sublime and the physical experience of vomiting, and his conclusions are apposite for reading Gaspar de Alba's story as well. In his analysis, disgust in some sense stands in for that which is unassimilable. Vomit is the reappropriation of negativity by which disgust lets itself be spoken:

> What it [the logo-phonocentric system] excludes ... is what does not allow itself to be digested, or represented, or stated. ... It is an irreducible heterogeneity which cannot be eaten either sensibly or ideally and which – this is the tautology – by never letting itself be swallowed must therefore *cause itself to be vomited*. Vomit lends its form to this whole system. (Derrida, 1981, p. 21)

Derrida concludes: 'The word *vomit* arrests the vicariousness of disgust; it puts the thing in the mouth' (Derrida, 1981, p. 25). Both literally and metaphorically, then, what the white man puts into the indigenous woman – his words in her ears, his water and semen in her body – provokes disgust at that unassimilable presence which nevertheless figures the hegemonic discourse that must somehow be taken in and made one's own. It is, as Derrida and Gaspar de Alba intimate, too much to be swallowed, and therefore must be thrown up. At the same time, the colonial woman needs to hold back the pressure to give her words into the conqueror's ears, to give anything of herself or her culture to him. Thus, while disgust and vomiting give form to the system, the retention of some quality of the unassimilable creates blockages – the blood clots that choke narrative even while they retain the chameleonic power of the native woman's unspoken, unspeakable secrets.

While for the colonial woman nausea is provoked by the need to contain the words of power in the face of an alien threat, in the modern woman's experience the immediate need is to eject the foreign presence from her body, to rid herself of an invader who is nonetheless at this point, nearly 500 years after the conquest, deeply of her own body and blood – the father to whom this story is explicitly addressed:

> Te eché en seguida. Abrí la boca sobre el excusado y te dejé salir. ... No me voy a disculpar. Cuando me avisaron de tu embolia, sentí una gran calma. El coagulo de palabras en mi garganta al fin se empezó a deslizar, al fin pude soltar la sangre de tu recuerdo. (Gaspar de Alba, 1993, p. 50; 'I got rid of you immediately. I opened my mouth over the toilet and allowed you to leave ... I am not going to ask for pardon. When I was told about your embolism I felt a great calm. The clot of words in my throat finally began to break up, at last I was able to get rid of the blood of your memory.')

Here the death of the father, and the visit to the grave that frames the narrative, serves to free up, finally, the clotted narrative; the language may have changed from the words of power Malinche caught back in her throat, but in any case the vomiting up of that unassimilable presence of the disgusting allows narrative to take shape.

There is another form taken by resistance to the master discourse, one even more closely aligned with the symbolic import of the story's title than the image of vomiting. Says the modern woman at her father's grave, 'He venido a traerte tunas' (Gaspar de Alba, 1993, p. 47; 'I came to bring you prickly pears'). The prickly pear is, of course, a sweetly delicious native fruit, but one whose delicate heart must be carefully uncovered because of the cactus spines covering the protective outer peel. If, in this story, what is foreign and cannot be assimilated causes disgust and must be vomited, it would seem that the cactus fruit would stand at the opposite pole as a native source of pleasure and nourishment. Nevertheless Gaspar de Alba's use of this fruit, with its blood-red secret core and prickly exterior, rests on a different and feminocentric metaphoric turn. At the end of the story the modern narrator clarifies: 'Estas tunas son los derechos que me violaste, las palabras secretas que me tragué' (Gaspar de Alba, 1993, p. 52; 'These fruits are the rights of mine which you violated, the secret words I swallowed').

Here too, there is a carefully articulated genealogical thrust, as the modern woman's evocation of the blood-red fruits echoes the colonial woman's resistance to the force of the conqueror, her strategy for a silent opposition to his violation. The enforced silence, the secret that also becomes the defining quality of her identity and her resistance to co-option, are figured in the internalization of the image of the prickly pear, by which the narrator and her foremother define those alienated rights, those coagulated narratives, that constitute them as excluded subjects from the masculinist-driven national enterprise. These women are raped and discursively rendered abjectly apologetic or voiceless precisely so that their tongue will not be disseminated within this hegemonic structure. Yet, paradoxically, their exclusion creates the possibility not only for rhetorical rendering of difference, but real oppositional strategy. Says Santiago Castro-Gómez: 'Observarse *como sujetos excluidos* conllevaba la posibilidad de desdoblarse, observar las propias prácticas y compararlas con las práctica de sujetos distantes en el tiempo y el espacio, establecer diferencias con otros sujetos locales y producir estrategias de resistencia' (Castro-Gómez, 1998, p. 210, author's emphasis; 'To observe *as excluded subjects* carries with it the possibility of unfolding, of observing one's own practices and comparing them with the practice of subjects distant in time and space, of establishing differences with other local subjects and producing resistance strategies').

If the prickly pear is what the modern woman swallows, and, in the unclotting of the narrative, it also represents the blood she spills on her father's gravestone, this metaphorical connection becomes even more deeply layered through reference to the colonial tale. There is a homology of mouth and genitals in this story, already established in the parallels between rape and vomit, violation and secrecy. Both sites on the body become overdetermined loci of what is forced on the woman, what is resisted, what is spat out in silence. In this resistant narrative the prickly pear serves an important function in a wincingly graphic attack on the master's power:

> La Malinche no dijo nada. ... Esa noche, Marina se preparó bien. Con la ayuda de Coatlicue y Tonantzín, se irritó las paredes de su sexo con el pellejo espinoso de unas tunas, dejando que el jugo rojo de la fruta le chorreara las piernas. ... Cuando él se encontró en aquella hinchazón, en aquel nido de espinas donde su miembro se había atrapado como una culebra, sus gritos le salieron a borbotones. Nunca se había sentido Doña Marina tan dueña de su destino' (Gaspar de Alba, 1993, pp. 51–52; 'La Malinche said nothing. ... That evening, Marina prepared herself well. With the aid of Coatlicue and Tonantzín she rubbed the walls of her genitals with the spiny peel of some cactus fruits, allowing the red juice to flow down her legs. ... When he found himself in that swelling, in that nest of spines where his penis was trapped like a snake, his shouts escaped in torrents. Never had Doña Marina felt so in charge of her destiny.')

This is not a utopic tale, however. Both for Malinche and her modern counterpart, defiance is reactive: a refusal to submit passively to a conquest that has already taken place. 'Los derechos de la Malinche' begins and ends at the father's grave, suggesting that in this circular narrative the feminine voice, whether clotted or free-flowing, is still doomed to repeat the structure of violation and vomit. Furthermore, the unclotting of narrative offers purging (vomiting) of the father's memory – but it is still the father's story, like the father's gravestone, that frames the tale and dominates its telling. Survival, when that survival is marked by the inescapable presence of the father's grave serving as the only opening onto narration, offers no clear, proactive solution for the future.

In 'Facing the Mariachis', the last story in volume, Gaspar de Alba comes closer to a structural alternative to narrative-as-vomiting, but one which still retains its stubborn anti-utopic quality. This narrative tells the story of Mercedes, a Mexican woman who unburdens herself of a guilty secret to her supportive and understanding husband José, a Chicano. Mercedes was raped at 14 and forced to marry her rapist, an abusive *curandero*'s assistant, and subsequently giving birth to a deformed son she describes as a monster. With the assistance of the *curandera* Estrella González, she first poisons her child, and later her abusive husband. Yet this secret crime is for Mercedes only the prelude to another, greater secret – the payment that the *curandera* demands for her assistance in the double murder is for Mercedes to give birth to a girlchild created by the old woman with the application of her mysterious powers. Thus, Mercedes has allowed herself to be made pregnant through the offices of the *curandera* with the daughter who, according to the wise woman, will represent the living memory of her culture. This secret of a pregnancy without male intervention is the deeper crime that Mercedes is unable to confess even to her loving husband. The story ends as Mercedes, nauseous with the burden of her unconfessed guilt and her new pregnancy, haunted by wails of her dead son, leans back in her husband's arms as the mariachis play 'El niño perdido' at his request.

If we can say that the Mexican proverb 'A people that loses its memory loses its destiny' serves as the organizing theme of this volume, the final story in the collection offers a critical rereading of this project. Mercedes's child, Xochitl, is the narrative voice explicitly structuring the whole of this loosely knit sequence, and she is directly associated with the memory piñata that will rescue the destiny of her people from oblivion. In conjuring this child, the *curandera* rubs an egg over Mercedes' womb and repeats, in Spanish and in English: 'Your womb shall be the piñata. The piñata shall carry the memory. When the piñata breaks, the memory will be the destiny of she who comes' (Gaspar de Alba, 1993, p. 100). Her immaculate conception is quite obviously meant to echo the Christ story, and Xochitl's birth is tied to a recuperation and rewriting of the immemorial founding tales of Western society as a strategy for future redemption.

However, what Gaspar de Alba provides in this almost allegorical tale is not just another renegotiation of tired concepts but a strategic operation to usher in a reconceptualization as well as a reinscription of the linguistic/cultural project intimated in the whole of this collection. The prehistory of Xochitl's conception and birth forces us to rethink the whole of the volume. There are two crucial steps involved in this breaking and reconstruction of previous presuppositions: first, the revelation of the originative crime; and second, the conception of a child without male participation.

Josefina Ludmer helps us to understand the import of a fictional structure organized around and through focus on a murder, and her study of this issue is applicable point by point to Gaspar de Alba's story. In her 'Mujeres que matan' ('Women Who Kill') she writes:

> El delito en la ficción puede afectar al conjunto de diferencias porque en realidad funciona como un instrumento (teórico, si se quiere) que sirve para trazar límites, diferenciar y excluir: *un línea de demarcación que cambia el estatus simbólico de un objecto,* una posición o una figura. (Ludmer, 1996, p. 781, author's emphasis; 'Crime in fiction can affect the body of differences because it really functions as an instrument (theoretical, if one wishes) that serves to trace limits, to differentiate, and to exclude: *a line of demarcation that changes the symbolic structure of an object*, a position or a figure.')

This quality of structural and symbolic difference underwriting crime narrative and distinguishing it from other narrative forms is given another twist (what Ludmer calls 'torsión') when the murderer is a woman: 'la cadena de mujeres que matan cuenta otra vez cada vez que un grupo nuevo, un sujeto-posición diferente, se abre camino entre los intersticios de los demás' (Ludmer, 1996, p. 793; 'the chain of women who kill tells once again each time that a new group, a different subject position, is opening a path in the interstices of the others'). In Gaspar de Alba's story, this exploration of theoretical positionings, this opening into a new and different subject position, explodes on to the page with Mercedes's revelation of her murder of her monstrous child and her abusive first husband with the collaboration and complicity of the *curandera* Estrella González. This criminal twist permanently alters our perception of the stereotypical, self-abnegating Mexican housewife, and forces us to reread the entire volume again, so as to re-evaluate the other stories of women's relationships to abusive men, from Malinche's time to the present, from another perspective: that of justifiable rage and deliberative action.

Ludmer notes that this symbolic and narratological twist in fiction about women who kill often finds an analogy in the distortion of the juridical field. Like the murders to which Mercedes confesses, women's crimes tend to be domestic, private: the so-called crimes of passion. Ludmer comments that these women, in their narrative representations at least, are seldom prosecuted by the state, and infrequently brought to 'justice' in any formal or informal sense. For Ludmer, this double torsion acts both as a distortion (of the narrative underpinnings of crime fiction, of the juridical structure) and a reconfiguration: 'la pone en contacto con otras "realidades"' (Ludmer, 1996, p. 793; 'it puts her in contact with other "realities"'). This too is the case of Gaspar de Alba's characters; for it is only through the acceptance of this strange new subject position, that of the woman who has deliberately killed other human beings, that Mercedes can be pressured into the other reality: that of serving as host mother for the *curandera*'s miracle conception.

Finally, this narrative twist has further consequences, ones that carry heavy implications for larger social structures. Ludmer concludes her lucid argument with the proposal that women who kill 'son delincuentes de la verdad y de la legitimidad, los valores del estado: ... se sitúan en el campo semántico de la duplicidad' (Ludmer, 1996, p. 795; 'are delinquent from truth and legitimacy, the values of the state: ... they are situated in the semantic field of duplicity'), and thus, curiously, 'Ese abrirse camino en las diferencias es el "delito": un instrumento que traza una línea de demarcación y transforma el estatus simbólico de una figura ... y también un instrumento fundador de culturas' (Ludmer, 1996, p. 793; 'This opening of paths among differences is the "crime": an instrument that traces a lines of demarcation and transforms the symbolic status of a figure ... and also an instrument that founds cultures'). Mercedes's crime inescapably projects her into this founding role, and even in the confession of murder, and her husband's absolution for this act, she retains the secret of the price she was required to pay for her actions: agreeing to carry the child who will recuperate lost memories of the last 500 years. In the *curandera*'s words, 'only by seeding the new world with the old names will the memories come back' (Gaspar de Alba, 1993, p. 101). Estrella González's concrete reference in this passage is, of course, to the name 'Xochitl' (Nahuatl for 'flower') that she gives the baby; however, by a narrative twist, the memories that return are also the memories of previous crimes, or justifiable acts of rebellion against conquerors past and present: vomiting words in various tongues, piercing the conqueror's member with cactus spines, poisoning the abuser, aborting or eliminating the monstrous fruit of rape.

Significantly, Mercedes finds it easier to confess and expiate the old crime than to explain the, for her, even more tormenting secret of her daughter's conception. The narrative makes it clear that Mercedes sees this old crime as merely the prologue to the real story she has to tell, and cannot confess. This unconfessed crime, more than anything else, seems to catalyse the crisis at the end of the story, in which Mercedes is simultaneously tormented by the wails of her ghostly son (her murdered husband causes no twinge of conscience) and the burden of her secret pregnancy. Throughout the collection, the folkloric/mythic figure of La Llorona, the weeping woman who murdered her children in a fit of madness, haunts such intimations of a mother's guilt for abandoning her child. Here, in this final story, the tale of murder and madness is once again given a twist. Xochitl María Espinosa (the prickly last name is entirely apposite) breaks open both the piñata and the Pandora's box, releasing all the messy complexities of memory and historical imaginings, but does so, importantly, in the context of a feminocentric (if vaguely sinister) genealogy that ties recuperated memory to cultural destiny.

Anne McLeod describes the effects of feminism for women as a process of unhinging, of imagining 'antithetical relations between the parts in such a way that the ontological framework within which they have been thought comes unhinged' (McLeod, 1985, p. 59). Likewise, Gaspar de Alba's inquiry into the twists and torsions of a Mexican-American woman's narration of her doubled and duplicitous histories point toward an unhinging of both US- and Mexican-based masculinist ontological frameworks. To take this step runs the risk of becoming unhinged in its second sense as well: thus the continual flirting with madness. Gaspar de Alba's literary practice challenges readers to rethink the category of the woman as discursive subject/object outside the essentialist frame into which she has so traditionally been cast, as she also forces us to return to a question relative to the field of literary study at large, that of the struggle with and against the power of words. In putting pressure on ignored and reinscribed histories of origins, she suggests not only a model for revitalizing national and cultural mythic structures, but also a method for dislocating the hinge between linguistic and extralinguistic binaries such as the one that has exercised us over the last few pages.

This, of course, brings us back to the original question of the canon and its theoretical twists and turns. The Gaspar de Alba who resists nostalgia for a universalizing, utopic, abstract borderness, is equally careful in her stories to resist co-option into another version of the North's hermeneutic map. In these powerful texts, it is through Gaspar de Alba's reinscription of concepts of gender right in an uncompromisingly bilingual context that she exposes the weakness and bias of much Mexican, Chicano and mainstream US theoretical meditations on borders. And that resistance, of course, makes her a problematic candidate for canonicity. At the same time, thinkers throughout the Americas have become disillusioned with canonical theoretical models that were created out of and for other cultural conditions. Most importantly, the last few years have seen a widespread recognition of cultural basis and bias of a theoretical structure formerly imagined to be transparent and universal. While the power/knowledge relations remain severely unequal between theory talk and any kind of border-grounded work, the most pertinent question seems to me to be *how* to rethink issues derived from both Euro-American and Latin American theoretical discourses so as to recontextualize them for a reality that we all know is vastly distinct. This work is going forward.

Works Cited

Anderson, Benedict, 1991. *Imagined Communities: Reflections on the Origin and Spread of Nationalism*, Revised edition, London: Verso.

Arteaga, Alfred, 1997. *Chicano Poetics: Heterotexts and Hybridities*, Cambridge: Cambridge University Press.

Avalos, David, with John C. Welchman, 1996. 'Response to The Philosophical Brothel', in Welchman, 1996, pp. 187–99.

Barrera, Eduardo, 1995. 'Apropiación y tutelaje de la frontera norte', *puentelibre, revista de cultura*, vol. 4, pp. 13–17.

Candelaria, Cordelia, 1993. 'Introduction: Piñatas of Memory: Alicia Gaspar de Alba's Stories of Survival', in Gaspar de Alba, 1993, pp. 1–5.

Castro-Gómez, Santiago, 1998. 'Modernidad, latinoamericanismo y globalización', *Cuadernos americanos*, vol. 12, no. 1, pp. 187–213.

de Certeau, Michel, 1981. 'Californie, un théâtre de passants', *Autrement*, vol. 31, pp. 10–18.

de Certeau, Michel, 1986. *Heterologies: Discourse on the Other*, trans. Brian Massumi, foreword Wlad Godzich, Minneapolis: University of Minnesota Press.

Derrida, Jacques, 1981. 'Economimesis', *Diacritics*, vol. 11, no. 2, pp. 3–25.

García Canclini, Néstor, 1989. *Culturas híbridas: Estrategias para entrar y salir de la modernidad*, Mexico: Grijalbo. Trans. Christopher Chiappari and Silvia L. López, *Hybrid Cultures: Strategies for Entering and Leaving Modernity*, Minneapolis: University of Minnesota Press, 1995.

Gaspar de Alba, Alicia, 1993. *The Mystery of Survival and other Stories*, Tempe: Bilingual Press.

Johnson, David E., 1997. 'The Time of Translation', in Michaelson and Johnson, 1997, pp. 129–65.

Johnson, David E. and Scott Michaelson, 1997. 'Border Secrets: An Introduction', in Michaelson and Johnson, 1997, pp. 1–39.

Ludmer, Josefina, 1996. 'Mujeres que matan', *Revista iberoamericana*, vol. 62, nos 176–77, pp. 781–97.

Lugones, María, 1990. 'Hablando cara a cara/Speaking Face to Face: An Exploration of Ethnocentric Racism', in Gloria Anzaldúa (ed.), *Making Face, Making Soul: Haciendo Caras: Creative and Critical Perspectives by Women of Color*, San Francisco: Aunt Lute, pp. 46–54.

McClintock, Anne, Aamir Mufti and Ella Shohat (eds), 1997. *Dangerous Liaisons: Gender, Nation, and Postcolonial Perspectives*, Minneapolis: University of Minnesota Press.

McLeod, Anne, 1985. 'Gender Difference Relativity in GDR-Writing or: How to oppose without really trying', *Oxford Literary Review*, vol. 7, pp. 41–61.

Michaelson, Scott and David E. Johnson (eds), 1997. *Border Theory: The Limits of Cultural Politics*, Minneapolis: University of Minnesota Press.

Mignolo, Walter D., 1998. 'Posoccidentalismo: El argumento desde América Latina', *Cuadernos americanos*, vol. 12, no. 67, pp. 143–65.

Monsiváis, Carlos, 1992. 'De la cultura mexicana en vísperas del TLC', in Gilberto Guevara Niebla and Néstor García Canclini (eds), *La educación y la cultura ante el tratado de libre comercio*, Mexico: Nueva imagen.

Olalquiaga, Celeste, 1996. 'Vulture Culture', in Welchman, 1996, pp. 85–100.

Paz, Octavio, 1959. *El laberinto de la soledad*, Mexico: Fondo de Cultura Económica, 1980. Trans. Lysander Kemp, *The Labyrinth of Solitude*, New York: Grove, 1961.

Saenz, Benjamin Alire, 1997. 'In the Borderlands of Chicano Identity', in Michaelson and Johnson, 1997, pp. 68–96.

Stoler, Ann Laura, 1997. 'Making Empire Respectable: The Politics of Race and Sexual Morality in Twentieth-Century Colonial Cultures', in McClintock et al., 1997, pp. 344–73.

Tabuenca Córdoba, María-Socorro, 1995/96. 'Viewing the Border: Perspectives from "The Open Wound"', *Discourse*, vol. 18, pp. 146–68.

Tabuenca Córdoba, María-Socorro, 1997. 'Aproximaciones críticas sobre las literaturas de las fronteras', *Frontera norte*, vol. 9, no. 18, pp. 85–110.
Trigo, Abril, 1997. 'Fronteras de la epistemología: epistemologías de la frontera', *Papeles de Montevideo*, vol. 1 (June), pp. 71–89.
Trinh T. Minh-ha, 1996. 'An Acoustic Journey', in Welchman, 1996, pp. 1–17.
Welchman, John C., 1996. 'The Philosophical Brothel', in Welchman, 1996, pp. 160–86.
Welchman, John C. (ed.), 1996. *Rethinking Borders*, Minneapolis: University of Minnesota Press.

14

Racialism and Liberation in Native American Literature

Lee Schweninger

In Gerald Vizenor's *Landfill Meditations* (1991b), as in the earlier *Bearheart* (1990), the mixed-blood pilgrim Belladonna Darwin-Winter Catcher adheres to 'terminal creeds', stating that Indians 'are children of dreams and visions. Our bodies are connected to mother earth, and our minds are the clouds, and our voices are the living breath of the wilderness' (Vizenor, 1991b, p. 109). For accepting such stereotypes and refusing to change, she is once again fed the lethal sugar cookie; she is poisoned because, according to one of the hunters, 'Surviving in the present means giving up on the burdens of the past and the cultures of tribal narcissism' (Vizenor, 1991b, p. 113). Belladonna is unable to give up those burdens.

Belladonna repeats her story, and Vizenor thereby evokes an oral tradition; various characters tell and retell their shared stories, stories Vizenor's audience has likely heard before. At the same time that Belladonna repeats her story, Vizenor challenges stereotypes in that the story his character tells continually changes, even if only slightly. With Belladonna, he challenges 'terminal creeds', those racialist beliefs that deny the dynamic nature of a culture or a people. Through her characterization as mixed-blood who embraces an invented identity, Vizenor identifies several of the stereotypes that are imposed on Native Americans. He demonstrates the danger of such creeds and insists that readers move beyond them because 'terminal creeds are terminal diseases' (Vizenor, 1991b, p. 113). It is not new to point out that the concept 'Indian' is an invention imposed upon the aboriginal peoples of the Western hemisphere. In *The Invented Indian* James Clifton suggests that the invention results from the imposition of dominant narratives (Clifton, 1990, p. 21). Elsewhere Bernard Fontana writes,

> The 'Indian' concept has engulfed notions of individual ethnic identities so that many Indian people themselves believe that to be 'Indian' is to dance

in powwows, to wear Plains Indian war bonnets, to live in tepees, to paddle birch-bark canoes, to carve totem poles, and to be at one with the universe and mother earth. (Fontana, 1998, p. 181)

Writing about artistic representation, Julie Schimmel makes a similar point about preconceived notions of what constitutes an Indian, writing that 'Indians were not seen at all' (Schimmel, 1991, p. 150).

Such preconceived formulations predispose readers of Native American texts to ignore individuals and contemporary issues. But unfortunately, popular culture continually reinscribes such stereotypes, especially Hollywood films and many contemporary historical novels about nineteenth-century Indians. In *The Pretend Indians: Images of Native American in the Movies*, Bataille and Silet point out such stereotypes. Similarly, Jenni Calder discusses how Indians have become imaginary enemies or noble savage figures in film (Calder, 1974, pp. 39–40). According to these stereotypes, Indians – if they survive at all in contemporary consciousness – survive dressed in buckskin, living in tepees, roaming the plains in search of bison, locked in the Stone Age, and fighting or fleeing the US Cavalry. These fictitious, demeaning and dangerous stereotypes inevitably get carried over into the reading of literature, and they are dangerous because, as Duane Niathum writes, 'Stereotypic expectations break down the free play between reader and writer' (Niathum, 1987, p. 554). In *Defeathering the Indian* Emma LaRocque makes the point that stereotypes perpetuate myths and thus not only hide the truth but also prevent it. In the same vein, according to Patricia Limerick, 'Savagery meant hunting and gathering, not agriculture; common ownership, not individual property owning; pagan superstition, not Christianity; spoken language not literacy; emotion, not reason' (Limerick, 1988, p. 190). Obviously, such misinterpretations, stereotypes and inventions deny history and complexity as they replace the actual. The effect is reciprocal; stereotypes result from and contribute to racialism.

Kwame Anthony Appiah defines racialism as the tendency to

> divide human beings into a small number of groups, called 'races', in such a way that all the members of these races [are believed to share] certain fundamental, biologically heritable, moral and intellectual characteristics with each other that they [are not believed to share] with members of any other race. (Appiah, 1990, p. 276)

Such an assignation, writes Vizenor, 'does not reveal the experiences of diverse native communities' (Vizenor, 1995b, p. 1).

Given the prevalence of racialism in the American consciousness, the purpose of this chapter is, first, to suggest the problematics of that racialism and, second, to note briefly ways in which a few Native American writers attempt to dismantle it. The challenge, as formulated by Dominick LaCapra in another context, is 'to avoid racial stereotyping or uncontrolled mythologizing and come to terms with race critically and transformatively without denying the historical and political need for people of color to find effective voices and to work out necessary subject-positions' (LaCapra, 1991, p. 1). In working out these subject positions, writers face a difficult challenge, however, in that, again as articulated by LaCapra, 'it is difficult to avoid the growing tendency to substitute a commercialized exoticism or an anodyne, commodified discourse on race for problems of racial stereotyping and oppression' (LaCapra, 1991, p. 2). In the context of literature, Vizenor makes the same contention: 'Native American Indian literatures have been pressed into cultural categories, transmuted by reductionism, animadversions, and the hyperrealities of neocolonial consumerism' (Vizenor, 1989, p. 5).

Novelist and critic Louis Owens makes a similar point when he suggests that several Native American authors themselves reinforce rather than challenge stereotypes and thus finally contribute to an essentialized notion of the Indian: 'Such fiction tells the reader that the Indian is a helpless, romantic victim still in the process of vanishing just as he is supposed to do' (Owens, 1998, p. 77). Beware of 'presold, commodified Indian fiction', Owens warns (1998, p. 78). Thus, despite the resistance that Simon Ortiz, for example, has found to be an integral part of a 'nationalistic voice' of Native American literature (Ortiz, 1993, p. 67), some Native American authors, Owens would assert, continue to perpetuate racialism.

Overcoming racial stereotyping is further challenging because simply by naming or identifying a work or a selection of works as Native American literature one invites stereotypes. Despite any resistance to it, the term 'Indian' itself – or any term whose intention is to group an immensely diverse population – is both racially loaded and reductive; hence 'Indian literature' (whether called 'Native American' or 'Indian') is a concept that can not help but tend toward racialism. 'Since the original inhabitants of the Western Hemisphere neither called themselves by a single term nor understood themselves as a collectivity, the idea and the image of the Indian must be a White conception' (Berkhofer, 1978, p. 3). Vizenor points out that the term 'Indian' 'is a simulation of racialism, an undesirable separation of race in the political and cultural interests of discover and colonial settlement of new nations' (Vizenor, 1995b, p. 1).

Theorists on race and difference argue that, because establishing a canon by authors of colour is political, we must be wary. Establishing a nationalistic or ethnic literature inscribes stereotypes that must again be overcome; after all, inclusion does not necessarily or automatically eradicate marginalization. In responding to a review of his novel *Wolfsong* Louis Owens asks why the rules concerning authenticity are 'different for authors who write about Native Americans' (Owens, 1998, p. 17). There exists a spoken assumption that Indian novels must be written by 'authentic' Indians (that is, by white inventions). Owens counters this assumption by arguing that 'any novel is an *authentic fiction*. It is a tropical figuration, not the "real" thing. ... The only "real" Indians in writing by Native authors are clichéd representations of the Euramerican-constructed Indian' (Owens, 1998, p. 22, his emphasis).

As noted above, LaCapra uses the terms 'stereotyping' and 'mythologizing'; Vizenor uses the term 'simulation', arguing that the term '"Indian" is a simulation of racialism'. Vizenor borrows from the French theorist Jean Baudrillard, who contends that 'Simulation is no longer that of a territory, a referential being or a substance. It is the generation by models of a real without origin or reality: a hyperreal. ... It is the real ... whose vestiges subsist here and there.' It is a 'question of substituting signs of the real for the real itself' (Baudrillard, 1988, pp. 167–68). In the context of Native American studies, one sees Baudrillard's concept of the simulacrum at every turn. In the re-creation of the historical Chief Seattle, for example, as Denise Low points out, 'the mediated image of Seattle, a "simulacrum", perpetuates non-Indian concepts of Indian people as noble savages without distinct tribal cultures or histories. Further, the generalized Indian figure is frozen in a nineteenth-century setting in which he is powerless' (Low, 1995, pp. 407–408). In his formulation of Indian history as a cultural fiction, James Clifton identifies such simulations as springing from invented speeches or dialogues: 'One of these imaginary actors often employed as a rhetorical foil is found in the much used Adario motif, which consists of a Wise Old Indian Uttering Marvelous Lessons for the Whiteman's Edification' (Clifton, 1990, p. 39). As Berkhofer points out, 'For most Whites ... the Indian of imagination and ideology has been as real, perhaps more real, than the Native American of actual existence and contact' (Berkhofer, 1978, p. 71).

Popular culture forces these simulations and stereotypes upon mainstream readers of Native American literature. From early childhood, Americans (both Indian and non-Indian) are inundated with stereotypical depictions of the continent's first inhabitants. Prevalent derogatory stereotypes cause Indian children to believe the image rather than themselves (see Mihesuah, 1996, p. 113), and thus the image influences the reality. According to Michael Dorris,

> Frozen in a kind of pejorative past tense, these make-believe Indians are not allowed to change or in any other way be like *real* people. They are denied the dignity and dynamism of their history, the validity of their myriad and major contributions to modern society, the distinctiveness of their multiple ethnicities. (Dorris, 1982, p. vii)

Vizenor makes a similar point in an interview: '[W]e're invented and we're invented from traditional static standards and we are stuck in coins and words like artifacts. So we take up a belief and settle with it, stuck, static' (Bowers, 1981, p. 47).

Arguing that stereotypes prevent readers or moviegoers from seeing individuals, Dorris insists that 'flesh and blood Indians have been assigned the role of a popular-cultural metaphor for generations. Today, their evocation instantly connotes fuzzy images of Nature, the Past, Plight, or Summer Camp' (Dorris, 1992). In 'Indians in Aspic', Dorris asks whether literary and cinematic depictions of Indians that 'generate a bubble of sympathy' will translate into practical support for religious freedom cases, restoration of Lakota sacred lands, tribal sovereignty.

> Or will it turn out, once again, that the only good Indians – the only Indians whose causes and needs we can embrace – are lodged safely in the past, wrapped neatly in the blankets of history, magnets for our sympathy because they require nothing of us but tears in dark theater? (Dorris, 1991)

Also challenging such easy encounters with Indians, Louis Owens argues that crossing conceptual horizons can be, in fact must be, hard work: 'It is our responsibility, as writers and teachers, to make sure that our texts and our classrooms are not "safe" spaces from which a reader or student may return unchanged of unthreatened' (Owens, 1998, p. 46).

Readers must undergo change as a result of reading ethnic literatures because ethnicity *is* itself change. Racialism, a racialist attitude, denies dynamism. As Frank Shuffelton and others have pointed out, 'Ethnicity is a dynamic relation between different cultural groups.' It changes over time; that is, 'ethnicity is not a constant but an index of a cultural group's continually changing self-understanding in the face of shifting relations to the larger world' (Shuffelton, 1993, pp. 7–8). The paradoxical effect of racialism, of stereotyping, then, is to make static an ethnicity, which by definition knows no stasis. The artefacts that result from such attempts are not ethnicity but simulacrum, something that stands for the real but which is finally fake, a representation that comes to stand for and actually be thought of as real.

Owens is acutely aware of the danger of stereotyping, and he articulates the challenge: Native American writers 'must demonstrate a dexterity with the "master's tools" while simultaneously bearing and baring sufficient traces of subservient savagery to provide a kind of "ethnostalgia", or literary tourism, for the white reader' (Owens, 1998, p. 59). Owens addresses this issue throughout his novel *Wolfsong* (1991). His main character, a full-blood Salish, imagines the 'old ones' who had followed the same mountain path he walks; he

> tried to imagine himself as one of them. An image of a Plains warrior padding silently through the forest came to him and he smiled. Books and movies seldom showed Indians who looked like the Salish people of these mountains. Short, dark people, dressed in woven cedar bark weren't as exciting as Sioux warriors in eagle-feather headdresses on horseback, the sun always setting behind them. (Owens, 1991, p. 83)

In challenging one of the stereotypes that confront Indians themselves, Owens describes one who does not lend himself to simple classification: 'at the urban pow wows would be guys like the kid from Laguna Pueblo who sang and drummed and, between songs, listened to heavy metal on his earphones. That was what real Indians were like. And he was a good singer and part of a family that was in demand for all the pow wows' (Owens, 1991, p. 127).

In the context of the complexity of portraying Native Americans in realistic fiction, Berkhofer points out that

> realism in the Indian novel means the treatment of Native Americans as individuals rather than as Indians, as human beings not assemblages of tribal traits. ... Humanness not race should be the essential criterion, neither nostalgia nor sympathy per se is a substitute for knowledge. (Berkhofer, 1978, p. 106)

According to Berkhofer 'only an accurate understanding of cultural diversity and tribal detail combined with first hand experience constitutes a true basis for the realistic depiction of Native American life' (Berkhofer, 1978, p. 104).

Thomas King challenges stereotypes by providing his readers with realistic depictions and with characters who stand at the centre of his fiction. In the novel *Medicine River* (1991) King presents complexities of life for specific individuals through whom he confronts stereotypes. The story-teller Lionel James, for example, laments that his white audiences around the world are not interested in stories about contemporary Indians; rather they 'want to hear stories about how Indians used to be. I got some real good stories, funny ones, about how things are now, but those people say, no, tell us about the olden days' (King, 1989, p. 173). The chapter about Lionel's encounters with racialist cultures is itself one such funny story. Through the telling of this story, the author himself (King) becomes a sort of trickster-story-teller, teasing the reader with contemporary characters who themselves challenge stereotypes and who do not fit preconceived notions of what Indians are 'supposed' to do and be.

Faced with the potential of creating stereotypical characters as helpless victims or as Indians in aspic – in her historical novel *Mean Spirit* (1992) – Linda Hogan creates the illusive Hill People who move between two worlds. They are mystical runners and criers who have 'learned the secrets of invisibility' (Hogan, 1992, p. 258); sometimes they are seen, sometimes not; and, if they will it, the 'clearly marked' road to their settlement can simply vanish: 'They had to hide it. Too many people coming up' (Hogan, 1992, p. 304). In their illusiveness the Hill People have a two-fold effect. Since they clearly do not 'really' exist – except in an imagined or 'other' realm – they tease the reader. They seem to fit the preconceived notions but finally challenge such preconceptions in that they do not themselves exist. In their allusive- and illusiveness they both evoke and frustrate the reader's expectations of Indian fiction.

Her enigmatic Hill People notwithstanding, like King and Owens, Hogan writes a basically realistic fiction that is also self-aware. These writers know the reader's tendency to expect Indian characters to fit certain stereotypes, and they consistently frustrate that expectation. Gerald Vizenor demonstrates the same awareness, and challenges the reader with post-Indian warriors in a postmodern fiction. He forces the reader to abandon preconceptions because he celebrates mixed-blood tricksters, as one reviewer puts it, 'with sufficient adaptability to transcend the rigidity of slavish adherence to an unchanging past and to resist total rejection of the structures of that past' (Clements, 1994). In the author's own words, his stories 'overturn the static reduction of native identities' (Vizenor, 1995a, p. 142). The trickster refuses to be pressed into a cultural category, and he thereby transcends such categories.

In a review of *Landfill Meditations* Lawrence Smith writes that 'Vizenor's crossblood tricksters ... are given the opportunity to reinvent the world – and that means synthesizing the most potent elements of European cultures and Native cultures, rather than relying on foolish stereotypes "invented by missionaries"' (Smith, 1994). Indeed, Vizenor often uses characters to liberate the reader's mind with trickster stories. His characters are in motion, sometimes literally, always metaphorically. And because they are in motion, in flux, never quite literal, never totally abstract, they cannot come to represent a particular stereotype. In the story 'Almost Browne', for example, the crossblood character of the title 'learned to see the wild world as deals between memories and tribal stories', and he also learned 'to liberate his mind with trickster stories' (Vizenor, 1991b, p. 5).

Vizenor's trickster can liberate his own and the reader's mind from debilitating, limiting stereotypes. As he contrasts *motion* with *museum*, the narrator in 'Heartlines' asserts that 'trickster stories are the natural reason of our independence' (Vizenor, 1995a, p. 143). Vizenor's metaphor for motion is the Naanabozho (Trickster) Express, a tribal railroad that travels borrowed lines from the White Earth reservation to the White House in Washington, DC. Gesture Browne, trickster and founder of the railroad, asks the paradoxical when he summons 'his heirs to declare motion a tribal island, a natural tribal state' (Vizenor, 1995a, p. 152). Motion serves as Vizenor's metaphor for the impossibility of pinning down or of imposing stasis on tribal stories and cultures. If readers, observers or anthropologists cannot stop the trickster-train, they cannot stereotype. This 'express train was natural reason in motion' and served as 'a nomadic survivance' (Vizenor, 1995a, p. 152). According to Vizenor, motion is natural sovereignty. Motion is autonomous. 'Natural reason and memories are motion, and motion can never be stolen', whereas in the museum 'the sacred objects in the collection were stolen and are [ironically] more secure than tribal families on reservations' (Vizenor, 1995a, p. 152).

By their very nature, museums – like stereotypes – do not change; they lack motion; they are the epitome of stasis. According to Vizenor, artefacts are stolen and made to represent a culture that does not actually exist. In the 'Prologue' to the play *Ishi and the Wood Ducks*, Ishi comments that Kroeber 'was lonesome, a museum talker' (Vizenor, 1995c, p. 303). And because anthropologists have no stories of their own, they start museums: 'That leaves museums with stolen stories' (Vizenor, 1995c, p. 305). Jim Northrup in the story 'Looking with Ben' also confronts the reader with the lies museums tell. As Luke Warmwater tours the Smithsonian in DC he comes upon an empty diorama, so he makes a sign that reads 'Contemporary Chippewa' and steps into the empty space behind the velvet rope. 'Pretty soon, some tourists came by. They read the sign and looked up at me. ... They looked at me a long time before they went on to the next display' (Northrup, 1993, p. 159). Like Northrup, whose realistic image of a living diorama unsettles and lingers with the reader, Vizenor writes a story that can be 'imagined as a real landscape, with historical documents, and the characters seem believable at first, but their interaction is given over to chance transformations' (Vizenor, 1995a, p. 142).

Vizenor avoids easy categories; he refuses stereotypes; he resists easy interpretation, denies closure. The very open-endedness of his fiction liberates his characters and his readers from reductive stereotyping. In describing Bagese, the story-teller in *Dead Voices*, the narrator writes that 'she would never be considered traditional, or even an urban pretender who treasured the romantic revisions of the tribal past. She was closer to stones, trickster stories, and tribal chance, than tragedies of a vanishing race' (Vizenor, 1992, p. 6). Similarly, in *The Heirs of Columbus*, a novel about rights concerning stolen artefacts, 'Samana was an island in the ocean sea that would be imagined but never possessed in the culture of death', the very culture museums present. Samana is island, she is motion, and she is also a hand talker who seduces Columbus by swimming to the *Santa Maria* and relieving the Admiral's pain: 'She was a hand talker and eased his pain with lust and wild rapture; she released the stories in his blood.' According to the heirs' stories, 'Samana conceived a daughter that night', and 'Samana was born the next summer at the stone tavern near the headwaters of the great river' (Vizenor, 1991a, p. 44). Samana the daughter, Samana the mother, Samana the island itself. With the character Samana, Vizenor problematizes easy categories. She is the daughter of Columbus and the hand talker and healer (also named) Samana. Samana is also a personification of the island Samana Cay. Her very mutability, her multiple identities, keeps the reader from being able finally to characterize and thus stereotype her. She is no Pocahontas.

If Samana and Almost Browne liberate the world in stories, other characters, as suggested in the opening of this essay, offer terminal creeds, debilitating stereotypes, which imprison the mind. But such characterizations also challenge stereotypical attitudes. With Belladonna, Vizenor presents a 'crossblood' who strings together invented characteristics applied to tribal peoples, but her opinions are so cliched that Patricia Haseltine calls her 'a symbol of pan-indianism' (Haseltine, 1985, p. 43). Belladonna presents herself as a spokesperson for Indians, and reiterates that Indians are stoic nature lovers who step lightly and do not often touch each other. As tribal people, she says, 'we are raised with values that shape our world in a different light because we are tribal' (Vizenor, 1991b, p. 109).

Vizenor does not allow such static assumptions to go unchallenged. One character calls out from the crowd, insisting that hunters say the same thing about the hunt. Belladonna is also challenged by a woman who asks how Indians are different from white people. Poor Belladonna. She fumbles with her beads and falls into mouthing platitudes about Indian children not being punished, about living in larger families, about not touching each other. Finally she is reduced to declaring that 'Indians have more magic in their lives' (Vizenor, 1991b, p. 110). Again she is challenged: '[I]f you are speaking for all Indians, then how can there be truth in what you say?' (Vizenor, 1991b, p. 110). The hunter argues that 'Indians are an invention'. He says,

> You tell me that the invention is different than the rest of the world when it was the rest of the world that invented the Indian. ... An Indian is an Indian because he speaks and thinks and believes he is an Indian. The invention must not be too bad because the tribes have taken it up for keeps. (Vizenor, 1991b, p. 110)

As Belladonna and the hunter make clear, reading Vizenor teaches us that we must avoid the deceptive ease of final determinations, that we must be willing to rearrange our own as well as a fictional character's identities. Like King, Hogan and Owens, Vizenor suggests that readers (and hence a culture) must open a dialogical space for continual questioning of those identities. And like Northrup, Vizenor teaches that as serious and important as it is to raise questions of racialism, we must remember the place of humour; we must not take ourselves or our reading too seriously. The writers discussed here expose the dangers of stereotyping, of the damages of racialism: as Marie Gee in 'The Last Lecture' says:

> My skin is dark ... you can see that much. But who, in their right mind, would trust the education of their children to mere pigmentation? ... Who knows how to grow up like an Indian? Tell me that. And who knows how to teach values that are real Indian? (Vizenor, 1991b, p. 57)

Works Cited

Appiah, Kwame Anthony, 1990. 'Race', in Frank Lentricchia and Thomas McLaughlin (eds), *Critical Terms for Literary Study*, Chicago: University of Chicago Press, pp. 274–87.

Bataille, G. M. and C. Silet, 1980. *The Pretend Indians: Images of Native Americans in the Movies*, Ames: Iowa State University Press.

Baudrillard, Jean, 1988. 'Simulacra and Simulations', in Mark Poster (ed.), *Selected Writings*, Stanford: Stanford University Press, 1988, pp. 166–84.

Berkhofer, R. F., 1978. *The White Man's Indian: Images of the American Indian from Columbus to the Present*, New York: Knopf.

Bowers, N. and C. Silet, 1981. 'An Interview with Gerald Vizenor', *MELUS*, vol. 8, no. 1, pp. 40–49.

Calder, Jenni, 1974. *There Must Be a Lone Ranger: The American West in Film and Reality*, New York: Taplinger Press.

Clements, W., 1994. Review of *Dead Voices*, *American Indian Quarterly*, vol. 18, no. 2, pp. 247–48.

Clifton, James A., 1990. 'The Indian Story: A Cultural Fiction', in *The Invented Indian: Cultural Fictions and Government Policies*, New Brunswick: Transaction Press, pp. 29–47.

Dorris, Michael, 1982. 'Foreword', in A. B. Hirschfelder (ed.), *American Indian Stereotypes in the World of Children*, Metuchen: Scarecrow Press, pp. vii–ix.

Dorris, Michael, 1991. 'Indians in Aspic', *New York Times*, 24 February, no. IV, p. 17, col. 1.

Dorris, Michael, 1992. 'Noble Savages, We'll Drink to That', *New York Times*, 21 April, A23.

Fontana, B. L., 1998. 'Inventing the American Indian', in S. Lobo and S. Talbot (eds), *Native American Voices: A Reader*, New York: Longman, pp. 178–82.

Haseltine, Patricia, 1985. 'The Voices of Gerald Vizenor: Survival through Transformation', *American Indian Quarterly*, vol. 9, no. 1, pp. 31–47.

Hogan, Linda, 1992. *Mean Spirit*, New York: Ballantine.

King, Thomas, 1991. *Medicine River*, New York: Penguin.

LaCapra, Dominic, 1991. 'Introduction', *The Bounds of Race*, Ithaca: Cornell University Press.

LaRocque, Emma, 1975. *Defeathering the Indian*, Agincourt: Book Society of Canada.

Limerick, Patricia, 1988. *The Legacy of Conquest*, New York: Norton.

Low, Denise, 1995. 'Contemporary Reinvention of Chief Seattle: Variant Texts of Chief Seattle's 1854 Speech', *American Indian Quarterly*, vol. 19, no. 3, pp. 407–21.

Mihesuah, D. A., 1996. *American Indians: Stereotypes and Realities*, Atlanta: Clarity International.

Niathum, Duane, 1987. 'On Stereotypes', in Brian Swann and Arnold Krupat (eds), *Recovering the Word: Essays on Native American Literature*, Berkeley: University of California Press, pp. 552–62.

Northrup, Jim, 1993. *Walking the Rez Road*, Stillwater: Voyageur.

Ortiz, Simon, 1993. 'The Historical Matrix Towards a National Indian Literature: Cultural Authenticity in Nationalism', in Richard F. Fleck (ed.), *Critical Perspectives on Native American Fiction*, Washington: Three Continents Press, pp. 64–68.

Owens, Louis, 1991. *Wolfsong*, Norman: University of Oklahoma Press.

Owens, Louis, 1998. *Mixedblood Messages: Literature, Film, Family, Place*, Norman: University of Oklahoma Press.

Schimmel, Julie, 1991. 'Inventing the Indian', in *The West as America* Washington: Smithsonian Institution, pp. 149–89.

Shuffelton, Frank, 1993. *A Mixed Race: Ethnicity in Early America*, New York: Oxford University Press.

Smith, Lawrence, 1994. Review of *Dead Voices, American Indian Quarterly*, vol. 18, no. 2, p. 247.
Vizenor, Gerald, 1989. *Narrative Chance: Postmodern Discourse on Native American Indian Literatures*, Albuquerque: University of New Mexico Press.
Vizenor, Gerald, 1990. *Bearheart: The Heirship Chronicles*, Minneapolis: University of Minnesota Press.
Vizenor, Gerald, 1991a. *Heirs of Columbus*, Hanover: Wesleyan University Press.
Vizenor, Gerald, 1991b. *Landfill Meditations: Crossblood Stories*, Hanover: Wesleyan University Press.
Vizenor, Gerald, 1992. *Dead Voices*, Norman: University of Oklahoma Press.
Vizenor, Gerald, 1995a. 'Heartlines', in *Native American Literature: A Brief Introduction and Anthology*, Berkeley: HarperCollins, pp. 142–57.
Vizenor, Gerald, 1995b. 'Introduction', in *Native American Literature: A Brief Introduction and Anthology*, Berkeley: HarperCollins, pp. 1–15.
Vizenor, Gerald, 1995c. *Ishi and the Wood Ducks*, in *Native American Literature: A Brief Introduction and Anthology*, Berkeley: HarperCollins, pp. 299–336.

15

Ants in the System: 'Thinking Strongly' about Native American Stories

Robert Gregory

> Was it your grandmother who taught you this art?
> It's no such a thing, art. It's spirit.
> (Sarris, 1994, p. 2)

Certainly when talking about American Literature we should include Native American Literature. But there are better reasons for this 'should' than simple inclusiveness. Native American literature incorporates a critical and theoretical tradition that is both profound and accessible (in two senses: it is jargon-free and it is included within the 'stories' themselves). But it is not accessible right away. It seems to me that 'text' is not the word for these things. For a number of reasons, one of which is that they are not like woven cloth, whole or otherwise, but more like jerky: very old and dried up, these sometimes funny-looking salty bits that take a lot of moistening and chewing on, but are full of nourishment and sometimes even a little sweetness.

One of the essential points is that stories are not stories and poems are not poems. This is something various Native American traditions understand quite well but that we often don't. Little Wagon believed this was an error in our schooling. He was an old Navaho man of whom the child of a travelling family taking shelter with him from the snow asked one night: Where does the snow come from?

> Little Wagon, in answer, began a long and involved story about an ancestor who had found a piece of beautiful burning material, had guarded it carefully for several months until some spirits [*ye'ii*] came to claim it, and had asked then that the spirits allow him to [keep] a piece of it. This they would not allow but would see what they could do for him. In the meantime he was to perform a number of complicated and dedicated tasks to test his endurance.

Finally, the spirits told him that [in reward for] his fine behavior they would throw all the ashes from their own fireplace down into Montezuma Canyon each year when they cleaned house. Sometimes they fail to keep their word, and sometimes they throw down too much; but in all, they turn their attention toward us regularly, here in Montezuma Canyon. When this story had been completed there was a respectful silence for a moment, and then the young questioner put in: 'It snows in Blanding, too. Why is that?'

I want to pause to mark the beauty and theoretical interest of Little Wagon's response.

> 'I don't know, the old man replied immediately. 'You'll have to make up your own story for that.'
> Little Wagon commented after the travellers' departure that it was too bad the boy didn't understand stories. I found that ... he [Little Wagon] did not consider it a [story about origins or causes] and did not in any way believe that was the way snow originated; rather, if the story was 'about' anything it was about moral values, about the [behavior] of a young [hero] whose actions *showed a properly [balanced] relationship between himself and nature*. ... our young visitor [had missed the point], a fact which Little Wagon at once attributed to the deadly influences of white schooling. (Toelken and Scott, 1981, pp. 73–74)

The important points here are, first, that a story is not something you read, a story is something you invent; second, a story is a way to express an ongoing relationship. Many commentators on Native American narratives say much the same thing as the latter. Keith Basso, for example, in his study of the Western Apache theory of 'stalking with stories', writes: 'Whenever Apaches describe the land – or, as happens more frequently, whenever they tell stories about incidents that have occurred at particular points upon it – they take steps to constitute it in relation to themselves' (Basso, 1996, p. 585). Again, Barre Toelken (in a volume called *Seeing with a Native Eye*) stresses the idea of behaviour (and stories *are* a form of behaviour) 'embodying the reciprocal relationships between people and the sacred *processes* going on in the world' (Toelken, 1976, p. 14). He mentions, as examples, rug-making not as making objects or artworks but as making itself, a process which can be a 'symbol of the relation between animal, man, and cosmos'; he also talks about beads made of the inside of the blue juniper seed, carried by Navahos to prevent nightmares. This practice 'works' because health in Navaho terms is a proper relationship to the world and to contemplate these beads (which 'represent a partnership between the tree, the animal, and man') is a way to maintain this healthy relationship. So far, so good, one might say: symbols – this is all familiar.

But this means we need to stress the fact that we are not talking about symbols. One of the clearest examples of the proper understanding of stories and all other sorts of representation is the initiation by disillusionment practised by the Hopi. As reported by Sam D. Gill, the crucial ceremony comes at a time when the young boys have been for years believing fervently in the reality of the kachinas they see before them now. Then the kachinas remove their heads: only masks, and now the laughing faces of fathers, uncles, and other relatives. The beauty of the ceremony is that it so effectively breaks the trap of the literal mentality faced by all traditions of representation, not just the Hopi. Here, the boys need to see that the kachinas are not 'THE KACHINAS'. As Gill puts it,

> What is shown to the Hopi child through this disenchanting experience is that things are not simply what they appear to be ... It places the child in a position to learn what is perhaps the most important lesson in his or her entire religious life: that a spiritual reality is conjoined with, and stands behind, the physical reality. (Gill, 1982, p. 92)

To say poems are not poems and stories are not stories is to say that poems and stories are not words but expressions of a feeling of relationship. This idea may sound familiar: to make this often forgotten distinction is simply to be faithful to explicit comments in the rest of American tradition, like those of Whitman and Stevens. For example, in the Preface to *Leaves of Grass*, Whitman makes a point of claiming the United States (an entity not made entirely of words, even after all our attempts to render it so) as a poem and of offering a way, not to write poems, but to become a poem, to make your flesh a poem. More obliquely perhaps, the ending of 'Song of Myself' tells us that the poem is not there to be words but to do something, is not the object of study but a pointer to the road. As the saying by Zen teachers reminds their students, 'Don't mistake the finger pointing at the moon for the moon.' Stevens says much the same: 'poetry means not the language of poetry but the thing itself, wherever it may be found' (Stevens, 1957, p. xiv). In his 'Adagia' (a series of apophthegms) for example:

> Poetry increases the feeling for reality.
> Poetry is a poetic conception, however expressed. A poem is poetry expressed in words.
> It is not every day that the world arranges itself in a poem.
> Poetry is the statement of a relation between a man and the world. (Stevens, 1957, pp. 157–58)

But 'relationship' is a vague word. What kind of relationship exactly? Barry Lopez has an excellent way of explaining this so I want to quote him at length:

> I think of two landscapes – one outside the self, the other within. The external landscape is the one we see – not only the line and color of the land and its shading at different times of the day, but also its plants and animals in season, its weather, its geology, the record of its climate and evolution. ... These are all elements of the land, and what makes the landscape comprehensible are the relationships between them. One learns a landscape finally not by knowing the name or identity of everything in it, but by perceiving the relationships in it. (Lopez, 1986, p. 61)

'The second landscape', he continues, 'is an interior one, a kind of projection within the person of a part of the exterior landscape' and its relationships. Therefore, story-telling of a certain kind brings those two 'landscapes' together; it does not express *a* relationship but a relationship of relationships. In that sense, telling is important for the health of the relationships of the people present at the telling. Lopez explains:

> Among the Navaho and, as far as I know, many other native peoples, the land is thought to exhibit a sacred order. That order is the basis of truth. Rituals themselves reveal the power in that order. Art, architecture, vocabulary, and costume, as well as ritual, derive from the perceived natural order of the universe – from observations and meditations on the exterior landscape. ... Each individual, further, undertakes to order his interior landscape according to the exterior landscape. To succeed in this means to achieve a balanced state of mental health. (Lopez, 1986, p. 63)

One more observation from Lopez, to close this long series of quotations: 'I believe storytelling functions in a similar way. The purpose of storytelling is to achieve harmony between two landscapes, to use all the elements – syntax, mood, figures of speech – in a harmonious way to reproduce the harmony of the land in the individual's interior' (Lopez, 1986, p. 64).

We could object that Lopez is describing stories told by a hunting culture and that none of our Western readers are hunters (or, if they are, not in a sacred manner). But the analogy I want to suggest is close to hunting. It is becoming what you seek. In that way, to understand the story is not to stand at a distance and discuss its verbal elements (though that can be a way of dressing the game). The story needs to be retold rather than understood, I think. You have to tell them to yourself and understand how people make them: not the structure but the feeling of relationship – of looking at something and then the story coming out of the looking. For example, consider these two moments of relation to the landscape from Willa Cather's *O Pioneers!*:

> Marie sat sewing or crocheting and tried to take a friendly interest in the game, but she was always thinking about the wide fields outside, where the snow was drifting over the fences; and about the orchard, where the snow was falling and packing, crust over crust. When she went out into the dark kitchen to fix her plants for the night, she used to stand by the window and look out at the white fields, or watch the currents of snow whirling over the orchard. She seemed to feel the weight of all the snow that lay down there. The branches had become so hard that they wounded your hand if you but tried to break a twig. And yet, down under the frozen crusts, at the roots of the trees, the secret of life was still safe, warm as the blood in one's heart; and the spring would come again. Oh, it would come again! (Cather, 1989, p. 79)

In this first passage the relationship is spelled out to some extent in the figures but that doesn't mean that we understand it. In a way, the second passage, because it is more withheld, makes the gap between Emil and us clearer: 'After [Emil] left Marie at her gate, he wandered about the fields all night, till morning put out the fireflies and the stars' (Cather, 1989, p. 92). At such a moment you have to become Emil like a hunter would become a deer and make a story yourself about what he saw in the stars and the fireflies and the fields he wandered through. A story (or a poem) is not just expressing a relationship, in the sense of the term as defined in legal documents, but is the result of an intimate contact. To make a story is like having a child: it is the result of intimate contact with another being (or animal or landscape). To merely read the story (decode the bare meanings of the words) is nothing like a relationship in this sense.

Greg Sarris comes at this point from an interesting direction when he stresses the way a story as told by Mabel McKay (the weaver and Dreamer) 'interrupts' the norms or expectations of the listeners and thereby initiates a fruitful relationship. The idea is that something that we find perfectly understandable is something that fits our norms so well that it vanishes when held up against them and no longer exists. Something, which doesn't match, doesn't vanish; we look at it again (and again) because it is still there.

> If Mabel's talk initiates in the interlocutors a kind of internal dialogue where the interlocutors examine the nature of their own thinking, that dialogue can be carried over to an ever-widening context of talk in stories and conversations, such that the inner dialogue can inform and be informed by new stories and conversations. (Sarris, 1993, p. 30)

In the same way, to read Marie's reverie about the snow or Emil's more enigmatic night of wandering is to encounter (not suppress) gaps and interruptions, to listen to one's own voice in consequence, and to enter into dialogue with the story (which itself is already in dialogue with Virgil's pastorals, Dante's story of Paolo and Francesca, and Wagner's *Tristan und Isolde*). That is, as Sarris points out, Mabel's 'stories' are not 'pure story' but are also comments on older versions of the event ('hers and others') and those in turn may have been comments also. He also cites Dennis Tedlock's remark about Zuñi stories that listeners 'are getting the criticism at the same time from the same person [who is telling the story]. The interpreter does not merely play the parts, but is the narrator and commentator as well' (Tedlock, quoted in Sarris, 1993, p. 44).

Therefore, we should realize that we need to remember (as Mabel McKay tells Greg Sarris),

> [W]hen you hear and tell my stories there is more to me and you that *is* the story. You don't know everything about me and I don't know everything about you. Our knowing is limited. Let our words show us as much so we can learn together about one another. Let us tell stories that help us in this. Let us keep learning. (Sarris, 1993, p. 46)

We can always offer Native American stories as analogues, of course; for example, stories of Corn Maidens who die to become the food may help to understand the connection between Alexandra (in *O Pioneers!*) and the land (she fears). For another example, Sam Gill retells the Hopi story of Sunset Crater kachina, Ka'nas, who marries a human woman and enriches her with gifts of food but then abandons her when the local sorcerers impersonate him and have sex with her. The story does not 'mean' x, y or z. The story is 'a portrayal of a way of life and the difficulties of living it. ... the story raises complex and difficult issues [but] ... these questions cannot be simply answered now, probably because this is not a story that provides answers' (Gill, 1993, pp. 302–303). That is, it is not a form of words that points to another form of words. That is not what it provides. Instead, 'the story, likely throughout its long tradition, has presented for contemplation the concerns of the peoples who told and heard it, peoples whose world was complicated and sometimes difficult to live in, yet rich in meaning'. In this way Gill and McKay might agree: Our knowing is limited. Let our words show us as much.

This approach offers us a different way of reading.

As Greg Sarris reminds us, 'Non-Indians often ask what this or that symbolizes, as if signs and semiotic systems were transcultural. ... It seems to me that the ways snakes are viewed by the Pomo vary from tribe to tribe and *even from person to person within a given tribe*' (Sarris, 1993, p. 43). Sarris goes on, sounding much like William Carlos Williams: 'So much depends on the situation, who is in the situation, who is telling about it, and who is listening' (Sarris, 1993, p. 43).

This kind of approach (involvement and dialogue, rather than distance and expertise) can create a certain confusion among beginning readers, but confusion is salutary in this case. Without a relationship, a story, the name is nothing much, just knowledge. This kind of knowing that is not knowing needs to be interrupted. That need is an imperative we can find (but often forget about) in Euro-Christian tradition also:

> And the disciples came to the opposite shore, but they forgot to bring any bread. Jesus said to them: 'Look, take care, and guard against the leaven of the Pharisees and Sadducees.'
> Now they looked quizzically at each other, saying, 'We didn't bring any bread' [that is, they are worried they are in trouble for forgetting to bring any literal bread].
> Because Jesus was aware of this, he said, 'Why are you puzzling, you with so little trust, because you don't have any bread? ... How can you possibly think I was talking to you about bread? Just be on guard against the leaven of the Pharisee ...
> Then they understood that he was not talking about guarding against the leaven in bread but against the teaching of the Pharisees. [(Matt. 16:5–12)

Perhaps I exaggerate the differences or similarities between cultures or kinds of stories or poems, or deliberately ignore the way in which poems and stories are very much the words of them. But at the same time, some useful interrupting can happen this way. I'd like to close with another example from *The Sacred*. It concerns a Navaho curing ceremony:

> A non-Navaho had a ceremony performed as part of the treatment for red ants in the system, an illness like pneumonia which he said he had 'no doubt picked up by urinating on an ant hill'. Some time after the successful treatment, he asked the *hataalii* if he had really had ants in his system. The singer answered, 'No, not ants, but ANTS'. He went on to explain what he meant by saying, 'We have to have a way of thinking strongly about disease. (Toelken and Scott, 1981, p. 90)

Equally, we need a way to think strongly about not just words but the world they exist in relation to – and the making of relations (poems and stories) with that world.

Works Cited

Basso, Keith H., 1996. '"Stalking With Stories": Names, Places, and Moral Narratives Among the Western Apache', in *Wisdom Sits in Places*, Albuquerque, NM: University of New Mexico Press.

Cather, Willa, 1989. *O, Pioneers!* New York: Penguin.

Gill, Sam D., 1982. *Native American Religions: An Introduction*, Belmont, CA: Wadsworth.

Gill, Sam D., 1993. 'Religious Forms and Themes', in Alvin Josephy, Jr. (ed.), *America in 1492: The World of the Indian Peoples Before the Arrival of Columbus*, New York: Vintage, pp. 277–304.

Lopez, Barry, 1986. 'Story at Anaktuvuk Pass', in Scott Walker (ed.), *The Graywolf Annual Three: Essays, Memoirs and Reflections*, St Paul: Graywolf Press, pp. 59–66.

Sarris, Greg, 1993. *Keeping Slug Woman Alive: A Holistic Approach to American Indian Texts*, Berkeley: University of California Press.

Stevens, Wallace, 1957. *Opus Posthumous: Poems, Plays, Prose*, ed. Samuel French Morse, New York: Random House.

Toelken, Barre, 1976. *Seeing with a Native Eye*, New York: Harper & Row.

Toelken, Barre and Tacheeni Scott, 1981. 'Poetic Retranslation and the "Pretty Languages" of Yellow Man', in Karl Kroeber (ed.), *Traditional Literatures of the American Indian; Texts and Interpretations*, Lincoln: University of Nebraska Press.

List of Contributors

Debra A. Castillo is Stephen H. Weiss Presidential Fellow and Professor of Romance Studies and Comparative Literature at Cornell University, where she also serves as Director of the Latin American Studies Program. She specializes in contemporary Hispanic literature, women's studies, and post-colonial literary theory. She is author of *The Translated World: A Postmodern Tour of Libraries in Literature* (1984), *Talking Back: Strategies for a Latin American Feminist Literary Criticism* (1992), and translator of Federico Campbell's *Tijuana: Stories on the Border* (1994). Her most recent book is *Easy Women: Sex and Gender in Modern Mexican Fiction* (1998).

Pauline Dodgson is Head of Subject for Languages and Cultural Studies at Thames Valley University. She worked in teaching, curriculum development and educational broadcasting in Zimbabwe from 1982 to 1988. She has published articles on Southern African and Caribbean literature and is currently writing a book on Zimbabwean war literature. She teaches contemporary British writing, American literature and post-colonial literatures.

Rosemary Feal is Professor of Spanish at the State University of New York at Buffalo. She specializes in Caribbean and South American literature and literary theory, including Afro-Hispanic studies, feminist criticism and queer theory. She is an Associate Editor of the *Afro-Hispanic Review*. Her books include *Novel Lives: The Fictional Autobiographies of Guillermo Cabrera Infante and Mario Vargas Llosa* (1986) and *Painting on the Page: Interartistic Approaches to Modern Hispanic Texts* (1995). Feal's latest research focuses on women's erotic writing *en español*. Her chapter in this volume incorporates, in revised and condensed versions, portions of two published articles that first appeared in *Afro-Hispanic Review* 10.3 (1991) and *Latin American Literary Review* 20.40 (1992). The material reprinted is used with permission.

Robert Gregory holds a PhD in Native American literature and is currently a research fellow at the University of Kentucky.

Candida Hepworth is Lecturer in American Studies at the University of Wales, Swansea, with funding from ALCOA (UK). She is Managing Editor of *Borderlines: Studies in American Culture* and a member of the Border Areas Research Group, which is currently researching the dynamics of the US–Mexico border. She has published on various aspects of Chicano/a literature.

Richard Lane is Lecturer in English at South Bank University, London, where he specializes in Canadian literature, critical theory and archival studies. He has published on such authors as Margaret Atwood, Bertrand William Sinclair, Malcolm Lowry and Robert Kroetsch.

Patricia Linton is Associate Professor of English at the University of Alaska, Anchorage, where she teaches courses on twentieth-century literature, narrative theory and film. She has published in *Studies in American Indian Literatures* and *MELUS* and has articles forthcoming in *Modern Fiction Studies* and in the volume *Multicultural Detective Fiction: Murder from the 'Other' Side* (Garland Press).

Gail Ching-Liang Low teaches post-colonial, contemporary British and American literatures and film at the University of Dundee. Her work has previously appeared in *New Formations*, *Women: A Cultural Review* and *Research into African Literatures*. She is the author of *White Skins/Black Masks: Representation and Colonialism* (1996).

Deborah Madsen is Professor of English at South Bank University, London. She has published extensively on American literature of the colonial and modern periods. Her publications include *The Postmodernist Allegories of Thomas Pynchon* (1991), *Rereading Allegory: A Narrative Approach to Genre* (1994), *Postmodernism, A Bibliography, 1926–1994* (1995), *Allegory in America: From Puritanism to Postmodernism* (1996) and *American Exceptionalism* (1998). She edited *Visions of America Since 1492* (1994) and several volumes of *The Year's Work in English Studies*. Her current research focuses upon post-colonialism and the multiethnic literature of the United States. She is working on a three-volume study of American ethnic women's literature, and is now completing the first book on contemporary Chicana writing.

Karen Piper is Assistant Professor in Post-colonial Literature and Theory at the University of Missouri-Columbia. She has published previously in journals such as *Cultural Critique*, the *American Indian Quarterly*, *MELUS*, and the *Journal of the Kafka Society of America*. She is currently completing a book entitled *Territorial Fictions: Postcolonial Literature and Cartography*.

Alan Rice is Lecturer in American Studies and Cultural Theory at the University of Central Lancashire. He has written widely on African-American literature and culture. His book *Liberating Sojourn: Frederick Douglass and Transatlantic Reform*, jointly edited with Martin Crawford, will be published in 1999. His chapter in this volume was completed during a research sabbatical granted by the University of Central Lancashire.

Suzanne Scafe is Senior Lecturer in English at South Bank University, London, where she specializes in Caribbean women's writing. She is editor of *Teaching Black Literature* (1989) and has published a number of articles and essays on literature and the multicultural curriculum. She is also the co-author of *The Heart of the Race: Black Women's Lives in Britain* and is a contributing editor of the journal *Changing English*.

Lee Schweninger is Professor of English at the University of North Carolina, Wilmington, where he teaches early American, ethnic and American Indian literatures. Author of *The Writings of Celia Parker Wooley* (1998) and *John Winthrop* (1990), he has also published recently in *Studies in American Literatures* and *MELUS*. He is currently at work on a study of American Indian literature of the land.

Gina Wisker is Principal Lecturer at Anglia Polytechnic University, Cambridge, where she is Divisional Head of Women's Studies. She has published widely on post-colonial literature and genre fiction, including *Insights Into Black Women's Writing* (1992), *It's My Party: Reading Twentieth-Century Women's Writing* (1994) and, with Lynne Pearce, *Rescripting Romance in Fiction and Film* (1998). She has written on educational issues, including *Empowering Women in Higher Education* (1996) and, with Sally Brown, *Enabling Student Learning* (1996); she is co-editor of the *Innovations in Education and Training* (SEDA) journal.

Marion Wynne-Davies teaches English Literature at the University of Dundee. She is the author of, among other works, *Women and Arthurian Literature: Seizing the Sword* (1996) and the editor of *Women Poets of the Renaissance* (1998).

Index

abolition, 107, 108
Aborigines, 2, 10, 11, 54–5, 60–2, 66–8, 72–85
academy, 19, 29, 148, 149, 151, 152, 153, 160, 186, 190, 210
Acuña, Rudolfo, 169
Adam, Ian, 5
Africa, 1, 3, 4, 5, 11, 16, 17, 25, 26, 73, 74, 76, 81, 84, 88, 89, 98, 99, 108, 120, 126, 137–40, 148, 149, 151, 152, 155, 158, 160, 161
African Americans, 2, 4, 5, 10, 23, 27, 34, 72, 80, 84, 117, 118, 133–45, 150
Afro-Hispanic literature, 2, 10, 148–61
Afro-Hispanic Review, 150
Afro-Hispanic Studies, 149–52
Alarcón, Norma, 193
allegory, 5, 200
Allen, Paula Gunn, 36
alterity, 30, 55
American literature, 2, 3, 4, 5, 6, 10, 36, 218
Americanization, 188
Americas, the, 113, 148–61, 183
Anaya, Rudolfo, 176
Anderson, Benedict, 189
Antigua, 155
Anzaldúa, Gloria, 8, 166, 169, 170, 171, 172, 176, 180, 183, 185, 193
apartheid, 72, 73, 75, 76, 82, 84
Appiah, Kwame Anthony, 207

appropriation, 79
Ardrey, Robert, 171
Armstrong, Louis, 137, 138
Arteaga, Alfred, 166, 167, 168, 169, 170, 172, 174, 175, 176, 190, 193, 194
Ashcroft, Bill, 4, 5, 6, 9, 20
Asia, south-east, 1, 4
assimilation, 20, 22, 32
Attridge, Derek, 83
Atwood, Margaret, 45, 51, 52
authenticity, 6, 9, 17, 75, 76, 89, 90, 114, 152, 153, 209
authorship, 29
Australia, 1, 2, 4, 5, 6, 9, 20, 61, 66, 69, 72, 79, 80, 84
Australasia, 3
autobiography, 11–12, 72, 74–81, 85, 90, 101, 108, 122, 130, 159
Avalos, David, 186
Aztecs, 166, 167, 174

Baker, Houston, 117, 160
Bakhtin, Mikhail, 141
Balsamo, Anne, 153
Bandler, Faith, 77, 80
Baraka, Amiri, 134, 135
Barrera, Eduardo, 186
Barrio, Raymond, 174
Bashir, Leyli Miller, 23–6
Basso, Keith, 219
Bataille, G. M., 207
Baudrillard, Jean, 45, 46, 49, 52, 53, 54, 183, 209
Bennett, Louise, 120

Berkhofer, R. F., 208, 209, 211
Bhabha, Homi, 15, 16, 55–6, 180, 186
biography, 77, 90
Bishop, Maurice, 126, 127
Blackburn, Robin, 105
blackness, 77, 148
Black Nationalism, 126
Black Power movement, 117, 120
black writing, 2
blues, 145
Boehmer, Elleke, 5, 7, 8, 10, 83
Booth, Wayne, 33
Border Art Workshop / Taller de Arte Fronterizo, 186
borders, 170, 171, 172, 176, 191
  writing, 3, 164, 180–203
Botswana, 73, 74, 81, 82
Boyce Davies, Carole, 98
Bradford, William, 4
Brathwaite, Edward, 105
Brink, André, 75
Britain, 24, 89, 104, 117, 118
Brown, Russell, 46–7, 55
Bruce-Novoa, Juan, 164, 165, 166, 168, 169, 172, 173, 174, 190
Bruzzi, Stella, 59
Brydon, Diana, 4, 6, 10
bush, the Australian, 69
Bush, Barbara, 108
Bush, Catherine, 45–6, 48–50, 52–4

Calder, Jenni, 207
Calderón, Héctor, 190, 191
Campion, Jane, 58–60, 62–5, 69, 70
Canada, 1, 2, 3, 4, 5, 6, 11, 20, 34, 35, 36, 40, 41, 45–56
Candelaria, Cordelia, 192
cannibalism, 135, 142, 143
canon, 1, 2, 5, 8, 11, 12, 29, 36, 55, 74, 89, 101, 149, 150, 151, 156, 157, 161, 180–203, 208
Carby, Hazel, 117, 160
CARD (the Campaign Against Racial Discrimination), 117
Caribbean, 1, 3, 4, 5, 6, 104, 108, 117, 120–31, 141, 150, 151, 154

Carmichael, Stokeley, 117
Carpentier, Alejo, 92
Case, George, 108
Castillo, Ana, 193
Castillo, Debra, 3, 6
Castro-Gómez, Santiago, 198
Cather, Willa, 222, 223
Caute, David, 89
Central America, 150, 151
Certeau, Michel de, 182, 185, 188–9
Chávez, Denise, 8, 175
Chávez, John R., 166, 169
Chicano Movement, 174
Chicano/as, 186, 193, 194, 195, 199, 203
  culture, 27, 192
  writing, 2, 3, 5, 10, 164–76, 190, 192–203
Chinodya, Shimmer, 95
Chodorow, Nancy, 128
Chopin, Kate, 100
Christian, Barbara, 160, 161
Cinco de Maya, 19
Cisneros, Sandra, 8, 169, 173, 174, 190
Cixous, Hélène, 23, 72, 97
Clare, Monica, 77
Clemens, Theresa, 77
Clements, W., 212
Clifford, James, 153
Clifton, James, 206, 209
Clinton, William (Bill), 24
Clitoridectomy, 16
Code switching, 9
Coetzee, J. M., 84–5
Collingwood, Luke, 106, 108
Collins, Merle, 2, 8, 120–31
Colonial literature, 5, 7
Colonialism, 8, 14, 16, 19, 20, 24, 25, 26, 27, 55, 67, 73, 75, 76, 84, 88, 89, 91, 98, 104, 123, 125, 130, 139, 140, 141, 155, 164–71, 173, 175, 176, 183, 194, 195, 208
  colonized, 2, 7, 8, 12, 122, 123, 124, 130, 133, 140, 141, 172, 173, 188, 196, 197

colonizer, 8, 59, 62, 63, 68, 85, 122, 130, 133, 141, 188
colonialist, 7, 9, 60, 63, 69, 149
Colombia, 150
Coltrane, John, 138
Columbus, Christopher, 190
commodification, 62
Commonwealth Literature, 1, 2, 3, 4, 5, 12
comparativity, 1, 2, 3, 5–11
Coronil, Fernando, 183
Cortés, Hernán, 167, 193
COSAW (Congress of South African Writers Collective), 75, 76, 81
Coser, Stelamaris, 133
Crawford, John, 173
creole, 9, 120, 122, 125, 126–7, 131
crime narrative, 200–1
cross-cultural identity, 54, 106
Crosse, Ronald, 50
Cuba, 150, 154, 155, 159
Cyrus, Stanley, 151

D'Aguiar, Fred, 2, 8, 104–18
Dabydeen, David, 105
Dangerembga, Tsitsi, 8, 89, 90, 94–5, 101
Dante, 223
decolonization, 121, 122, 123, 124, 125, 126, 131, 173
DeCosta-Willis, Miriam, 151, 159, 160
deconstruction, 99, 144
democracy, 18, 27
Delany, Paul, 48
Deleuze, Gilles, 18, 19, 55
Delillo, Don, 55
Derrida, Jacques, 196
dialect, 9, 67
dialogism, 12, 140, 141, 142, 214
diary, 80
diaspora, 55, 106, 114, 156
  black, 2, 5, 117, 118, 139, 155, 160
discontinuous narrative, 5
diversity, 16, 18
Dodgson, Pauline, 2
Dominican Republic, 154, 155, 159
Donaldson, Laura E., 39

Dorris, Michael, 209–10, 214
Douglass, Frederick, 114
Du Bois, W. W. B., 114

Ecuador, 150, 154
Ellison, Ralph, 145
empire, British, 4, 16, 106
England, 20, 61
English, language, 4, 84, 91, 107, 174, 175, 176, 190, 191, 192, 193, 195
'Englishes', 10
Enlightenment, 105, 106
Equiano, Olaudah, 108
Esquivel, Laura, 180
essentialism, 17, 18
ethics, 33, 43, 52, 128, 148
ethnicity, 12, 21, 50–1, 54, 63, 64, 69, 115, 151, 155, 160, 176, 208
ethnic literature, 1, 2, 5, 29, 30, 31, 32, 33, 43, 164, 210
Eurocentrism, 31, 39, 112
Europe, 8, 22, 69, 74, 79, 88, 89, 105, 107, 109, 113, 114, 139, 150, 151, 152, 156, 160, 212, 224
extinction, 62

Fanon, Frantz, 6, 8, 121, 122–3, 125, 126, 127, 130, 131, 173, 174
false consciousness, 99
Faragher, John Mack, 165
Feal, Rosemary, 2
female genital mutilation (FGM), 14, 16, 17
feminism, 4, 34, 59, 60, 70, 72, 98, 99, 133, 148–61, 202
Ferrier, Carole, 78
fetishization, 65, 153, 184
First Nations, 11, 53
Fischer, Michael M. J., 176
folklore, 145, 202
Fontana, Bernard, 206
Foucault, Michel, 94, 184
Fraginals, Manuel Moreno, 159
Francis, Daniel, 55
frontier, 22, 23, 52
Fryer, P., 107

Fuentes, Carlos, 180
fundamentalism, Muslim, 26
Furman, Nelly, 164
Fuss, Diana, 157

Gaidzanwa, Rudo, 89, 99
García Canclini, Néstor, 183, 185, 186, 188, 189
Gaspar de Alba, Alicia, 181, 190–203
Gates, Henry Louis, Jr., 117, 137, 138, 159, 160
gender, 30, 42, 59, 60, 62, 72–85, 88–101, 120–31, 142, 149, 152, 154, 156, 157, 158, 159, 189, 193, 200, 202, 203
genre, 9, 67, 78, 79, 80
genocide, 22, 77
Ghana, 25
Gill, Sam D., 220, 223
Gilligan, Carol, 128
Gilroy, Paul, 104, 105, 114, 115, 117
globalization, 5, 7, 19
Gómez Peña, Guillermo, 186
Gonzales, Rodolfo, 172
Goolagong, Evonne, 77
gospel, music, 138
gothic, 58
Governor, Jimmie, 60
Govinden, Betty, 75
Grenada, 121, 122, 126, 127, 130, 131
Griffiths, Gareth, 4, 5, 7, 20, 66
Gregory, Robert, 3, 10
Gregson, William, 108
Guadalupe Hidalgo, Treaty of, 168, 169
Guam, 20
Guatemala, 166
Guattari, Félix, 18, 19
Guillén, Nicolás, 158
Gunner, Liz, 93

Hall, Stuart, 114, 115
Haraway, Donna, 153
Hartsock, Nancy, 74
Haseltine, Patricia, 214
Hawthorne, Evelyn, 139

Head, Bessie, 8, 73–4, 75, 76, 81–3, 84
Heath Anthology of American Literature, 4, 190
Hebdige, Dick, 120
Henderson, Stephen, 135, 136
Hepworth, Candida, 3, 6
Herrera, Albert S., 165
heteroglossia, 30
Hicks, D. Emily, 164, 170, 171
Hidalgo y Costilla, Miguel, 167
Hinojosa, Rolando, 168, 175, 190
Hispanic writing, 2, 3, 4, 151
Hogan, Linda, 31–2, 37, 212, 214
Holocaust, 115
homosexuality, 64
Hood, Thomas, 58, 59
hooks, bell, 72, 117, 148, 149, 159, 160, 161
Houston, Samuel, 168
Hove, Chenjerai, 89, 90–5, 101
Huggins, Jackie, 78
Hughes, Robert, 171, 176
Hutcheon, Linda, 55
hybridity, 6, 15, 21, 22, 23, 30, 59, 63, 106, 114, 170, 171, 175, 181, 183, 186
hyperreality, 46

idiom, 91, 125
immigration, 15, 16, 19, 20, 22, 23, 24, 25, 168, 169
imperialism, 4, 8, 9, 10, 11, 12, 19, 20, 52, 73, 85, 104, 166, 167, 172
India, 1
Indians, see Native Americans
indigeneity, 3, 5, 9, 11, 12, 18, 19, 20, 56, 61, 63, 65, 66, 67, 69, 70, 74, 85, 151, 155, 167, 169, 171, 185, 191, 192, 193, 195, 196
internationalism, 16, 32
intertextuality, 117, 122
invader-settler cultures, 5, 7, 10, 12, 19, 73, 169
irony, 5, 66, 70, 80, 108, 138

Jabavu, Noni, 76
Jackson, Richard, 149, 150, 152

Jamaica, 120, 131
Jameson, Fredric, 171
jazz, 134, 135, 136, 137, 138, 140, 144
Jolly, Rosemary, 83
Johnson, Charles, 118
Johnson, David, 181, 182, 183, 185, 190, 191
Jones, Eldred, 88
journalism, 75, 82
Joyce, Joyce, 160

Kant, Emmanuel, 196
Kassindja, Fauziya, 14–17, 23–7
Kelsall, James, 106, 107, 108
Kendall, K. Limakatso, 84
Keneally, Thomas, 8, 60–2, 65–70
Kennedy, Marnie, 77
King, Bruce, 5
King, Martin Luther, Jr., 117
King, Thomas, 2, 3, 8, 9, 34–43, 211–12, 215
Kincaid, Jamaica, 155
Krupat, Arnold, 11–12
Kuzwayo, Ellen, 76, 81
Kwanzaa, 19

Labarlestier, Jan, 79
LaCapra, Dominick, 208, 209
La Llorona, 202
Lane, Richard, 2
Langford, Ruby, 77
language, 5, 9, 10, 25–6, 30, 54, 59, 61, 62, 66, 78, 84, 91, 92, 100, 105, 107, 109, 114, 117, 120, 122, 123, 133, 136, 140, 141, 143, 157, 161, 174, 175, 176, 180, 190, 192, 194, 195, 196, 200, 202, 207
LaRocque, Emma, 207
Latin America, 150, 152, 158, 190, 203
Latinas, 34
Leal, Luis, 166
Ledent, Benedicte, 104
Lee, John, 108
Leon-Portilla, Miguel, 166, 167

Lesotho, 75, 84
Lewis, Anthony, 24
Lewis, Marvin, 151
liberation struggle, 88
Lima, Maria Helena, 122
Limerick, Patricia, 207
Linton, Patricia, 2, 3, 8, 10
Lipsitz, George, 145
Little Wagon, 218–19
Lomelí, Francisco A., 165
Lopez, Barry, 221
López de Santa Anna, General Antonio, 168
Loomba, Ania, 66
Lorde, Audre, 149
Low, Denise, 209
Low, Gail, 2, 6, 63, 114
Lowry, Malcolm, 47
Lucashenko, Melissa, 78
Ludmer, Josefina, 200
Lugones, María, 33

McDowell, Deborah, 160
McFarlane, Brian, 68, 69
McKay, Mabel, 222–3
McLeod, Anne, 202
McLintock, Anne, 20
Mackenzie, Craig, 73
magic realism, 5
Mailman, Stanley, 24
Makhalisa, Barbara, 88
Malinche, 192–6, 199, 201
Manifest Destiny, 168
Manzano, Juan Francisco, 159
Maoris, 2, 11, 60, 63–5, 70
Marechera, Dambudzo, 8, 88, 89
marginality, 5, 34, 35, 81, 90, 101, 121, 122, 124, 140, 149, 161, 174, 175, 209
Marshall Islands, 20
Martínez, Julio A., 165
'mascon words', 135, 136
masculinity, 21, 23, 123, 128, 198, 202
  gaze, 59
Mazorodze, I. V., 95
Meier, Matt, 169

Memmi, Albert, 6
metanarrative, 68, 69, 110
Mexican Americans, 23
Mexico, 170, 171, 174, 175, 181, 182, 183, 186, 187, 190, 193, 194, 203
Mexicanness, 188
Mexican literature, 191
Michaelson, Scott, 181, 182, 183, 185, 191
Mignolo, Walter, 183, 184, 185
migration, 106, 117, 128, 129, 182
minority literature, 15, 16, 27, 156
Miller, Stephen E., 47–8
mimicry, 151
Miner, Madonne M., 142
Mintz, Sidney, 142
Mirandé, Alfredo, 166, 169
miscegenation, 167, 170
mixed-blood, 206, 212
Mntuyedwa, Nomakhosi, 84
Modernism, 4, 136, 137
modernity, 90, 105, 106, 114, 187, 189
Mohanty, Chandra Talpade, 152
Molina, Silvia, 180
Monsiváis, Carlos, 188
Monson, Ingrid, 137, 138
Morejón, Nancy, 155
Morgan Sally, 8, 77, 78, 79–80
Morrison, Toni, 2, 8, 72, 79, 80, 84, 93, 117, 133–45
motherhood, 98
Mphahele, Eskia, 82
multiculturalism, 2, 6, 15, 16, 17, 18, 19, 22, 26, 27, 50, 171, 176, 185
multiethnicity, 3, 164, 170, 171, 176
Mungoshi, Charles, 88
Muñoz, Carlos, 165, 166
music, 61, 114, 120, 121, 123, 134, 145
mutilation, 15, 23
myth, 36–7, 77, 117, 144, 145, 193, 202, 208, 209

Narogin, Mudrooroo, 77, 78
National Parks, 21, 23

nationalism, 8, 11, 22, 26, 52, 88, 89, 117, 130, 185, 188, 193, 194, 202, 208
nationality, 11, 30, 170, 171, 186, 191, 192
Native peoples, 7, 8, 9, 15, 24, 123, 126, 169, 193, 207
  Americans, 2, 3, 4, 5, 10, 11, 18, 21, 22, 23, 27, 30–43, 50–1, 206–15, 218–24
  land claims, 50
  resistance, 50–1
Neel, David, 50–1
négritude, 5, 98
neo-colonialism, 4, 19, 25, 130, 208
New England, 3, 4
New Zealand, 1, 2, 4, 5, 6, 9, 20, 58, 63, 69
Ngcobo, Lauretta, 76, 81
Niathum, Duane, 207
Nichols, Grace, 105
Nietzsche, Friedrich, 22, 23
Nkosi, Lewis, 82
noble savage, 64, 207
Norton Anthology of American Literature, 4
nostalgia, 136, 137, 203, 211
novel, 29

O'Callaghan, Evelyn, 120, 121, 122
O'Meally, Ralph, 143
Oka Crisis, 50–1
Olalquiaga, Celeste, 188
Olivella, Manuel Zapata, 161
Onuru, Oku, 131
orality, 30, 36, 38, 73, 75, 77, 78, 81, 120, 122, 137, 190, 206
Ortiz, Adalberto, 154
Ortiz, Simon, 208
Owens, Louis, 30–1, 208, 209, 210, 211, 212, 215

Pakeha, 63, 64, 65, 69, 70
parody, 49, 50, 64, 120, 138
Parry, Benita, 24
pastiche, 67
paternalism, 130

INDEX

patriarchy, 14, 26, 60, 64, 69, 82, 89, 100, 152
Paz, Octavio, 170, 171, 172, 185, 193–4
Peñalosa, Fernando, 175
Pettinger, Alastair, 115, 116
Phillips, Caryl, 104, 113, 114, 115, 117
Phillips, Mike, 117
Phillips, Trevor, 117
Piper, Karen, 2, 6
Plasa, Carl, 104
pluralism, 56
Polk, James K., 168
Pollard, Velma, 121
Portalatín, Aída Cartagena, 154, 159, 160
post-colonial literature, 5, 7, 8, 9, 10, 16, 20, 29, 32, 33–4, 43, 62, 70, 96, 101, 176
post-colonialism, 4, 7, 12, 19, 22, 27, 50, 55, 56, 66, 67, 69, 70, 104, 122, 126, 130, 150, 153, 156, 164, 172
 canon, 1, 2, 3–5
 cultures, 6, 170
 studies, 3, 149
postmodernism, 4, 48, 49, 55, 67, 73, 74, 75, 89, 212
postmodernity, 183
poststructuralism, 1, 53, 55
prostitution, 77
psychoanalysis, 115
publication, 74, 75
Puerto Rico, 20

Quebec, 50, 51

Rabinowitz, Peter, 29–30
race, 59, 60, 62, 70, 72, 77, 79, 80, 82, 83, 106, 115, 142, 143, 145, 149, 152, 154, 155, 157, 158, 160, 176, 193, 206–15
reading, 2, 29–43
realism, 5
Reddy, Jayapraga, 76, 81
reggae, 120

regionalism, 53
Reichstein, Andreas, 168
relativism, 56
religion, 31
reminiscence, 80
representation, 11, 80, 84, 85, 157, 209
reservations, 18, 22, 35, 43, 213
Rhodesia, 88
Ribera, Feliciano, 169
Rice, Alan, 2
Richards, Henry, 151
Ricou, Laurie, 53, 55
Rieff, David, 170
Rigney, Barbara Hill, 142, 143
Ring, Betty, 104
Rodríguez, Joe, 176
Rodriguez, Richard, 167, 172, 175
Romanticism, 54
Romero, Rolando J., 170
Rooney, Caroline, 100
Roosevelt, Franklin Delano, 165
Roosevelt, Theodore, 21–3
Rose, Jacqueline, 115
Rousseau, Jean-Jacques, 64
Rushdie, Salman, 17

Saenz, Benjamin Alire, 185
Said, Edward, 20, 164, 166, 172, 173
Saldívar, José David, 190, 191
Sam, Agnes, 76
Samupindi, Charles, 95
Sarris, Greg, 222–4
savagery, 11, 16, 17, 211
Scafe, Suzanne, 2
Schepisi, Fred, 60, 61, 65, 66, 68, 69
Schimmel, Julie, 207
Schlesinger, Arthur, 173
Schweninger, Lee, 3, 8, 9
science fiction, 51
Scott, Tacheeni, 219
Searle, Chris, 127
segregation, 18
self-reflexivity, 39, 68, 91, 114
semiotics, 54, 95, 100, 223
settler culture, 2, 7, 19, 20, 63, 66, 95, 123

sexuality, 15, 16, 23, 62, 64–5, 77, 157, 160, 187, 189, 193, 194, 195
Sharp, Granville, 107, 108
Sharpe, Jenny, 20
Shuffleton, Frank, 210
silence, 9, 15, 33, 59, 60, 61, 62, 70, 72, 73, 74, 75, 80, 81, 84, 97, 108, 122, 152, 172, 176, 198
Silet, C., 207
Simmens, Edward, 166
slave narratives, 27, 75, 108, 117
slavery, 2, 104–18, 130, 138, 143, 159, 161
Smart, Ian, 151
Smith, Andrea Lynn, 175, 176
Smith, Lawrence, 212
Smith, Shirley C., 77
Smitherman, Geneva, 137
Softing, Inger-Ann, 143, 144
Sommer, Doris, 32–4, 42, 43
South Africa, 2, 72–85
South America, 150, 151
Southern Africa, 89
South Pacific, 4
sovereignty, 50, 210, 213
Spanish, 151, 156, 174, 175, 176, 180, 190, 191, 192, 194, 195
Spillers, Hortense, 160
Spivak, Gayatri Chakravorty, 9, 14, 26, 59–60, 65, 66
Spurr, David, 16
Staunton, Irene, 96, 97
Stead Eilerson, Gillian, 83
Stearns, Marshall, 138
stereotypes, 64, 65, 89, 99, 154, 182, 187, 188, 201, 206–14
Stevens, Wallace, 220
Stoler, Ann Laura, 187, 189
structuralism, 53
subaltern, 9, 14, 15, 26, 59–60, 61, 62, 64, 65, 66, 67, 70
suttee, 14
Swaziland, 84
Sykes, Bobbi, 77

Tabuenca Córdoba, María-Socorro, 181, 182, 186, 191
Taller de Arte Fronterizo / Border Art Workshop, 186
Tedlock, Dennis, 223
testimony, 79, 90, 91, 108
textuality, 7
Thieme, John, 4
Thiong'o, Ngugi wa, 84
Third World, 90, 141, 150, 153, 170, 183
Tiffin, Helen, 4, 5, 6, 10, 20
Tlali, Miriam, 8, 76, 84
Toelken, Barre, 219
Togo, 14, 24–5
Toure, Sekou, 126
transculturalism, 180, 181, 191, 223
transnationalism, 1, 16, 20, 26, 30, 180
Treichler, Paula, 156–7
tribal culture, 62, 69, 114, 116, 214
trickster, 35, 39, 212, 213, 214
Trigo, Abril, 184, 185
Trinh, T. Minh-ha, 187
Tucker, Margaret, 77
Turner, Frederick Jackson, 21–3
Turner, J. M. W., 107

United States, 1, 2, 3, 4, 6, 9, 12, 14–27, 40, 45–56, 69, 89, 124, 127, 139, 143, 144, 145, 148, 150, 154, 155, 159, 164, 167, 168, 170, 171, 172, 173, 174, 176, 182, 185, 187, 188, 189, 190–4, 203, 220
universalism, 48
Unsworth, Barry, 104

Vaca, Cabeza de, 190
Veit-Wild, Flora, 89, 91
Venezuela, 183
Vera, Yvonne, 8, 90, 96–101
vernacular, 9, 133, 136
Vicioso, Sherezada (Chiqui), 155
Villagrá, Pérez de, 190
Viramontes, Helena María, 190
Virgil, 223
Vizenor, Gerald, 3, 8, 9, 206–15

voice, 7, 9, 11, 14, 59, 67, 76, 78, 85, 122, 152, 157, 158, 199
violence, 62, 122, 123, 125, 126, 131, 169, 187, 193, 195

Wagner, Richard, 223
Walcott, Derek, 92, 104, 105, 106, 111, 112
Walker, Alice, 72, 81, 84
Wallace, Michele, 152
Walvin, James, 105, 107
Ward, Glenyse, 77, 79
Welchman, John C., 183
West, the, 187
West Africa, 84
White, J. P., 112
whiteness, 21, 22, 23
Whitlock, Gillian, 78
Whitman, Walt, 220
Wicomb, Zoë, 75, 76, 81, 84
wilderness, 21, 22, 23, 65
Williams, Sherley Anne, 118, 148, 149, 156
Williams, William Carlos, 224
Willis, Susan, 133, 136, 137, 142, 143
Wilson, Betty, 121
Winchell, Mark Royden, 173
Winthrop, John, 4
Wisker, Gina, 2, 8, 9
Wittig, Monique, 156
women's studies, 89, 156–7
Wong, Shelly, 143
world literature, 1
Worsley, Peter, 172
Wright, Alexis, 78, 79
Wright, Richard, 114
writing, 6, 159
'writing back', 8
Wynne-Davies, Marion, 2, 6, 9

X, Malcolm, 117

Zhuwarara, Rino, 91
Zinyemba, Ranganai, 88
Zimbabwe, 2, 88–101